A Concise Companion to
Milton

Blackwell Concise Companions to Literature and Culture
General Editor: David Bradshaw, University of Oxford

This series offers accessible, innovative approaches to major areas of literary study. Each volume provides an indispensable companion for anyone wishing to gain an authoritative understanding of a given period or movement's intellectual character and contexts.

A Concise Companion to
Milton

Edited by Angelica Duran

Blackwell
Publishing

BLACKWELL PUBLISHING
350 Main Street, Malden, MA 02148-5020, USA
9600 Garsington Road, Oxford OX4 2DQ, UK
550 Swanston Street, Carlton, Victoria 3053, Australia

First published 2007 by Blackwell Publishing Ltd

1   2007

Library of Congress Cataloging-in-Publication Data

A concise companion to Milton / edited by Angelica Duran.
    p. cm.—(Blackwell concise companions to literature and culture)
  Includes bibliographical references and index.
  ISBN-13: 978-1-4051-2271-9 (hardback : alk. paper)
  ISBN-10: 1-4051-2271-4 (hardback : alk. paper)
  1. Milton, John, 1608–1674—Criticism and interpretation.   I.   Duran,
Angelica.   II.   Series.

PR3588.C59 2006
821'.4—dc22

                                                                2006006917

A catalogue record for this title is available from the British Library.

Set in 10/12pt Meridien
by Graphicraft Limited, Hong Kong
Printed and bound in Singapore
by COS Printers Pte Ltd

The publisher's policy is to use permanent paper from mills that operate
a sustainable forestry policy, and which has been manufactured from pulp
processed using acid-free and elementary chlorine-free practices. Furthermore,
the publisher ensures that the text paper and cover board used have met
acceptable environmental accreditation standards.

For further information on
Blackwell Publishing, visit our website:
www.blackwellpublishing.com

To harp-fingered Jacqueline and mild-eyed Paul

Contents

Contents

Notes on Contributors

Paul Alpers (1953 B.A., 1959 Ph.D. English, Harvard.). His first book, *The Poetry of the Faerie Queene* (1967), remains a must-read; and his most recent one, *What is Pastoral?* (1996), well earned three prestigious prizes: a Guggenheim Fellowship to fund its research, and the Christian Gauss Award of Phi Beta Kappa and the Harry Levin Prize of the American Comparative Literature Association to recognize its merits. Paralleling his distinguished publishing career, he has earned teaching awards and the undying gratitude of his former students, including this volume's editor, teaching Elizabethan and seventeenth-century literature from 1962 to 2000 at the University of California at Berkeley, where he is Class of 1942 Professor Emeritus. Having relocated from the west coast to the east coast to Smith College, he is now Professor-in-Residence, and his wife, Carol Christ, is President.

Juliet Lucy Cummins (1994 L.L.B., 1995 B.A. English, 2001 Ph.D. English, University of Sydney). She lectured in English and Law at the University of Western Sydney from 2000 to 2003 and has been an adjunct fellow in Law at that university since 2004. She held the position of Research Associate to the President of the Administrative Decisions Tribunal of New South Wales in 2004 and 2005, and is now practicing law part-time, working as an independent scholar, and looking after her three children, James, Oliver, and Harriet. She edited and contributed to a collection of essays called *Milton and the Ends of Time* (2003), and is co-editor of another collection of essays, *Science,*

Literature and Rhetoric in Early Modern England, which is forthcoming. She also writes in the areas of administrative and privacy law.

Angelica Duran (1987 B.A. English with Spanish minor, 1988 M.A. English, University of California at Berkeley; 2000 Ph.D. English, Stanford). Her English and Comparative Literature courses at Purdue University reflect the research concerns of her first book projects, *The Age of Milton and the Scientific Revolution* (2007) and studies of Miltonic influence in Hispanophone literature. These and other shorter projects reveal her interest in showing points of unity between groups that are often seen as antagonistic and oppositional, and in extending the readership of seventeenth-century literary texts. Having been born and schooled in California, she (nevertheless and thoroughly) enjoys living in the US Midwest during the school year with her husband, Sean, daughter, Jacqueline, and son, Paul, and traveling nationally and internationally in the summers, most recently to Costa Rica, Mexico, Spain, and Thailand.

Karen L. Edwards (1973 B.A. English and Comparative Literature, Brown; 1978 M.A., M.Phil., 1979 Ph.D. English, Yale). After teaching for 12 years at Kenyon College in Gambier, Ohio, she moved to England and is now a Senior Lecturer in the School of English at Exeter University. There she teaches courses on sixteenth- and seventeenth-century English literature in general, and on Milton, Shakespeare, and the Bible and Literature in particular. Her first book is *Milton and the Natural World* (1999) and she has just finished a study of the animals that have a presence in Milton's poetry and prose. Entitled *Milton's Reformed Animals: An Early Modern Bestiary,* the book is being published as a series of special issues of *Milton Quarterly.* By what seems an inevitable progression, she is now working on a study of early modern insults.

Katsuhiro Engetsu (1980 B.A., 1982 M.A. English, Doshisha; 1985 M.A. English, Indiana University). Professor of English at Doshisha University (Japan), he has contributed chapters to *Milton and the Terms of Liberty* (2002) and *The Cambridge Companion to John Dryden* (2004), and translated into Japanese Roy Strong's *Renaissance Garden in England* and Christopher Hill's *Collected Essays.* He has written extensively on early modern British literature and history in both English and Japanese in order to examine the politics of reading and misreading in intercultural issues. He teaches British literature as well as translation theory to his undergraduate and graduate students in Kyoto, one of the most historic cities of Japan, where he lives with his wife and two daughters. He often travels internationally to join academic conferences, most recently invited by the Wordsworth Trust to give a lecture on Milton and the Romantics.

J. Martin Evans (1958 B.A., 1963 D.Phil. English, Oxford). A native of Cardiff, he emigrated to the United States in 1963 to teach at Stanford University, where he has been on the faculty ever since, most recently as the William R. Kenan Professor of English. His publishing record spans 30 years, starting with *Paradise Lost and the Genesis Tradition* (1968) and leading to *The Miltonic Moment* (1998). He shared his familiarity with Renaissance and Milton criticism, which emerges so clearly in the "Select Bibliography" of this volume, in editing the five-volume *John Milton: Twentieth Century Perspectives* (2002); and in teaching courses in the English Department as well as the Introduction to the Humanities and Overseas Studies programs. He has earned numerous, well-deserved awards for his service to his students, including the editors of the *Cambridge Companion to Milton* and this volume. He is the 2004 Milton Society of America Honored Scholar.

Robert Thomas Fallon (1949 B.S. Engineering, USMA; 1960 M.A. History, Canisius College; 1965 Ph.D. English and Comparative Literature, Columbia). After a career as a commissioned officer in the US Army (1949–70) he joined the English faculty at LaSalle University in Philadelphia, Pennsylvania, retiring in 1995 as Professor Emeritus. He has published three books on John Milton, *Captain or Colonel* (1984), *Milton in Government* (1993), and *Divided Empire: Milton's Political Imagery* (1995), and served as President of the Milton Society of America. He is a contributing editor to two volumes of *A Variorum Edition of the Poetry of John Donne: The Songs and Sonnets* (in progress) and *The Holy Sonnets* (2005). Since retirement from LaSalle, he has published four books on Shakespeare, the three *Theatergoer's Guide* volumes (2001, 2002, 2004) and *How to Enjoy Shakespeare* (2005), as well as *The Christian Soldier* (2003), an edition of English Civil War political and religious tracts.

Roy Flannagan (1960 B.A. English, Washington and Lee; 1966 Ph.D. English, University of Virginia). Roy Flannagan spent 32 years at Ohio University, Athens, avoiding being Chair of his English Department only to retire and assume that position at the University of South

Carolina, Beaufort. The Milton Society of America has recognized his great contributions to Milton studies – founding the *Milton Quarterly*, editing *The Riverside Milton*, and directing the 7th International Milton Symposium in Beaufort, South Carolina, for example – through the Irene Samuel Award and 2001 Honored Scholar award. Listed in *Who's Who in America* for the last ten years, he has also been President of the Council of Editors of Learned Journals and an active member of the Renaissance English Text Society. He is a member of the Parris Island Masters' Swimming Team (which hasn't lost a meet in 12 years) and a regular columnist and photographer for *The Lowcountry Weekly*.

David Gay (1977 B.A., 1981 M.A. English, Queen's University; 1989 Ph.D. English, University of Alberta). David Gay teaches at his *alma mater*, the University of Alberta, and researches Milton specifically and early modern literature generally. He also continues to develop interdisciplinary courses in biblical-literary studies and religion and literature. He is drawn to writers like Milton, Blake, and Frye in part because of the central place they give to the creative imagination in both education and religion. He has authored *The Endless Kingdom: Milton's Scriptural Society* (2002) and co-edited *Awakening Words: Bunyan and the Language of Community* (2000). Since 1995, he has served as Secretary of the International John Bunyan Society. Like the Milton Society of America, the Bunyan Society affirms a global sense of community among teachers, students, and the general public, and encourages scholarly work that deepens our understanding of the legacy of early modern literature.

Achsah Guibbory (1966 B.A. English, Indiana University; 1970 Ph.D. English, University of California at Los Angeles). After teaching at the University of Illinois from 1970 to 2004, she joined Barnard College's English Department in 2004. Guibbory is a recipient of many honors and awards, including a national Endowment for the Humanities Senior Research Fellowship (2001–2) and the Harriet and Charles Luckman Undergraduate Distinguished Teaching Award at the University of Illinois (1995). She has served as the President of the Milton Society of America and the John Donne Society. Her books include *The Map of Time: Seventeenth-Century English Literature and Ideas of Pattern in History and Ceremony* (1986) and *Community from Herbert to Milton: Literature, Religion, and Cultural Conflict in Seventeenth-Century English Literature* (1998). Author of many essays and articles on seventeenth-century literature from Donne through Milton, she is editor of *The Cambridge*

Companion to John Donne (2005) and is currently writing a book on the uses of Judaism, Jews, and the Hebrew Bible in early modern England.

Edward Jones (1974 B.A. English, Central Connecticut State University; 1978 M.A., 1985 Ph.D. English, Ohio University). An Associate Professor of English at Oklahoma State University, where he received the President's Distinguished Service Award (1999), a Regents Distinguished Teaching Award (1998), and the Outstanding Teacher Award in the College of Arts and Sciences on two occasions (1996 and 1993), Jones is the author of *Milton's Sonnets: An Annotated Bibliography, 1900–1992* (1994). In addition to publishing several articles on Milton's biography, he is completing a study of Milton and the Parish Chest and the commentary for Books 7 and 8 of *Paradise Lost* for the Milton Variorum. In 2005, Jones was appointed the editor of the *Milton Quarterly*, was asked to serve as the volume editor of Milton's Letters of State for the Oxford Milton, and was elected the President of the Milton Society.

Annabel Patterson (1961 B.A. English, University of Toronto; 1963 M.A. with distinction, 1965 Ph.D. English, University of London). Annabel Patterson was born in England and emigrated to Canada in 1957. She returned to the University of London for her M.A. and Ph.D. She has taught in Canada at the University of Toronto and at York University, and after moving to the US, at the University of Maryland and Duke University. She has spent the last 12 years at Yale, from which she is now retired as Sterling Professor of English, Emeritus. She is a Fellow of the American Arts and Sciences and the 2002 Honored Scholar of the Milton Society of America. She has written or edited about 20 books, and about a hundred articles, many of them on Milton, Marvell, and Donne. She herself is most fond, for ideological reasons, of *Early Modern Liberalism* (1997), now reprinted in paperback, and considers the two-volume *Prose Works of Andrew Marvell* (2003) – a collaborative venture – her most lasting contribution to the field.

Louis Schwartz (1984 B.A. English, New York State University–Albany; 1985 M.A., 1989 Ph.D. English and American Literature, Brandeis University). As Associate Professor of Sixteenth- and Early Seventeenth-Century English Literature at the University of Richmond (in Virginia), he teaches widely in the Literature of Early Modern

England and in the History of English Poetry and Poetics. He is also a contributing editor to the Milton Variorum Project, has published articles on Milton, Shakespeare, and Thomas Wyatt, and has recently finished a book-length study of Milton's responses to problems surrounding maternal mortality in the seventeenth century.

John T. Shawcross (1948 B.A. English and Mathematics, Montclair State University, 1950 M.A. English; 1958 Ph.D. English, New York University; 1975 Litt. D. Montclair State University; 1995 Litt. D. St Bonaventure University). A prolific and careful author and editor, his most recent books are *Paradise Lost* (2002); *Milton and the Grounds of Contention* (2003); *"The Arms of the Family": John Milton and the Significance of Relatives and Associates* (2004); *Thirteen Watercolor Drawings by William Blake Illustrating Paradise Lost by John Milton* (with Robert Essick, 2004); and *Rethinking Milton Studies: Time Present and Time Past* (2005), with other books, volumes, and articles in press. His position as a driving force in Renaissance studies is expressed in various forms, including the publication of *John Donne's Religious Imagination: Essays in Honor of John T. Shawcross* (1995) and his induction as the 1981 Honored Scholar of the Milton Society of America. He is Professor Emeritus of English at the University of Kentucky.

Introduction

Angelica Duran

A Concise Companion to Milton is the second in the Blackwell Concise Companions to Literature and Culture series (General Editor: David Bradshaw) dedicated to a single author rather than to a literary period or theory. The aim of this volume is to provide readers with key guides to understanding the great influence and endurance of the works of the seventeenth-century British writer John Milton. Introductory and succinct without being cursory, it is intended to complement the award-winning, 29-chapter *A Companion to Milton* (Blackwell, 2001), edited by Thomas Corns and used for advanced study.

The cover illustration speaks to the vitality of interpretations of Milton's complex works and life. Similarly, the essays in this collection provide readers not with one coherent line of interpretation but rather with diverse, authoritative interpretations that will greatly amplify their appreciation of that complexity. Indeed, diversity is one of the hallmarks of this volume's 12 newly commissioned chapters and two reference sections, penned by a wide range of scholars – from exciting neophytes to respected veterans, from native English speakers in England, Australia, Canada, and the United States to non-native-English-speaking scholars in Japan and the United States. The careful selection of the contributors is express recognition of the global network of scholars and institutions that contribute to the transmission of literary works that should not simply endure but thrive.

Because of its brevity, depth, and structure, *A Concise Companion to Milton* can serve as the one companion text to Milton's collected works required for undergraduate and graduate Milton courses. Its accessibility also makes it an ideal companion for the general reader and for college and university survey courses. This volume's chapters are purposefully brief and written with a minimum of scholarly jargon so that readers at any level can have time to read them alongside weekly primary reading. There are 12 chapters so that those on 10-week quarters and 15-week semesters can easily schedule reading them all, either skipping or doubling up readings assignments – chapters 1–3 will work particularly well for the introductory week(s). In the case of survey courses, an individual chapter can be assigned from a copy kept in library reserve.

In a text dedicated to a single author yet authored by many, it would be remiss to ignore the authors of each chapter. I mention the often bypassed section "Notes on Contributors" in hopes of encouraging readers to perceive of the chapters as written portions of conversations with fellow readers interested in the same author. The subsection titles of my "Chapter 4: First and Last Fruits of Education" – passion, gratitude, hope, and compassion – encompass only some of the emotions that have propelled each of the contributors' immense and humane contributions to both literary studies and this volume. They each care about texts, they care about students, they care about their world. I thank them heartily for making my job as editor so delightful.

The volume is divided into three parts, with titles that reflect the idea of this volume acting as a guiding *companion* to readers on an exciting educational journey. "Part I: Surveys" explains how and why Milton's works established and continue to maintain their central position in the English and international literary canon. Its three chapters survey the relationship of Milton's works to historical, literary, sociopolitical, and theoretical trends. The nine chapters in "Part II: Textual Sites" clarify important issues that emerge in specific texts or sets of texts, and that are particularly relevant to contemporary society: cultural encounters, ecology, gender, religion, and the value of scholarship. These chapters follow Milton's poetry primarily in chronological order, reflecting the customary organization of college and university syllabuses and the reading practices of general readers. Some chapters focus on a number of texts from various periods of Milton's life, related by topic (education in chapter 4), genre (sonnets in chapter 5), or character (Jesus in chapter 11). Additionally, most chapters incorporate Milton's prose works into their discussions – and by extension into current reading practices and future Milton studies – where those prose works warrant attention. "Part III: Reference Points," comprised of the "Select Chronology" and "Select Bibliography," helps readers in contextualizing the readings in terms of biography, history, literary studies, and Milton studies.

In *Areopagitica*, Milton wrote that "Books are not absolutely dead things, but doe contain a potencie of life in them to be as active as that soule was whose progeny they are." When books have led such public lives as have Milton's, they contain also the lifeblood of the many readers, scholars, and institutions that have dedicated their energies to preserving them, including the collaborators of this volume. In an important sense, the collaboration of this volume extends to its readers. As such, this introduction does not conclude in closure but rather in prospect. Please contact me through Blackwell Publishing at www.blackwellpublishing.com/contacts with descriptions of your successes and challenges in using this volume so that we may improve subsequent editions. Together, we will continue to work towards clearer visions of Milton and his works.

Part I

Surveys

Chapter 1

A Reading of His "left hand": Milton's Prose

Robert Thomas Fallon

It should be noted at the outset that John Milton thought of himself primarily as a poet, one who wrote prose, as he put it, with his "left hand," reserving the right for his chosen calling (1.808; all quotations are from Milton 1953–82 [*CPW*]). Milton's first prose works were his *Prolusions*, performed as school exercises during his studies at Cambridge. During his mature years, the English press, released from strict government control, experienced an explosion of printing, and he joined in the lively debate over his country's fortunes, publishing both as a private citizen and a public servant. Much of his mature prose could well serve as a chronicle of two turbulent decades of English history, the 1640s and 1650s. Milton entered into public print with tracts that ranged widely over issues of his day, publications that, for the purpose of discussion, can be roughly divided into two categories, the religious and the political.

Milton's seventeenth-century contemporaries looked upon these two spheres of human concern as intimately intertwined: political actions were seen as profoundly influencing the fate of their immortal souls. The poet's prose works identify him as very much a man of his age since religion is always close to the surface of his political works and politics ever a factor in his vision of religion. But he was ahead of his time in his insistence on the separation of church and state. He returned to the issue time and again during the decades of warfare and governmental innovation, often seizing occasions when England was going through transitional crises to urge his countrymen to end the state's control over the content and ceremony of their worship. He addressed them during the contentious years at the beginning and the end of the Civil Wars, and again in the early months of the Protectorate. He returned to the cause in 1659 during the final days of Richard Cromwell's Protectorate Parliament and continued his appeal with that body's successor, the restored Rump. He addressed the issue one final time during the last years of his life in the tumultuous aftermath of King Charles II's "Declaration of Indulgences." Each transition, he hoped, provided an opportunity for England to emancipate spiritual belief and religious worship from political oversight, but he was disappointed in each instance, as his countrymen could conceive of no alternative to governmental support of religious institutions.

"[R]egaining to know God aright"

Some of Milton's works are predominantly religious in content. His first prose ventures into public print were his five Anti-Prelatical tracts, *Of Reformation, Of Prelatical Episcopacy, Animadversion upon the Remonstrants Defence, The Reason of Church Government,* and *An Apology against a Pamphlet,* published successively from May 1641 to April 1642. These were the troubled years prior to the English Civil Wars, when the Long Parliament and King Charles I were locked in a struggle over, among other matters, the shape and authority of the Church of England. The English monarch since the reign of Henry VIII (1509–47) had been recognized as the head of the Church, and Charles I took his responsibilities seriously. He authorized his Archbishop of Canterbury, William Laud, to regularize the doctrine and ceremony practiced throughout the kingdom; but Laud met with impassioned resistance from the various reformed congregations who saw his edicts as a campaign to restore English worship to the control of the Church of Rome, reviled as the dreaded, soul-corrupting Anti-Christ.

The poet joined in Parliament's campaign to wrest power from Charles I, writing to contest the crown's authority over the Church. Parliament contended that Charles had overstepped his prerogative when he authorized Archbishop Laud to impose rigid adherence to the dictates of *The Book of Common Prayer* as the ultimate authority for religious practice in the kingdom. The more radical members of the body endorsed a "Root and Branch Bill," which proposed to sweep aside the traditional ecclesiastical structure of the Church by abolishing the hierarchical offices of the prelates, the archbishops, bishops, deans, and lower orders that held sway over church affairs, and instead to reserve to individual congregations the right to determine the content and manner of their worship according to the collective conscience of their members. The bill did not pass, but the debate was underway.

Milton's argument against "prelatical episcopacy" was that the hierarchy had no sanction in Scripture and, further, that it was harmful to the religious and political health of the kingdom, its members "the only seducers and mis-leaders of the State" and "the greatest underminers and betrayers of the Monarch" (1.878, 858). At the time, Milton expressed no opposition to the secular power of the king, though his views in that regard changed dramatically after several years of civil war. The pamphlet wars grew acrimonious with disputants engaging in personal assaults, accusing one another of all manner of intellectual deception and personal corruption. In *A Modest Confrontation*, an answer to Milton's *Animadversions*, for example, the anonymous writer characterizes the work as "*a Slanderous and Scurrilous Libell*" and its author as a man who "haunts Playhouses and Bordelloes" (1.862–3, 886). Milton's biographers have reason to be grateful for these personal attacks, since the poet was quick to defend himself with passages relating details of his life experiences, his studies, and his literary ambitions, details that would have otherwise remained unknown (see, e.g., 1.808–23 and 883–93, as well as *A Second Defence*, 4.612–29).

In June 1642, soon after the publication of the political pamphlet *An Apology against a Pamphlet* Milton left London intent upon collecting rents due him from his father's properties near Oxford. A month later he returned, with a wife! – Mary, the young daughter of his tenant Richard Powell. Another month later, she left London for a visit with her family, but larger events intervened to prevent her return to her husband, even should she have wished to, about which there is considerable doubt. On August 22, 1642, Charles I raised the royal standard at Nottingham Castle, signaling the start of the English Civil Wars, and for years thereafter hostile armies tramped back and forth across the downs and pastures between London and Oxford, the King's capitol, effectively isolating the two cities from one another.

Milton, stung by what he could only conclude was his wife's desertion (the Powells were ardent Royalists), turned his creative energies for two years, 1643–5, primarily to the composition of four tracts arguing for the legality of divorce: *The Doctrine and Discipline of Divorce*, *The Judgement of Martin Bucer*, *Tetrachordon*, and *Colasterion*. In these works, he contends from the evidence of Scripture, theology, and philosophy that a husband and wife who have become spiritually and physically incompatible should not be forced by law to remain in their marriage (see also chapter 9). The poet was roundly condemned for his views. All but the most radical of reformers held that marriage vows were inviolable, and he was branded by his enemies for years after as the notorious "divorcer" – in fact, Mary and he reconciled in 1645. (Milton vented his scorn of his detractors in Sonnets 11 and 12, discussed in chapter 5.) It was the charge and countercharge of this controversy that prompted the poet to compose what is perhaps his best known and most widely admired prose work, *Areopagitica*.

The Doctrine and Discipline of Divorce was unlicensed. That is, it did not receive official state approval prior to publication, this because government censorship of the press had been suspended since 1641. On June 14, 1643, in a bill designed to reestablish the state's authority to regulate printing, the English Parliament passed the "Ordinance to prevent and suppress the licence of printing." In response, the poet published *Areopagitica*, subtitled *A Speech of Mr. John Milton For the Liberty of Unlicenc'd Printing, To the Parlament of England*, a tract couched in the form of a respectful speech to that Parliament, in which he deplored the statute. The primary title reminds the Members of Parliament that they sit in the tradition of the ancient Greek court of Areopagus, the august judicial body of Athenian elders that met on the rocks beneath the sacred heights of the Acropolis. In the work, Milton proposes that, "the knowledge of good and evil as two twins cleaving together leapt forth into the World," hence that humans experience difficulty distinguishing one from the other. It is only in the free play of ideas, he argues, that we can discern and embrace the good (2.514).

Milton imagines that good and evil are engaged in perpetual state of warfare for dominance of the human spirit. Truth, he says, will prevail only if allowed free expression to arm itself against its insidious enemy, and if left unfettered, it will invariably triumph: "Let her and Falsehood grapple; who ever knew Truth put to the wors, in a free and open encounter" (2.561). God left human beings free to choose between good and evil; but only when they are open to controversy, the poet insists, can they gain enlightened understanding and align themselves with justice and virtue. If printing is left unlicensed, Milton prophesies, England will be a beacon to the world in its fearless determination to allow this struggle to be waged in a free press, and London will become the model of a city where "disputing, reasoning, reading, inventing, discoursing, ev'n to a rarity, and admiration" are a source of strength rather than a danger to civic order (2.557).

Shortly thereafter, in 1644, Milton took the time to compose a short tract that touched on yet another aspect of civic order, *Of Education*. He published his recommendations for the best books and exercises "of a vertueous and noble Education" as a letter to Samuel Hartlib, a contemporary advocate of education reform, in answer to his request for the poet's views on the subject (2.376). In Milton's vision, the end of learning in general is "to repair the ruins of our first parents by regaining to know God aright" (2.366). On a more pragmatic level, but still grand in scope, he defines the specific goal of "a compleate and generous Education" designed for English youth "from twelve to one and twenty" as a course of studies that prepares them "to perform justly, skilfully and magnanimously all the offices both private and publike of peace and war" (2.378, 406). Milton's program lays heavy emphasis on Greek and Roman authors, as well as sixteenth-century Italian commentaries on "what the laws are of a true *Epic* poem, what of a *Dramatic*, [and] what of a *Lyric*" (2.405). The curriculum is daunting, and made more so by Milton's description of his students' "Exercise." Influenced by the Civil War, then at its height, the poet proposes a program that "shall be equally good both for Peace and warre" (2.408). Included is intense training in the military arts, everything from the students' "exact use of their weapon" to "the rudiments of their Souldiership in all the skill of embattailing, marching, encamping, fortifying, besieging, and battering" (2.409, 411).

During these years of warfare and political upheaval, Milton conducted a school in his home for a select few students. Some time in the late 1640s, Milton wrote, perhaps for his school, the first four (of six) chapters of *The History of Britain*, a chronicle of events from the mythological landing of the Trojan Brutus on the island's shores to the Norman Conquest. The *History* was not published until 1670, and at that time it omitted some few pages in which the poet had digressed from the historical account to comment on the political and religious controversy raging in England during, it is generally agreed, the early months of 1648. The first Civil War resulted in a total victory for Parliament, which then turned its attention to the settlement of the English Church. The Westminster Assembly of Divines had been convened for the purpose as early as 1643 and after lengthy deliberations the body submitted its proposal to Parliament some four years later. But the structure agreed upon favored retention of state control over worship to a degree entirely unacceptable to the more radical Independents, to John Milton, and, of even more significance, to the New Model Army. Both Parliament and the Assembly were dominated by the Presbyterian party, whose adherents were conservative in their approach to the political and religious issues that divided the country at the end of the war; and the situation in 1648 was complicated by the fact that both Parliament and the army were engaged in negotiations with Charles I in an effort to reach an accord on those issues. The King played one against the other, vacillating and procrastinating while secretly appealing to the Scots to intervene militarily on his behalf. Milton feared that all the blood and treasure sacrificed in the Civil War would prove a fruitless waste if the Presbyterian settlement were put in place.

The *Digression* to the *History* was not published until 1681, several years after the poet's death, under the title *Mr. John Milton's Character of the Long Parliament and Assembly of Divines*. In it, Milton excoriates both bodies. The Members of Parliament, he charges, have performed their public duty "like Children of the Devil, unfaithfully, unjustly, unmercifully, and where not corruptly, stupidly" (5.448). Further, the "*Church-men*" of the Assembly are "Timeservers, Covetous, Illiterate Persecutors, not lovers of the Truth," and he accuses them of "setting up a Spiritual Tyranny by a Secular power, to the advantage of their own Authority above the Magistrate" (5.448, 446; Milton's view of the Assembly is also reflected in his tailed sonnet, "On the New Forcers of Conscience under the Long Parliament," which ends in the memorable line, "*New Presbyter* is but *Old Priest* writ Large"). The *Digression* was considered too incendiary for publication in 1670, but appropriate for print 11 years later, significantly during yet another national crisis, the uproar over the royal succession, in England's long, contentious church–state controversy.

Milton wrote specifically about the religious doctrine of his times in the 1640s as well. One of Milton's students, his nephew Edward Phillips, later wrote a biography of the poet, describing him as continually at work collecting "from the ablest of Divines [. . .] A perfect System of Divinity" (Darbishire 1932: 61). Milton's anonymous biographer confirms that he was "framing a *Body of Divinity* out of the Bible" (Darbishire 1932: 29). This "System of Divinity" was apparently a lifelong labor, resulting in the end in a bulky manuscript entitled *De Doctrina Christiana*, a work with a history as controversial as its content. It was not published during Milton's life, indeed was not recovered until 1823, when it was found in London's Public Record Office in the company of a packet of his state letters. Recent scholarship has questioned how much of *De Doctrina Christiana* is actually Milton's, that is, to what extent it represents his thought on Christian belief. It is mentioned here because, if it is Milton's, it casts further light on his opposition to state control of religion, especially during the contentious decade of the 1640s.

The poet, like many reformers, considered Holy Scripture the ultimate authority on such subjects as the nature of God, the Son, the Holy Spirit, salvation, and the practice of religious worship. Humankind, as *De Doctrina* contends, will always have an imperfect perception of God and therefore "ought to form just such a mental image of him as he, in bringing himself within the limits of our understanding, wishes us to form," that is, one that corresponds to "his representation and description of himself in the sacred writings" (6.133). Faith was for Milton a matter to be settled only between God and the individual conscience, and from that belief grew his conviction that the manner of worship should not be determined by an ecclesiastical hierarchy endorsed by the state, not by "Romish" priests, nor by Church of England prelates, nor by the presbyters proposed by the Westminster Assembly of Divines.

Milton regularly injected the issue into his political works, in *A Second Defence of the English People*, for example, advising Oliver Cromwell, the newly installed Lord Protector, to "leave the church to the church" (4.678). He returned to the subject during the unsettled year 1659, when England experienced constant turmoil, coming under the rule of four successive governing bodies while suffering through a Royalist uprising (referred to as the second Civil War), and the army's seizure of power on two separate occasions. He first addressed Richard Cromwell's Protectorate Parliament with *A Treatise of Civil Power in Ecclesiastical Causes*, in which he argues that, "it is unlawfull for the civil magistrate to use force in matters of religion" (7.255). When the Protectorate was replaced by the restored Rump Parliament, he urged that body, in *Considerations Touching the Likeliest Means to Remove Hirelings out of the Church*, to discontinue the practice of assessing tithes, the state-imposed taxes on parishioners for the support of the clergy. He argues from the evidence of Scripture and history from antiquity to his own time that the Bible does not sanction tithes and that the wealth accumulated through them has always been a source of corruption in the church. His pleas went unheeded, however, at a time when his country was preoccupied with the political chaos that preceded the Restoration of Charles II in 1660.

In 1673 Milton took up the cause one final time in *Of True Religion, Heresie, Schism, and Toleration*. The tract appeared in the wake of the political upheaval that followed Charles II's "Declaration of Indulgence," the King's attempt to lift the severe religious, political, and social restrictions that Parliament had imposed on those of his subjects who failed to swear an oath of adherence to the doctrine and practice of the Church of England. Parliament, convinced that the King's chief intent was to emancipate English Catholics, forced him to withdraw the Declaration, but the controversy continued to fester for years thereafter. In *Of True Religion*, Milton joins vigorously in the outcry against "Popery," warning against "the growth of the Romish weed" in the kingdom and branding "the Romish Church *Mother of Error, School of Heresie*" (8.417, 421). At the same time, however, he defends the various dissident sects, the "Anabaptist," the "Arian," and the "Socinian," among others, against the charge of heresy, urging that they be tolerated in their "Arguing, Preaching in their several Assemblies, Publick writing, and the freedom of Printing," unfettered by state restraint (8.424, 426).

A "Commonwealth [. . .] of many Commonwealths"

In his political works Milton makes liberal use of Scripture and ancient learning to record contemporary history and bolster his arguments for liberty of conscience and freedom from tyranny. The works are devoted to a number of causes. In his Regicide tracts, the poet justifies Parliament's trial and execution of Charles I. In *A Defence of the People of England* and *A Second Defence of the English People*, he answers foreign attacks on, first, the Commonwealth government set up to replace the monarchy and, later, the Protectorate settlement that succeeded it. And then, he offered a *Defence of Himself*. In the closing days of the English Republic, after a five-year silence, he returned to the political arena with two editions of *The Readie and Easie Way*, warning of the ills that would befall the nation should it readmit the King. All the while, he was busily engaged in preparing and translating the Letters of State exchanged between his government and the nations of Europe in his governmental position as Secretary of Foreign Languages (or Tongues).

After the failure of the Royalist uprising in the summer of 1648, events moved swiftly to a revolutionary outcome. The army lost all confidence in the possibility of achieving a settlement with the King and bristled at the hostility of the Presbyterian-dominated Parliament. In December, the soldiers expelled from the body those members who opposed bringing the King to trial and closely confined him in Windsor Castle. Those left sitting in the "Rump" Parliament, as it was called, convened a special court that indicted Charles I, found him guilty of tyranny, and had him beheaded on January 30, 1649. The Rump then selected, largely from among its own ranks, a number to sit on a Council of State to act as the Republic's executive body, though it remained under strict Parliamentary control. It was this Council that in March 1649 appointed John Milton to serve as its Secretary of Foreign Languages, an office he filled dutifully for the next ten and a half years.

Prior to his appointment, however, Milton had published the first of his two Regicide tracts, *The Tenure of Kings and Magistrates*; indeed it may well have been this work that brought him to the attention of the Council. In *The Tenure* he defends Parliament's conduct in the war against the King and the decision to place him on trial for tyranny. Milton cites scriptural and historical precedent for the removal of a monarch who has proven himself a tyrant, whom he defines as "he who regarding neither Law nor the common good, reigns onely for himself and his faction" (3.212). And in the process, he continues his attack on the church prelates, "Mercenary noisemakers," as he calls them, and the Presbyterians, those "Ministers of Mammon instead of Christ" (3.236, 242).

Milton's principal duty as Secretary of Foreign Languages, as mentioned, was the preparation and translation of the government's correspondence with foreign states, which was conducted in Latin, the official language of international exchange, hence his more colloquial title, Latin Secretary. He was engaged in numerous other activities, however, chief among them the composition of lengthy tracts defending the Republic from attacks upon its legitimacy. Immediately after his appointment, he was assigned the task of condemning a treaty of peace between the Royalist forces in Ireland, led by the Earl of Ormond, and the Irish rebels. This *Observations Upon the Articles of Peace* is a tract of some 60 pages, two-thirds of which are devoted to the treaty itself and "the Insolent and seditious Representation of the *Scotch* Presbytery of Belfast," in which the Scottish settlers of northern Ireland deplored the revolutionary settlement in England. Milton's contribution to the tract refutes selected articles of the treaty "made with those inhumane Rebels and Papists of *Ireland* by the late King" (3.300–1).

Milton's second regicide tract, *Eikonoklastes*, published in October 1649, was a much longer labor, written in response to the publication of the incendiary book *Eikon Basilike*. The work appeared shortly after the execution of Charles I and was purported to be the King's account of his long contention with Parliament, from the calling of the Long Parliament in August 1641 to his pious meditations prior to his trial. In fact the "combined editor and ghost writer" of the book was William Gauden, but Milton could not have known this (3.152). This "King's book" depicted Charles I as a royal martyr, an unwavering servant of his people and devout defender of his Church, and it proved enormously popular, going through 35 editions during the first year of publication despite Parliament's efforts to suppress it. The work demanded an answer and the Council of State's Secretary of Foreign Languages was assigned the task.

Milton's *Eikonoklastes* is a point by point refutation of the *Eikon*'s claims. Milton's answer is divided into 28 chapters to match the like number in "the King's book." It represents Parliament's account of the turbulent decade, the first 12 chapters dealing with events prior to the Civil War from the King's calling *"this last Parlament"* (November 3, 1640) to the *"Nineteen Propositions"* (June 1, 1642) and the Irish uprising (3.350, 456). The next 14 chapters are a record of events during the war and the subsequent negotiations in which Parliament and the army attempted to reach a settlement with Charles I in a series of frustrating exchanges that resulted finally in the army's seizure of the King's person at Holmby House on June 4, 1647. *Eikonoklastes* concludes with responses to the last two chapters of *Eikon*, moving the account forward to the trial of the King and events thereafter. (*Eikon* makes no mention of the execution of the King, though it appears to have been published after the event.) The first of these chapters is said to be a letter composed by Charles I to his son, the second a transcript of his thoughts and prayers during his imprisonment. Milton names his chapters *"Intitl'd to the Prince of Wales"* and *"Intitl'd Meditations upon Death,"* as if to question their provenance (3.568, 582). *Eikonoklastes* depicts the monarch as devious and hypocritical from beginning to end, in his final years dragging out negotiations with Parliament and the army while secretly treating with the Scots to come to his aid. During this entire period, in Milton's judgment, Charles I meant "no good to either Independent or Presbyterian" (3.562).

Milton's first entry into international debate was in response, once again, to the publication of a book, the *Defensio Regia, Pro Carolo I*, which appeared in late 1649. The Council of State appointed their Secretary to answer the work in January of the following year, a task that took him until December to complete, since as he remarks, his "precarious health" required him to "work at intervals and hardly for an hour at a time" (4.307). It was not until February 1651 that *A Defence of the People of England* appeared, but it immediately established Milton as an influential voice in the learned international community.

Both the *Defensio Regia* and *A Defence* were composed in Latin, the language of scholarly debate throughout Europe, and both were apparently widely read as opposing arguments on the authority of kings. The *Defensio* was the work of Claude Salmasius, a distinguished member of the faculty at the University of Leyden, widely known and respected as a prolific writer on a variety of subjects, the author according to one account of 70 volumes during his lifetime (4.964). His book is a defense of monarchy and an expression of the anger and dismay shared by many in Europe at the time that the English should have taken it upon themselves not only to remove a king but to try, convict, and execute him as well. Milton's *A Defence* justifies the act, largely by dismantling Salmasius's arguments, questioning his logic, his learning, and his reading of Scripture and history.

Scholarly debate in this era could become personal, with disputants challenging not only the reasoning of opponents but their integrity as well, and Milton was not above the use of invective against his adversary. He characterizes Salmasius's argument as "full of words and as lacking in substance" and its author as "an empty windbag," a "trifler," and the "prince of liars," a man "notorious for ignorance and vice," and the unkindest cut of all, a mere "grammarian" (4.301, 325, 462, 404, 453, 306). These personal slurs aside, Milton mounts a serious rebuttal to the *Defensio*'s argument for divine right, one or two instances of which will give some flavor of the debate.

Salmasius divides his work into 12 books and Milton counters with a like number of chapters, each taking issue with a central theme of the controversy. In Book 4, for example, Salmasius argues that "the sanctity of kings is inviolable and dependent upon no other than divine power," and further that once the people have surrendered authority to the king, "that gift is made irrevocably; nor at the wish of the donor may it sometimes be voided" (4.986, 994). He cites Scripture, history, literature, and the church fathers to this effect and Milton turns each of his examples against him, ending with a string of instances when "Christians warred on tyrants, used arms in their own defence, and frequently punished the crimes of tyrants" (4.414). The poet concludes therefore that when a "king turns tyrant or degenerates through his worthlessness," the people may indeed revoke their agreement, for "they are released from their bond by his faithlessness, by justice herself, and by the very law of nature" (4.421).

Again, in Book 7 Salmasius insists that, "kings cannot be judged" (4.1007). "In a kingdom," he argues, "no one is higher than the king, no one is equal to him, no one is on the same level with him." "By whom, therefore," he asks, "will he be accused of crimes? By whom will he be judged?" (4.1011). Milton jumps on Salmasius: "What is this? Has the king no peer within his realm?" He then draws on history to refute the claim, noting that the "twelve most ancient peers of France" were equal to their king. He quotes Cicero on the early Romans who expelled their kings and "set up the Senate as guardian, guide, and champion of the state." And he cites Scripture to illustrate the Sanhedrin's power to try judges, who were also called kings (4.463–5). The people have always been superior to kings, Milton insists, and by "the people" he means "all citizens of every degree" (4.471). By Salmasius's definition, he concludes, the people are "to be counted as part of the property and possessions of their master and his son and heir," no different from "slaves or cattle" (4.472). Milton goes on in this vein for 172 quarto pages, denouncing Salmasius as a dunce, a liar, and a traitor, while drawing on the immense learning accumulated over the years to create a work that he would later describe as one "Of which all *Europe* talks from side to side" (Sonnet 22, "To Mr. Cyriack Skinner upon his Blindness").

The year 1652 was a trying one for Milton. His labors took their toll on his eyesight and within a year after the publication of *A Defence of the People of England* he was totally blind. Aside from the loss of sight, he suffered the death of his first wife Mary and infant son John. He continued to perform such tasks as his impairment permitted, however, translating and preparing letters and long treaties for the Council of State in steadily mounting numbers as the nations of Europe were compelled to accept Parliament as the *de facto* governing body of England. In the ensuing years, 1653–4, that government went through dramatic transitions. In April 1653, Oliver Cromwell and the army, impatient at the Rump's lack of progress with reform, dismissed the body. After a half-year of political experiment with a Nominated or "Barebones" Parliament (named after one of its most colorful and vocal members, Praisegod Barebones), England inaugurated yet another form of government. Cromwell was appointed Lord Protector and entrusted with the powers of a monarch in all but name.

Milton, meanwhile, was collecting material in anticipation of a response from Salmasius, but when that gentleman died in September 1653, he was asked to reply to a book that had appeared anonymously a year earlier, *The Cry of the Royal Blood to Heaven against the English*

Parricides (Salmasius's *Responsio* was published posthumously in 1660). The poet labored over the task during the early months of the Protectorate, finally publishing *A Second Defence of the English People* in May 1654.

As he had in earlier works, Milton undertook a point by point rebuttal to *Cry*'s accusation of parricide, but two other aspects of *A Second Defence* are of more interest to the poet's biographers and students of his political philosophy. *Cry* launches vituperative attacks on Milton himself, at one point describing him as "a monster, dreadful, ugly, huge, deprived of sight [. . .] Yet not huge, for there is nothing more feeble, bloodless, and pinched" (4.582). As mentioned earlier, we can be grateful for these personal assaults, for on this occasion they prompted Milton to defend himself with a lengthy account of his life, a record, as he says, of "Who I am, then, and whence I come" (4.612–29). Milton is not reticent about replying in kind, however. He identifies the author of *Cry* as "a certain More," whom he describes as "faithless, treacherous, ungrateful, foulmouthed, a consistent slanderer of men and women, whose chastity he is wont to spare no more than their good name" (4.564). He goes on with an account of Alexander More's disgraceful behavior, which caused him, a cleric, to be dismissed from church positions, especially one such episode when he had "cast lustful eyes" on a maidservant and, after fathering a child by her, abandoned them both (4.568–9).

The second element of interest in *A Second Defence* lies in its digressive passages of praise for the leaders of the English Revolution, prominent among them John Bradshaw, who presided over the trial of Charles I and served for a time as president of the Commonwealth Council of State, and Sir Thomas Fairfax, the commander-in-chief of the New Model Army during and after the Civil Wars (4.637–8, 669–70). Milton names others but reserves his most effusive praise for Oliver Cromwell (4.675–8, 666–72). After describing his exemplary character, his statesmanship, and his military victories, he addresses the Lord Protector himself, then in office for only a few months: "Cromwell, we are deserted! You alone remain. On you has fallen the whole burden of our affairs. On you alone they depend" (4.671).

As it turns out, Alexander More was not the author of *Cry*, and it seems that some of Milton's close associates tried to persuade him of his error prior to publication of *A Second Defence* (the author was closer to home, an Anglican priest, Peter du Moulin). Milton insisted that it be published nonetheless, and the work received a prompt reply from More, his *Fides Publicae*, in which he denies authorship of *Cry* and accuses the poet of all manner of deceit and egregious misrepresentation. Milton shot back with his *Defence of Himself*, which consists largely of further attacks on More. The poet stubbornly insists that More is the author of *Cry* and marshals further evidence of his depravity, embellishing his former accounts with even more damning details. The work need not delay us, except to note that its exuberant language of invective sounds to some attentive ears like a renewed vigor in the poet's pen. Kester Svendsen, for example, draws attention to his pervasive use of "mock-heroic prose epic similes, extended metaphors, and the other materials and modes of poetry," foreshadowing the style of his later great works. Svendsen concludes that in the composition of the tract "surely [. . .] the right hand knew what the left was doing" (4.693). It might be added that in dictating these lengthy tracts the blind Milton honed the skills that made his great poems possible.

Milton was silent on political events in England for the next five years, though it was a period of startling developments on the national and international scene. Cromwell built a fleet and maintained an army that gained the country a reputation as a major European power. He died unexpectedly in September 1658 and was succeeded by his son Richard, who had none of his father's energy, vision, or prestige. The new Lord Protector called a Parliament early the following year and was soon at loggerheads with the body over matters of church and state. The army broke what was a political stalemate by dismissing Parliament and compelling Richard to abdicate his office, but the officers were forced by public outcry to recall the Rump Parliament that Cromwell had dissolved six years earlier. After the Royalist uprising in the summer of 1659, the Republic experienced further political turmoil. The New Model Army had marshaled under General John Lambert to oppose the Royalists and, still displeased with the Rump, marched on Westminster and dissolved the body. A military Committee of Safety ruled England briefly but again public pressure forced them to recall the Rump in late December. Distraught at these developments, Milton composed two short documents, "A Letter to a Friend" and *Proposalls of Certaine Expedients for the Preventing of Civill War*, in an effort to heal the breach between the two bodies, but they proved to be irrevocably at odds.

The Rump embarked on a concerted effort to demobilize the army by cashiering officers and disbursing units in small garrisons throughout the country. In Scotland, General George Monk avoided the worst effects of this "remodeling" and retained a cohesive force loyal to him. He began a slow march south, stopping along the way to sample public opinion, and arrived in London to discover that the people were no more pleased with the Rump than they had been with the army's Committee of Safety. He compelled Parliament to dissolve itself and call for new elections, which all were well aware would result in a body disposed to restore the monarchy. This they did and Charles II returned triumphantly to England in May 1660.

It was during these chaotic months that Milton composed his final prose work on the political life of his country, *The Readie and Easie Way to Establish a Free Commonwealth*. It appeared in two editions, the second in April as the Convention Parliament was assembling. In warning of the dangers of restoring the monarchy, Milton renews many of the arguments of his former works and describes with biting derision the royal court that would ensue. There will be a king, he scoffs, who "must be ador'd like a Demigod, with a dissolute and haughtie court about him, of vast expence and luxurie, masks and revels, to the debaushing of our prime gentry both male and female." There will be a queen and a queen mother as well, and in time the "royal issue," all surrounded by their own "sumptuous courts; to the multiplying of a servile crew, not of servants only, but of nobility and gentry, bred up then to the hopes not of public, but of court offices; to be stewards, chamberlains, ushers, grooms, even of the close-stool [the royal chamber pot]" (7.425).

Of special interest is Milton's visionary sketch of a proposal for an English Republic (7.432–44, 458–61), a government that in its broad outline is a federation, not "one Commonwealth," as he puts it, "but many Commonwealths under one united and entrusted Sovrantie" (7.461). He discards the discredited title "Parliament" in favor of a "Grand or General Counsel" to perform the function of a central government, selected by only those electors "who are rightly qualifi'd" (7.443). The body will be limited in its powers, however, concerned principally with "forein affairs" while jurisdiction over domestic matters, including divine worship, will be reserved largely to county assemblies and local congregations. He is curiously indefinite as to how the armed forces will fit into the scheme, implying that they will exist as an independent element in the republic. The General Council will "dispose of Forces, both by Sea and Land" but they will remain, as he proposes in an accompanying letter to General Monk, "under the conduct of your Excellency" (7.394; there is no evidence that the letter, "The Present Means, and Brief Delineation of a Free Commonwealth" [7.392–5] was ever delivered to Monk).

The Readie and Easie Way is a quixotic work, since the country was moving inexorably toward the Restoration, but Milton is fearless – one might say foolhardy – in his final effort to save the Republic, while at the same time all too aware that his labors are to no avail. He opens the second edition asking for a pause in the fateful rush to monarchy, "a little Shroving-time first, wherin to speak freely, and take our leaves of Libertie" (7.408–9). And he closes with a plaintive coda in which he acknowledges that he may be addressing only "trees and stones; and had none to cry to, but with the Prophet, *O earth, earth, earth!* to tell the very soil it self [these] last words of our expiring libertie" (7.462–3).

After the Restoration, the poet was imprisoned briefly and feared for his life. He was ultimately released through the intercession, it is said, of at least two poets, William Davenant and Andrew Marvell, the latter a Member of Parliament and, just as importantly, Milton's former associate in the Republic's office of the Secretary of Foreign Languages. Milton thereafter wisely assumed a life insulated from the political arena.

Mention should be made of several works Milton published in his later years, when he seemed to be emptying his archives of projects he had labored over during periods of leisure during his busy life. We know of these works because some were published before and some after his death on November 9 or 10, 1674, and others were mentioned by his early biographers. These include an edition of Sir Walter Ralegh's *The Cabinet-Council* (1658), a second edition of *A Defence of the People of England* (1658), *The History of Britain* (1670), *Letters Patents of the Election of this Present King of Poland*, a translation (1674), and *A Brief History of Moscovia* (1682). Some of these works seem to be texts and reference books for students engaged in the demanding curriculum he designed in *Of Education*, among them a Latin dictionary (1693), a Greek thesaurus, a book on grammar (1669) and another on logic (1672) (see chapter 4). We can add to this list his private correspondence (1674) and Letters of State (1676).

During his mature years, then, John Milton assumed many roles: an innovative educator, a diligent public servant, a political polemicist passionately committed to liberty of conscience and freedom from tyranny, a visionary in his opposition to state control of the church, and finally a courageous advocate of the English Republic in its dying weeks. It is rare, indeed unique, to find a literary figure so intimately engaged in the political life of his country. He is remembered chiefly, however, as a consummate poet who in his youth was eager to create works that would "survive [their] master's funeral pyre" ("Ad Patrem" 116–17), an ambition realized early in his collection of poems of 1645. In later years his resolute spirit overcame the tragic burden of blindness to compose *Paradise Lost*, *Paradise Regained*, and *Samson Agonistes*. It is primarily to these timeless achievements of his right hand that we turn in the pages to follow.

References and Further Reading

Ashley, Maurice (1974). *The English Civil War: A Concise History*. London: Thames and Hudson.
Ashton, Robert (1978). *The English Civil War: Conservatism and Revolution, 1603–1649*. London: Weidenfeld and Nicolson.
Barker, Arthur E. (1942). *Milton and the Puritan Dilemma, 1641–1660*. Toronto: University of Toronto Press.
Bennett, Martyn (1997). *The Civil Wars in Britain and Ireland, 1638–1651*. Oxford: Blackwell.
Cust, Richard and Hughes, Ann (1997). *The English Civil War*. London: Arnold.
Darbishire, Helen (1932). *The Early Lives of Milton*. London: Constable.
Fallon, Robert Thomas (1984). *Captain or Colonel: The Soldier in Milton's Life and Art*. Columbia: University of Missouri Press.
Fallon, Robert Thomas (1993). *Milton in Government*. University Park: Pennsylvania State University Press.
Fallon, Robert Thomas (1995). *Divided Empire: Milton's Political Imagery*. University Park: Pennsylvania State University Press.
Fallon, Robert Thomas (2003). *The Christian Soldier: Religious Tracts Published for Soldiers on Both Sides During and After the English Civil Wars, 1642–1648*. Tempe: Arizona Center for Medieval and Renaissance Studies.
Fissel, Mark C. (1994). *The Bishops' Wars: Charles I's Campaign against Scotland, 1638–1640*. Cambridge: Cambridge University Press.
Fraser, Antonia (1974). *Cromwell, The Lord Protector*. New York: Knopf.
Gardiner, Samuel Rawson (1962). *The Constitutional Documents of the Puritan Revolution, 1625–1660*. 3rd edn, rev. Oxford: Clarendon Press.
Gardiner, Samuel Rawson (1965). *History of the Commonwealth and Protectorate, 1649–1656*. Reprint. 4 vols. New York: AMS Press.
Gardiner, Samuel Rawson (1965). *History of the Great Civil War, 1642–1649*. Reprint. 4 vols. New York: AMS Press.
Haller, William (1957). *The Rise of Puritanism*. New York: Columbia University Press.
Kenyon, John and Ohlmeyer, Jane (1998). *The Civil Wars: A Military History of England, Scotland, and Ireland, 1638–1660*. Oxford: Oxford University Press.
Kishlansky, Mark A. (1979). *The Rise of the New Model Army*. Cambridge: Cambridge University Press.

Lieb, Michael (2002). *"De Doctrina Christiana* and the Question of Authorship." *Milton Studies* 41: 172–230.

Manning, Brian (1976). *The English People and the English Revolution, 1640–1649*. London: Heinemann.

Milton, John (1953–82). *Complete Prose Works of John Milton* [*CPW*]. Edited by Don M. Wolfe. 8 vols. New Haven and London: Yale University Press.

Milton, John (1957). *John Milton, Complete Poems and Major Prose*. Edited by Merritt Y. Hughes. New York: Odyssey Press.

Morrill, John (1993). *The Nature of the English Revolution*. London: Longman.

Wedgwood, C. V. (1955). *The King's Peace, 1637–1641*. New York: Macmillan.

Wedgwood, C. V. (1959). *The King's War, 1641–1647*. New York: Macmillan.

Wolfe, Don M. (1941). *Milton and the Puritan Revolution*. New York: T. Nelson and Sons.

Chapter 2

"Shedding sweet influence": The Legacy of John Milton's Works

John T. Shawcross

The influence of an author on others can be direct or subtle, wide-spread or local, in many venues or few; but for John Milton it has long been demonstrated that he has been and still is one whose influence has been direct and subtle, widespread and also concentrated in specific eras and locales, in literature, art, and music, and in religious "knowledge," political theory, and social thinking. Current concerns of struggles between good and evil in the world have led to such a movie as *The Devil's Advocate* where the main character is called John Milton and the Satan-as-clever-fellow interpretation of his epic poem *Paradise Lost* pervades. Terroristic world action, particularly for religious reasons, has brought Milton's dramatic poem *Samson Agonistes* before the public seeking understanding of "suicide bombers" with a reading of Samson's destruction of the Philistines as his condoning of jihad (discussed further in chapter 12). The great advances of science and space travel which a movie such as the first *Matrix* exploits have reminded viewers of Satan's voyage in *Paradise Lost* through Chaos and later his circling the equinox three times, crossing the meridians of longitude four times, and returning to Earth on the eighth day. The Blind Neo has thus been seen as a counterpart of Milton. Then too, whenever some group attempts to remove certain literary works from a library or an academic syllabus, someone is sure to counter with Milton's argument that he "who kills a Man kills a reasonable crea-ture, Gods Image; but hee who destroyes a good Booke, kills reason it self, kills the Image of God" (*Areopagitica* 4). And scholars who have examined the thought behind the eighteenth-century revolutions of the American colonies against England and of the French people against monarchy have revealed Milton's influence, particularly through authors like John Locke and Algernon Sidney, on such prime movers as John Adams and Thomas Jefferson, and Claude Adrien Helvetius and Honoré Gabriel Riquetti, Comte de Mirabeau, among others. Here it is Milton's "republican" *Tenure of Kings and Magistrates, Pro Populo Anglicano Defensio*, and *A Treatise of Civil Power*, as well as his stand against Charles I in *Eikonoklastes* and his position on separation of church and state that have had lasting effect. But also of significance, though less recognized, is the federated governmental structure that Milton espoused in *The Readie and Easie Way to Establish a Free Commonwealth*, with a central authority and multiple local jurisdictions, allowing for a variety of social and religious differences.

For discussion of Milton's legacy, I employ an apt Miltonic image. In the Creation of the universe depicted in *Paradise Lost* 7.370–84, Milton describes "the glorious Lamp [. . .] Regent of Day" and the Pleiades (daughters of Atlas and Pleione, implying a conjunction of earth and ocean) who dance before the Sun, "Shedding sweet influence." The "less bright [. . .] Moon" borrows her light from him and "With thousand lesser Lights dividual holds." Metaphoric implications in these lines tell us much about the nature of Milton's influence. The influence of the Regent of Day is "shed," that is, "divided," "scattered" as its etymology (from Old English "sceaden") tells us, through those "thousand thousand Starrs" which the Moon "dividual" holds. This single word, "shed," means that those thousand lesser lights, whose rays are reflections of the bright rays of the Sun, are "divided," "scattered," like the extensive and varied influences from Milton one finds everywhere, some directly, some by reflected/borrowed/subtle light. The genderization makes clear that these productive orbs are "Communicating Male and Femal Light," direct and reflected light, "Which two great Sexes animate the World" (8.148–52). The image is continued and humanized in Adam's description of his leading Eve, "blushing like the Morn," to their Nuptial Bower, when "all Heav'n,/ And happie Constellations on that hour/ Shed thir selectest influence" (8.510–13). Milton employs this image as an ideal for all sorts of relationships in the fallen world, referring to "the influence of heav'n [. . .] which hath rarify'd and enlightn'd our spirits" in discussing the relationship of the government to its people, and invoking "the pure influence of peace and love, whereof the souls lawfull contentment is the onely fountain" in defining the relationship of husband and wife (*Areopagitica* 34;

Doctrine and Discipline of Divorce 8). When we apply the image to Milton's works in relation to other works, we can cast his influence, with hoped-for ultimate "lawful contentment," as peaceful and loving, as potentially pregnant with provoked thoughts, as influence that anyone can use literally or through adaptation. The history of the world, indeed, has exhibited those thousands of lights – bright and faint – generated by Milton's works in the three and a half centuries since he wrote. My selections, then, will not prioritize Miltonic influence on major writers over lesser writers, on literature to the exclusion of other disciplines, or on one period over another. Like the Miltonic image, Miltonic influence evades systemization and demands appreciation.

Neither can my discussion be exhaustive, as we may see from just a short glance at Milton's modern argument for divorce in *Doctrine and Discipline of Divorce*. The work bypassed the generally acceptable pleas of adultery or desertion. While it immediately brought opprobrium upon Milton, it later became a source for pleas of incompatibility or what today we call irreconcilable differences. An early literary example of this influential thought is seen in Mary Walker, Lady Hamilton's 1778 novel *Munster Village*, in the character of Mrs Lucy Lee, who quotes a passage from *Doctrine and Discipline of Divorce* in which Milton "proves, that a contrariety of mind, destructive of felicity, place, and happiness, are greater reasons for divorce than adultery" (1.92–7). The influence of Milton's argument, however, is not restricted to literary domains. It was reported that a Mistress Attaway, citing this divorce tract, ran away with another woman's husband in 1644 (Masson 1946: 3.189–92); and there is the court case of John Manners, Lord Roos, against his wife for adultery, concerning which Milton is reported to have been consulted in 1670 by a member of the House of Lords (French 1949–58: 5.11–15). We might note that the Attaway case and Milton's ideas about divorce found their way to the popular, rather than academic, *Gentleman's Magazine* 55 (1785), pp. 20–3. Its influence then crossed from England to France. Toward the end of the eighteenth century, Milton's tract had also made favorable impression in such anonymous and undated tracts as *Opinion sur le divorce* [*Opinion Concerning Divorce*] and *Réflexions d'un bon citoyen en faveur du divorce* [*Reflections of a Loyal Citizen in Favor of Divorce*].

A broader example of Miltonic influence should be noted. Many in the eighteenth century and later seem to have learned their Bible not from the Bible itself but from *Paradise Lost* and, for a few, from *Paradise Regain'd*. There are those who believe that the angels Uriel and Ithuriel and Abdiel appear in the Bible, but of course they do not. Indeed,

Milton made up Abdiel (whose Hebraic name means "servant of God"), just as he did the "palace" of the Fallen Angels, Pandæmonium (which means "place of all the demons"), and just as he did Jesus's soliloquy in the Wilderness in Book 1 of *Paradise Regain'd*. Yet many people do not know that Milton is their source. It is hoped, then, that the following selection and discussion will provide a sense of the breadth and depth of Miltonic influence, that it will provoke readers to assess its various permutations, to appreciate the brighter lights, and learn about fainter ones.

Illustrative, Musical, and Dramatic Arts

Influence in the arts begins early with the illustrations of the 12 books of *Paradise Lost* in 1688 by the Spanish baroque artist Sir John Baptist de Medina and the British artists Bernard Lens and Henry Aldrich. The first two artists provide epitomes of what happens narratively in the poem's respective books rather than a descriptive focus on one scene only. The paintings of the well-known French illustrator Gustave Doré in 1866, on the other hand, stay quite close to a single action and text of the poem, offering little commentary upon it. Doré's are widely known, reprinted, and loved; William Blake's, however, are also well-known and frequently reproduced designs. Illustrations of Milton's texts often afford an interpretation, and this is particularly evident in Blake's. An obvious case is the eight watercolors for *A Mask*: the serpent coiled around the Lady's chair, for one instance, makes clear Blake's reading of a relationship in Milton's mind between the temptation motif of the poem and the story of Adam and Eve. As Irene Tayler writes, Blake has shown us "the whole complex of human error resting in our mistaken notions about the nature of the generative life" (Tayler 1973: 249). The more imaginative illustrations of the American painters Carlotta Petrina (1936), who also produced four for *Paradise Regain'd*, or Mary Groom (1937), who also depicted *Samson Agonistes* (1939), create attitudes toward the texts, the characters, and the events. The abstract and impressionistic rendition of concepts of the dramatic poem by the British artist Robert Medley (1979) and of the selectively focused sketches of *Paradise Lost* by the Spanish artist Gregorio Prieto (1972) move away from literal relationship, instead yielding a primarily emotional understanding of the poem.

Yet Milton has also provided allusiveness for artists wishing on the one hand to make a public statement and on the other to induce attitudes toward the subject of a painting. James Gillray produced, as one example, *Alecto and her Train, at the Gate of Pandæmonium: – or – The Recruiting Sarjeant enlisting John Bull, into the Revolution Service* (July 4, 1791), where the Fury who represents constant anger satirizes the argument for the entry of Great Britain into the French Revolution (the American Revolution had closed in 1783), which soon after brought the Reign of Terror (war with France finally began in 1793). The Miltonic allusion casts all such revolutionaries as puny devils and implies the numerous revolutionary actions that would pop up here and there in Europe through the Year of Revolutions, 1848. Or another example, *An Angel, gliding on a Sun-beam into Paradice. Milton* (October 11, 1791), giving a pastiche of *Paradise Lost* (5.555–6; 5.266–7; 4.649; 9.151), where a fat Uriel or Raphael or Satan, loaded with gems, money, and a cross, descends from Heaven to Hanover, the origin of the then ruling monarch, George III. Through this sarcastic use of *Paradise Lost*, Gillray views the important struggle at this time between Edmund Burke and John Fox over French–British relationships as being ignored by the monarchy (there are black clouds of battle and death on the other side of the channel that separates the two countries, in the right lower corner of the drawing), which is filling its own coffers (that is, the Hanoverians', not Great Britain's) through its policies.

Allusion is the underpinning of George Romney's paintings *Mirth* and *Melancholy*, said to be renditions of Milton's companion poems; they were exhibited in 1770 at the Free Society of Artists. They aim at communicating the attitude of each concept, not any kind of illustration of the poems. His *L'Allegro and Il Penseroso*, together in one painting with no representation of anything in the poems, acts as an allusion for those who know the poems but there is no interpretative directive. Robert Smirke's two ovals (ca. 1780) depicting scenes from "L'Allegro" contrast Romney's by showing, not Milton's visions, but the artist's fleshing out of lines as Milton could have seen them: *The Village Festival* and *Walking in the Woods*. Such influence from a line or an image is frequent in nineteenth- and twentieth-century art, such as Samuel Palmer's or H. M. O'Kane's.

Milton's poems have repeatedly been rendered musically as well: through settings of the texts, stage adaptations, operas and oratorios, and compositions inspired by the subject. Only a very few can be mentioned here. While no music for it is known, *The State of Innocence, and Fall of Man* (1677) by John Dryden inaugurated operatic renditions of *Paradise Lost*, being confined usually to the action of Book 9, "the Fall Book." Andrew Marvell objected to the "tinkling Rhime" that

Dryden's "tagging" produced, but Nathaniel Lee praised his "mighty Genius" that "refin'd" Milton's "Golden Ore." As we move to the European Continent, we find Jean-Nicholas Servandoni's setting *Le Chute des anges rebelles* [*The Fall of the Rebellious Angels*] (1758). While Richard Jago's "adaptation to music," "Adam; or, The Fatal Disobedience" (1768), lacks the music, Benjamin Stillingfleet reworked the epic into an oratorio with music by John Christopher Smith in 1760. The best known employment of Milton's epic is Franz Josef Haydn's *Die Schöpfung; ein Oratorio* [*The Creation*] (1798, performed the next year). The libretto was by Thomas Lidley (Lindley, Liddell), revised by Baron Gottfried van Swieten. The attraction of the biblical story and Milton's version of it has continued through the intervening centuries. The world premiere of Krzysztof Penderecki's opera with libretto by Christopher Fry was given by the Lyric Opera of Chicago on November 29, 1978, with the narrative voice of Milton included, spoken by Arnold Moss who also played God's role. A dramatic reading of Books 1 and 2 by The Lark Ascending, directed by Nancy Bogen, in New York City, offered in its 2001 performance three preludes by Richard Brooks, which create atmosphere and characterize Hell and Satan, Pandemonium, and Chaos. Incidentally, there is also a published but unproduced film scenario from 1973, *Milton's Paradise Lost: Screenplay for Cinema of the Mind* by John Collier. As with influence in the illustrative arts, musical adaptations have varied in their focus. Specific passages rather than the epic's full sweep have been repeatedly treated by composers. Among these, "The Morning Hymn" (5.155–208) has often been interpreted, for example, by Johann Ernst Galliard (1728), Philip Hart (1729), Benjamin Cooke (in 1773), Johann F. Reichardt (ca. 1800), and Sir George Dyson (1958, called "Hail Universal Lord").

Just as with their fate in academic study, Milton's other works have not been particularly popular with composers. *Paradise Regain'd* was rendered in music by Carl Barbandt in 1756 and again in 1868 by Walter Leigh. Among the oratorios that Georg Friedrich Händel produced, *Samson* (1742) has frequently been performed, including a staging at the Lyric Opera of Chicago in 1985. The librettist was Newburgh Hamilton, who incorporated passages from "On the Morning of *Christs* Nativity" and "At a Solemn Music" into his text. Händel employed sections from Milton in other oratorios as well: *Alexander Balus*, *Jephtha*, and *An Occasional Oratorio*. His composition of *L'Allegro ed il Penseroso* (1740), not an oratorio though sometimes so labeled, has a text by Charles Jennens and often appeared on the stage in the eighteenth century. Jennens misunderstood Milton's poems and produced as a middle section "Il Moderato." In 2005, Mark Morris choreographed a full-length ballet of *"L'Allegro, il Penseroso ed il Moderato,"* based on "the music of Handel and the words of John Milton and Charles Jennens." It was performed in New York and elsewhere for the twenty-fifth anniversary season of the Mark Morris Dance Group. A number of the shorter poems have moved composers to set their texts or to create musical impressions of them. "Song: On *May* Morning" is a favorite, beginning with Michael C. Festing's award-winning composition in 1740; and, for other examples, James Battye's "Hail Bounteous May" (1840) and Arnold Cooke's (1967). Other versions of Milton's companion poems "L'Allegro" and "Il Penseroso" exist as music, as well as "At a Solemn Music," part of "Arcades," *Lycidas*, Psalms 8, 82, 84, 136, and the Nativity Ode (which includes Ralph Vaughan-Williams's *Hodie*, 1954).

Another important Miltonic piece with music is *A Mask*. Its revision named *Comus* – popularizing its most common and misleading title (see chapter 7) – by John Dalton, with music by Thomas Arne, was performed and published in 1738. Dalton's text is very different from the original. Elaborated and amplified, it incorporates a section from "L'Allegro" spoken by Euphrosyne. Again and again, songs were excerpted from this text in succeeding years and assigned to Milton although they were totally the work of Dalton. Performances and editions were numerous during the eighteenth century but a revision by George Colman in 1772 simplified and shortened the earlier version and held the stage often in the last quarter of the century. There have been a few successful productions of the Dalton/Arne work, as well as a recording. *Comus* also became the source for three ballets, one in 1930 with choreography by Frederick Ashton, another very important presentation by Sadler's Wells in 1942, this by Robert Helpmann, and another in 1946 by the International Ballet Company. Just as the Bible was understood by Milton's employment of it in *Paradise Lost*, so his own poems have often been known by musical and stage works that frequently do not offer *his* texts.

Imitations and Appropriations

We can learn much about Milton's poems from what later creative writers have discovered in them. Influence in literary materials takes many forms. It may be simply through allusion, through use of a quotation for a work's title; through epigraphs drawn from Milton's prose or poetry; often by quotation, even just a phrase or much of the time an adapted line; and, most subtly, by reaction to a subject or theme or emotional response. Such influence begins during Milton's lifetime, with Robert Baron's *Erotopaignion or the Cyprian Academy* (1647, 1648) and *Pocula Castalia* (1650), which have appropriations from various items in Milton's first collection of poetry, *Poems* (1645). The emergence of Milton's prosodic achievements have long been recognized in works by well-known writers: Andrew Marvell's *The First Anniversary of the Government Under His Highness the Lord Protector* (1655), "Last Instructions to a Painter" (1667), "The Garden," "Fleckno, an English Priest at Rome," "Upon Appleton House," "A Poem upon the Death of O. C." (these published in 1681); and John Dryden's *Absalom and Achitophel* (1681), *The Duke of Guise* (1683), and *Aureng-Zebe* (1685), with its imitation of a passage in *Samson Agonistes*.

But lesser known, and even unknown (anonymous), writers of the next century reveled in "Miltonicks," that is, blank verse, although many of these inferior efforts were only decasyllabic lines without rhyme. At times, titles only were appropriated for whatever allusive quality they might bring to an author's endeavors, for example, the anonymous *Paradise Lost and Paradise Regained by the Wonderful Works in God. In Verse* (1720?), H. T.'s "Paradise Regain'd" in *The Christians Magazine, or a Treasury of Divine Knowledge* (1761), or Ivan Vladykin's *Poteryannyi i priobretennyi rai. Poema* [*Paradise Lost and Regained*] (1776), erroneously thought of as a translation when it is, in fact, 17 books of Russian verse that show little influence from Milton. Structure and prosody are evident in William Mason's imitations of "L'Allegro" and "Il Penseroso" entitled "Il Pacifico" and "Il Bellicoso" (1764); and imaginative extension is seen in William Shenstone's "Eve's Speech in Milton, Upon Her Expulsion out of Paradise" (1737). The dramatic revision of *Paradise Lost* by Alexandre Tanevot, *Adam et Eve, tragédie nouvelle. Imitée de Milton* [*Adam and Eve, a New Tragedy, Imitated from Milton*] (1742), like Dryden's "opera," lies somewhere between translation and imitation and new work on a well-known theme.

One expression of the importance of Milton and his high evaluation by many in literary and religious matters will be seen in Mary O'Brien's "Ode to Milton" in *The Political Monitor: or Regent's Friend* (1790) (Shawcross 1972). "Hail, happy bard! With glorious thoughts inspir'd!/ Immortal themes thy lofty judgment fir'd," she begins; mortal themes belong to Greece and Rome, "More perfect truths beam forth in Milton's song." Her final lines raise the issue of his blindness, but his "orbs [. . .] Blaz'd in meridian flame beyond the sky." Milton's employment in political argument is represented in Conrad Ferdinand Meyer's "Miltons Rache" ["Milton's Revenge"] (written during the 1870s). Citing the numerous times (die "Stunde[n]") that have allowed the sons of Belial to wander forth in darkened streets, "flown with insolence and wine" (*Paradise Lost* 1.500–2), as the blind but visionary poet sang, the poem proclaims that the avenging poetry ("Miltons Rächerveerse"), inspired by the Celestial Patroness, remains, century after century, to counter the destruction of a republic (das "Grab der Republik") in his everlasting song, interwoven with truth and fiction ("Verwoben in sein ewig Lied"). Meyer's poem was written against the backdrop of the Franco-Prussian War.

Milton's influence has been shed productively not only on poetry but also upon drama and the novel. George Farquhar's *The Beaux Stratagem. A Comedy* (1707), a most popular and performed play even up to today, employs Milton's language a number of times, and William Mason's *Caractacus, A Dramatic Poem: Written on the Model of the Ancient Greek Tragedy* (1759, with an epigraph from "Manso," 38–41) reflects the structure, title character, and language of *Samson Agonistes*. The twentieth century has seen Clifford Odets's *Paradise Lost* (1935), which recounts the significance of the loss that besets a Jewish family in New York City with the cloud of the Depression upon them, and yet, as the title underscores, the characters can face a world all before them with Providence their guide. As Leo Gordon's final speech declares, "There is more to life than this! [. . .] That was the past, but there is a future. [. . .] Yes, I want to see that new world [. . .] Oh, yes, I tell you the whole world is for men to possess [. . .] The world is beautiful." As Harold Clurman says in his introduction, "The end of the play is a prologue" (Odets 1936: xii). Milton's epic also emerges in Samuel Beckett's deservedly commended *En attendant Godot* [*Waiting for Godot*] (1948–9), which Albert Labriola has demonstrated owes so much to *Paradise Lost*: their "ironic similarities [. . .] emphasize[] dialogue, characterization, tableau, and imagery [. . .] along with the intricacies of their interaction [. . .] Beckett may be participating in a dialectical encounter with Milton" (Labriola 1988: 216).

Two modern novels that really demand recognition of Milton's presence in them (there are many more) are Aldous Huxley's *Eyeless in Gaza* (1936) and Walker Percy's *Love in the Ruins* (1971). Aside from the title quotation from *Samson Agonistes* and its autobiographical nature, Huxley's negatively criticized novel (for both its structure and its philosophic stance) reflects Milton's message of a kind of mystical philosophy that understands the good life as the spiritual life, and a self-enlightenment that can derive from goodness and love. The stars shedding peace, mentioned earlier, have fallen upon Huxley's un-chronological treatment, as scenes and times shift back and forth, as do the interplay of past and present in Milton's dramatic poem and even more so in the unchronological treatment of *Paradise Lost*. Huxley demonstrates the interrelationships of everything that occurs in life or to a person, leading onward blindly but also repeating the past. Percy's *Love in the Ruins* sees at least a kind of religious hope persisting through the ruins that life has become. Its protagonist, Dr Tom More, is a wayfarer in life who registers the obliviousness of the "Paradise Estates" that he has passed through to the deterioration all around them. One must escape the "New Fall" experienced in the office of Monsignior Schliefkopf (the "sleepyhead") by employment of the "proper bronze sword" of the "somewhat prissy bronze archangel" Michael to unscrew the grill of the air conditioner in this hellish place. Percy, like Milton, hopes to educate us to the result of our misreading life and of the traps of our fallibility, and to suggest the means to overcome both "bestialism" and "angelism."

Attention to such major poets as British Romantics like Blake, Wordsworth, Shelley, and Keats has been repeatedly paid in critical examinations, and thus is not repeated here. As Peter Kitson remarks, "For the Romantic writers, Milton was, to a greater extent than Shakespeare, the prime precursor poet" (Corns 2003: 463). In certain ways *Paradise Regain'd*, particularly with its fourfold book structure, was as important as *Paradise Lost* to them, which along with some of their prose put Milton in the forefront of political thinking. Unfortunately William Godwin, William Blake, Mary Shelley, and her husband advanced the reading of Satan as hero first posited by John Dryden. While such a reading is perhaps an outcome of political/social issues of the time, the power of Satan's speeches, and the attraction that evil so regularly seems to provoke, it provides a faulty and incomplete view. The limitations of that view become clear when read alongside the texts discussed briefly above and those offered below in the "Further Reading" section.

A Close Look at Two Recent Examples of Influence

Quotations or adaptations and influence from Milton in later poetry will sometimes come upon a reader most unexpectedly. Those unexpected influences reinforce the extent and nature of Milton's importance for a variety of authors and demand that we evaluate which writers matter, which texts we pay attention to, and why we prioritize some influences over others. Some answers can be found in considering two late twentieth-century examples that supply allusion, greater understanding of the influenced work, quotation, and a redounding upon Milton's writing that may not always have been perceived and that certainly have been overlooked. Many readers might not think of the modernist US poet Louis Zukofsky (1904–78) as a Miltonist, but they would be wrong – even though the index to the complete 1978 edition of Zukofsy's major poem *A* does not cite Milton. The Miltonic influence, however, is clear at the verbal and ontological level in this 24-poem epic. "Poem 14," written in 1964, includes as a stanza, "Fly which/ way shall/ I fly" (319), and we remember Satan's "which way shall I flie/ Infinite wrauth, and infinite despair?/ Which way I flie is Hell; my self am Hell" (*Paradise Lost* 4.73–5). We are not then surprised that Zukofsky follows the stanza with "whose eye/ views all/ things at// one view" and for which we need no annotation as to whose eye: God's. The "precincts of/ light" that ensues recalls the Father's sighting of Satan as "he wings his way/ Not farr off Heav'n, in the Precincts of light" (3.87–8), flying ultimately toward Paradise. In Milton's Paradise, Satan will find "without Thorn the Rose" (4.256); in "Poem 14" the narrator finds that the "old/ Ocean smiles// without thorn." Two stanzas later "the neighboring/ moon Paradise/ of Fools" (320) continues Satan's journey in Book 3. Both poems point frankly to "embryos and/ idiots" ("14" 321; *Paradise Lost* 3.474), and the poet remarks that "space may/ produce new// worlds" and "Thee// Tsiyon feet/ nightly visit," echoing the narrator of *Paradise Lost* who told us of the Celestial Patroness who "deignes/ Her nightly visitation unimplor'd" (9.21–2).

Those verbal echoes reveal an intense conversation between these poets about the issue of vision: poetic and readerly. The poet of "Poem 14" remarks: "I started/ back it// started back/ what thou/ seest what// there thou/ seest thyself/ with thee// it came/ and goes/ but follow// me" (320); and is then asked and answered, "Whom/ fliest thou?/ who thou// fliest of / him thou/ art." In Milton's poem, it is Eve who recounts her first sight of herself in the smooth lake: "I started back,/ It started back [. . .] a voice thus warn'd me, What thou seest,/ What there thou seest fair Creature is thy self,/ With thee it came and goes" (4.462–9). But then Adam cries aloud, "Return fair *Eve*,/ Whom fli'st thou? whom thou fli'st, of him thou art" (4.481–2).

Marking the difference of source and influenced text, of influence and originality, Zukofsky's modern narrator is both Satan and Eve, and his quandary is answered by the godhead within him. This long poem with various other echoes or adaptations from various authors investigates the "lost Paradise" (324) of life and of the self in various locales, at numerous times, over years, through many countries and languages, through events and people from the past and from the present, and ends:

> (one:
> three)
> Sun
> eye   (358)

The clue to the poem's substance and organization lies in the influence seen from Milton's *Paradise Lost*, the depiction of where it all began: the omniscience of God, the evil of Satan, the Fall of the first parents and the woe that it brought, but there *is* "Praise/ Coming forth by/ day *on* earth" and there is always song, music. There is the "eye" that sees all and its pun "I" that places life's answer within the self.

The reader may feel that some of the lines quoted above do not finish a thought. That technique, I would suggest, points us to the indirections of life and, aptly enough for this discussion, to the nature of influence, with unstated cognitions that we may (or should) discern. As Basil Bunting wrote to Zukofsky in a letter dated February 3, 1951, he, like Milton, had a "fit audience, though few" (MS, Harry Ransom Humanities Center). Mark Scroggins (1998) relates the technique of highlighting the unstated to Ronald Johnson's 1977 poem *Radi Os*, a version of Milton's epic that has been "erased" (Shawcross 1982). That is PARADISE LOST with PA SE L T erased. The technique is used throughout, as in the poem's ending: "For proof look up,/ And read/ Where thou art" remains from erasures in *Paradise Lost* 4.1010–13: "for proof look up,/ And read thy Lot in yon celestial Sign/ Where thou art weigh'd, and shown how light, how weak,/ If thou resist." Little has been written about this specific poem from *A*, although Milton is cited when references to it do appear. Barry Ahearn astutely emphasizes its "isolation," the "matter of the reclusive poet's relation to the larger world," in which he finds himself "upside down in a public role," for this becomes an inventory that illuminates the poet's life as he talks to himself (Ahearn 1983: 160–1). Indeed, one can find

Milton in *Paradise Lost* as one in isolation, one upside down in his public life, one trying to convince himself that *his* "solitarie way" will finally find a "place of rest."

Translations of Milton's works have been needed for the most part to bring them to non-English-speaking lands; these begin in 1682 with Ernst Gottlieb von Berge's *Das Verlustigte Paradeis*. Primarily it has been *Paradise Lost* that has appeared in (among others) German, Latin, French, Italian, Spanish, Portuguese, Dutch, Swedish, Danish, Russian, Polish, Hungarian, Hebrew, Chinese, Japanese, Korean, and Urdu, but selections from the shorter poems as well as *Paradise Regain'd* and *Samson Agonistes* have also appeared, adding Norwegian and Greek. As one significant example that has not been acknowledged adequately, we can point to the major Argentinean author Jorge Luis Borges (1899–1986). Borges was decidedly a Miltonist, often commenting upon or quoting him in prose and poetry and in interviews (the numerous "conversations" that have been published). *The Literary Universe of Jorge Luis Borges: An Index to References and Allusions to Persons, Titles, and Places in his Writings*, compiled by Daniel Balderston (1986), notes Milton many times in 14 different publications. Among these, Borges remarks that one might initiate the study of English in order to appreciate the *intrinicados* [involvements] of Milton in *El libro de arena* [*The Book of Sand*] (1975). In the Prologue to *La rosa profunda* [*The Insightful Rose*], he counsels that we must read what the Hebrews and Milton called Spirit and what "nuestra triste mitología llama lo Subconsciente" ["our melancholic mythology calls the subconscious"]. Of this poem, which few people seem to have read, Borges asserted, "It's a poem about the last rose that Milton had in his hand and then I think of Milton holding the rose up to his face, smelling the perfume; and of course he wouldn't be able to tell whether the rose was white or red or yellow. I think that's quite a good poem. Another poem about a blind poet" (Burgin 1969: 78). He had previously written "Una rosa y Milton" (*El otro, el mismo* [*Another, yet the same*], 1964), which is immediately preceded in the volume by "El otro" with its reference to Milton and shadow, and uniting and interrelating the two poems. The rose of his "shining verse" is mesmerizingly "Gold, blood red or ivory or dark/ Like an invisible rose in his hands."

Four poems arise from the interfacing of the two poets' blindness: "On His Blindness" from *El oro de los tigres* [*The Tigers' Gold*] (1972), "El ciego" ["The Blind Man"] and "Un ciego" ["A Blind Man"] from *La rosa profunda*, and again "On His Blindness," which Borges wrote shortly before his death in 1986. The English title is, of course, the title that has been assigned to Milton's sonnet "When I consider how my life is spent." In the first of Borges' sonnets "las rosas/ Invisibles y [. . .] las silenciosas/ Multitudes de oros y de rojos" ["the invisible roses and [. . .] the silent multitudes of golds and reds"] appear as in the above conversation but within specific reference to Milton. In the first poem on the blind man, a double sonnet, Borges is again saddened by the lack of dawn, of setting sun: there is night only, nothing else. "Con el verso/ Debo labrar mi insípido universo" ["By verse I am obliged to build my insipid universe"] ends the first sonnet. Now, the second laments, only the constant yellow shapes that he is allowed to see make seeing his *pesadillas* [nightmares] possible. Perhaps in the background here is Milton's sonnet "Mee thought I saw my late espoused saint," which ends with the unforgettable lines: "But O as to imbrace me she enclin'd,/ I wak'd, she fled, and day brought back my night."

Milton is specifically named in "Un ciego," as are the "silenciosa" and "las rosas." Borges' self-reflective blind poet may be able to see his dear Sabría on this extraordinary evening: needed only are the comfort and the braveness of Milton. Borges' return to this subject shortly before his death in 1986 records his experience of lost sight "After many years": "circling near/ me is an obstinate and luminous haze"; and this becomes formless and colorless, "almost a mere idea," "a blur of light." Milton described his experience with the "sovran vital Lamp" of the Heavenly Muse that gives spiritual heat if little ocular clarity thus: "thou/ Revisit'st not these eyes, that rowl in vain/ To find thy piercing ray, and find no dawn;/ So thick a drop serene hath quencht thir Orbs,/ Or dim suffusion veild" (*Paradise Lost* 3.21–6). Borges recasts Milton's words in these four poems, as we can observe, ending his last dejected truth, like Milton once again, "For others there remains the universe;/ in my half-light: the habit of my verse."

These last two authors illustrate the shedding of sweet influence that Milton and his works have affirmed over the years: through allusion, through quotation, through adaptation of feelings and experience, language itself and belief, through literary composition and imitation. Although Milton's influence may have created anxiety for some authors, as Harold Bloom has seen, it also has been the power behind compositional form and substance, and a source of philosophic and political reflections. That influence may be patent or subtle, superficial or deep, but it exists and cannot be ignored. We read other authors more astutely by knowing the Miltonic influence that may have existed for them, for seemingly unrelated occurrences in life and different worlds, but also we identify in Milton and his works perceptions that otherwise may have been missed without the dancing of the Pleiades before the Sun.

References

Ahearn, Barry (1983). *Zukofsky's "A": An Introduction*. Berkeley: University of California Press.

Balderston, Daniel, compiler (1986). *The Literary Universe of Jorge Luis Borges: An Index to References and Allusions to Persons, Titles, and Places in His Writings*. Westport: Greenwood Press.

Borges, Jorge Luis (1977). *Obra poética 1923–1977*. Buenos Aires: Emecé Editores.

Borges, Jorge Luis (1988). "On his Blindness." Trans. Willis Barnstone. *American Poetry Review* 17.5: 21.

Burgin, Richard (1969). *Conversations with Jorge Luis Borges*. New York: Holt, Rinehart and Winston.

Corns, Thomas (ed.) (2003). *A Companion to Milton*. Malden: Blackwell.

French, J. Milton (1949–58). *The Life Records of John Milton*. 5 vols. New Brunswick: Rutgers University Press.

Labriola, Albert C. (1988). "'Insuperable highth of loftiest shade': Milton and Samuel Beckett." In Albert C. Labriola and Edward Sichi, Jr (eds), *Milton's Legacy in the Arts* (pp. 205–17). University Park: Pennsylvania State University Press.

Masson, David (1946). *The Life of John Milton*. 7 vols. New York: Peter Smith.

Milton, John (1643–4). *Doctrine and Discipline of Divorce*. London: T. P. and M. S.

Milton, John (1644). *Areopagitica*.

Milton, John (1971). *The Complete Poetry of John Milton*. Edited by John T. Shawcross. Garden City: Anchor.

Odets, Clifford (1936). *Paradise Lost: A Play in Three Acts*. New York: Random House.

Scroggins, Mark (1998). *Louis Zukofsky and the Poetry of Knowledge*. Tuscaloosa: University of Alabama Press.

Shawcross, John T. (1972). *Milton 1732–1801: The Critical Heritage*. London: Routledge and Kegan Paul.

Shawcross, John T. (1982). "*Paradise Lost*: 'Erased'." *Milton Quarterly* 16: 80–1.

Tayler, Irene (1973). "Say First! What Mov'd Blake? Blake's *Comus* Designs and Milton." In Stuart Curran and Joseph Wittreich (eds), *Blake's Sublime Allegory: Essays on The Four Zoas, Milton, & Jerusalem* (pp. 233–58). Madison: University of Wisconsin Press.

Walker, Mary, Lady Hamilton (1779). *Munster Village, a Novel. In Two Volumes*. Dublin: Peter Hoey.

Zukofsky, Louis (1978). "*A*". Berkeley: University of California Press.

John T. Shawcross

Further Reading

Bloom, Harold (1973). *The Anxiety of Influence: A Theory of Poetry*. New York: Oxford University Press.

Bond, Richmond Pugh (1932). *English Burlesque Poetry, 1700–1750*. Cambridge, MA: Harvard University Press; repr. New York: Russell and Russell, 1964.

Boss, Valentin (1991). *Milton and the Rise of Russian Satanism*. Toronto: University of Toronto Press.

Cass, Jeffrey (2003). "Miltonic Orientalism: *Jane Eyre* and the Two Dalilas." *Dickens Studies Annual* 33: 191–213.

Curran, Stuart A. (1971). "The Mental Pinnacle: *Paradise Regained* and the Romantic Four-Book Epic." In Joseph Wittreich (ed.), *Calm of Mind: Tercentenary Essays on* Paradise Regained *and* Samson Agonistes *in Honor of John S. Diekhoff* (pp. 133–62). Cleveland: Case Western Reserve University Press.

Damrosch, Leopold, Jr (1981). *God's Plot & Man's Stories: Studies in the Fictional Imagination from Milton to Fielding*. Chicago: University of Chicago Press.

Di Salvo, Jackie (1983). *War of Titans: Blake's Critique of Milton and the Politics of Religion*. Pittsburgh: University of Pittsburgh Press.

Dowden, Edward (1908). *Milton in the Eighteenth Century (1701–1750)*. London: Proceedings of the British Academy; repr. Folcroft, PA: Folcroft Library Editions, 1969.

Gillet, Jean (1975). *Le Paradis perdu dans la litterature française de Voltaire à Chateaubriand*. Paris: Librairie Klincksieck.

Griffin, Dustin (1986). *Regaining Paradise: Milton and the Eighteenth Century*. Cambridge: Cambridge University Press.

Grey, Robin (1992). "Surmising the Infidel: Interpreting Melville's Annotations on Milton's Poetry." *Milton Quarterly* 26: 103–13; rev. in Grey, *The Complicity of Imagination: The American Renaissance Contests of Authority, and Seventeenth-Century English Culture* (pp. 213–27). Cambridge: Cambridge University Press, 1997.

Grey, Robin (ed.) (2002). Special Issue: Melville and Milton, *Leviathan: A Journal of Melville Studies* 4; repr. as *Melville and Milton*. Pittsburgh: Duquesne University Press, 2004.

Havens, Raymond D. (1922). *The Influence of Milton on English Poetry*. Cambridge, MA: Harvard University Press; repr. London: Russell and Russell, 1961.

Keeble, N. H. (1987). *The Literary Culture of Nonconformity in Later Seventeenth-Century England*. Athens: University of Georgia Press.

Kelley, Mark, Lieb, Michael and Shawcross, John T. (eds) (2003). *Milton and the Grounds of Contention*. Pittsburgh: Duquesne University Press. See esp. John T. Shawcross, "The Deleterious and the Exalted: Milton's Poetry in the Eighteenth Century" (pp. 11–36); David Norbrook, "John Milton, Lucy Hutchinson and the Republican Biblical Epic" (pp. 37–63); Sharon Achinstein, " 'Pleasure by description': Elizabeth Singer Rowe's Enlightened

Milton" (pp. 64–87); Annabel Patterson, "Inventing Postcolonialism: Edmund Burke's Paradise Lost and Regained" (pp. 88–114).

Kreuder, Hans-Dieter (1971). *Milton in Deutschland: Seine Rezeption im latein- und deutsch-sprachigen Schrifttum zwischen 1651 und 1732*. Berlin: Walter de Gruyter.

Labriola, Albert C. and Sichi, Edward, Jr (eds) (1988). *Milton's Legacy in the Arts*. University Park: Pennsylvania State University Press.

Low, Lisa and Harding, Anthony J. (eds) (1994) *Milton, the Metaphysicals, and Romanticism*. Cambridge: Cambridge University Press.

Moore, Leslie E. (1990). *Beautiful Sublime: The Making of* Paradise Lost, *1701–1734*. Stanford: Stanford University Press.

Myers, Robert Manson (1956). *Handel, Dryden, and Milton*. Cambridge: Bowes and Bowes.

Nardo, Anna K. (2003). *George Eliot's Dialogue with John Milton*. Columbia: University of Missouri Press.

Nelson, James G. (1963). *The Sublime Puritan: Milton and the Victorians*. Madison: University of Wisconsin.

Newlyn, Lucy (1993). *"Paradise Lost" and the Romantic Reader*. Oxford: Clarendon Press.

Parker, William R. (1940). *Milton's Contemporary Reputation*. Columbus: Ohio State University Press.

Pointon, Marcia R. (1970). *Milton & English Art*. Toronto: University of Toronto Press.

Pommer, Henry F. (1950). *Milton and Melville*. Pittsburgh: University of Pittsburgh Press.

Rajan, Balachandra (ed.) (1978). "The Presence of Milton," special issue of *Milton Studies* 11.

Redman, Harry, Jr (1994). *Major French Milton Critics of the Nineteenth Century*. Pittsburgh: Duquesne University Press.

Robertson, J. G. (1908). *Milton's Fame on the Continent*. London: Proceedings of the British Academy; repr. Folcroft, PA: Folcroft Library Editions, 1970.

Scherpbier, H. (1933). *Milton in Holland: A Study in the Literary Relations of England and Holland before 1730*. Amsterdam: H. J. Paris.

Schulz, Max (1985). *Paradise Preserved: Recreations of Eden in Eighteenth Century England*. Cambridge: Cambridge University Press.

Sensabaugh, George (1952). *That Grand Whig, Milton*. Stanford: Stanford University Press.

Sensabaugh, George (1964). *Milton in Early America*. Princeton: Princeton University Press.

Shawcross, John T. (ed.) (1970). *Milton: The Critical Heritage* [1624–1731]. London: Routledge and Kegan Paul.

Shawcross, John T. (1991). *John Milton and Influence: Presence in Literature, History and Culture*. Pittsburgh: Duquesne University Press.

Shawcross, John T. (1994). "Milton and Epic Revisionism." In Steven M. Oberhelman, Van Kelly and Richard J. Golsan (eds), *Epic and Epoch: Essay on the Interpretation and History of a Genre* (pp. 186–207). Lubbock: Texas Tech University Press.

Shawcross, John T. (1995). "Fruitful Region, Splendorous Vegetation: Some Remarks on *Rasa* and Sir William Jones, and the Influence of John Milton." In K. Venkata Reddy (ed.), *M. V. Rama Sarma: His Mind and Art* (pp. 13–24). New Delhi: Prestige.

Shawcross, John T. (1998). "John Milton and his Spanish and Portuguese Presence." *Milton Quarterly* 32: 41–52.

Van Anglen, K. P. (1993). *The New England Milton: Literary Reception and Cultural Authority in the Early Republic.* University Park: Pennsylvania State University Press.

Vogler, Thomas A. (1971). *Preludes to Vision: The Epic Venture in Blake, Wordsworth, Keats, and Hart Crane.* Berkeley: University of California Press.

Williams, Meg H. (1982). *Inspiration in Milton and Keats.* London: Macmillan.

Wittreich, Joseph (ed.) (1970). *The Romantics on Milton.* Cleveland: Case Western Reserve University Press.

Wittreich, Joseph (1975). *Angel of Apocalypse: Blake's Idea of Milton.* Madison: University of Wisconsin Press.

Wittreich, Joseph (ed.) (1975). *Milton and the Line of Vision.* Madison: University of Wisconsin Press.

Wittreich, Joseph (1987). *Feminist Milton.* Ithaca: Cornell University Press.

Wittreich, Joseph (1997). " 'Under the seal of silence': Repressions, Receptions, and the Politics of *Paradise Lost.*" In Peter E. Medine and Joseph Wittreich (eds), *Soundings of Things Done: Essays in Early Modern Literature in Honor of S. K. Heninger Jr* (pp. 293–323). Newark: University of Delaware Press.

Chapter 3

"The world all before [us]": More than Three Hundred Years of Criticism

Roy Flannagan

In the year he died, 1674, Milton could not have been at all be sure what would become of his poetry or if he would become famous as a poet. He was in disgrace as a regicide who had endorsed the killing of the reigning monarch Charles II's father, and he was in disrepute among respectable Christians as someone who wrote pamphlets defending what his opponents called "divorce at will." Between the first edition of *Paradise Lost* in ten books in 1667 and its second edition in 12 books in 1674, Milton surely received personal compliments on his masterwork, but he could not be sure that its memory (and that of his other poetry and prose) would not quickly die because of his reputation as a king-killer and domestic troublemaker.

Milton saw to it that *Paradise Lost* was well printed, despite his blindness, in an accurate, if simple and modest, quarto rendition of his text, absent of either the ornamental trappings or prestige of a "great book." We have the manuscript of Book 1, now in the J. P. Morgan Library in New York City, and we can see in it the process of the printer's marking off sections for each day's composition. Because Milton was friendly with so many printers, stationers, and booksellers, and because he seems to have seen pamphlets like *Areopagitica* through the press, we can assume that, even though he had been blind for many years before the publication of his epic, he might have attended to such things as spelling, punctuation, and perhaps even the spacing between the lines. The epic as it was originally printed is not crowded on the page and is easy to read. Though *Paradise Lost* was printed modestly, on the scale of a first novel by an unknown author in the twentieth century, Milton must have intended for his text to gain fame on its own, but he did not live to see his fame as the great English epic poet. Sales were tepid, initially. Not long after the epic was first published, the printer asked Milton to provide prefatory matter and poetry by the political chameleon Andrew Marvell and by royal physician Samuel Barrow in support of the epic; and the publisher, Samuel Simmons, may also have requested that Milton convert the less conventional ten books to 12, in order to satisfy the poetry-reading public that *Paradise Lost* was indeed a proper epic.

There is evidence that in his last years Milton was trading on his goodwill with publishers. After *Paradise Lost* had appeared in 1667, the epic must have gained at least enough momentum for the poet's published work to cause Milton to send *Paradise Regain'd* and *Samson Agonistes* to the licensor in 1671 for joint publication. Shortly thereafter, in 1673, he also reedited his own *Poems*, originally published in 1645, to which he added *Of Education*, one of the most important "fillers" to a slender volume in publishing history. The publication of these poetic works and the prose of the early 1670s that Robert Fallon notes in chapter 1 of this volume form a kind of media blitz. All signs indicate that Milton was trying to raise money or raise his chances of immortality by getting as much of his work into print or back into print at the end of his life.

Canonization

It was not until 1688 that any of Milton's texts was honored by a form of publication best known now for its association with William Shakespeare and Ben Jonson, the folio volume. Larger than most modern coffee-table books and composed of a single printer's sheet folded just once, the folio of *Paradise Lost* in Milton's honor made the poet a star worthy of immortality. Over 500 worthy and wealthy citizens of England's "Nobility and Gentry" subscribed to Jacob Tonson's expensive and impressive 1688 folio, signing their names in support of the man and the poet Milton. Illustrators were hired who could copy Michelangelo's Adam and Eve from the Sistine Chapel for the illustration that accompanies Book 12 and who could pay close attention to the narrated events in the epic. The illustrations provide some of the best early critical commentary on the events of the poem, while also giving pictorial validity to such hard-to-imagine figures as Sin and Death.

With the publication of a folio, Milton joined the ranks of poets like Shakespeare and Jonson, and Queen Elizabeth I's historian William Camden and King James I's sometime favorite Sir Walter Ralegh, each of whom deserved folio publication of a masterwork. In the 1688 folio, published 14 years after his death, Milton's chief work became a classic, worthy of being compared by England's first official poet laureate John Dryden to the glories of classical Greece and imperial Rome – to the epics of Homer and Virgil. Dryden's prefatory poem sets a generic line of succession from Greece to Rome to England:

> *Three* Poets, *in three distant Ages born,*
> Greece, Italy, *and* England *did adorn.*
> *The* First *in loftiness of thought Surpass'd;*
> *The* Next *in Majesty; in both the* Last.
> *The force of* Nature *cou'd no farther goe*:
> *To make a* Third *she joynd the former two.*

In 1667, Dryden had tried to tag his own work on Milton's growing fame by publishing his operatic play based on *Paradise Lost, The State of Innocence, and Fall of Man* (1677), written not in Milton's blank verse but in the heroic couplets fashionable during the Restoration.

There is the danger of complacency or boredom as soon as one's work is put on a shelf of classics. The danger of being lost in bookshelf oblivion was even greater for *Paradise Lost* because its author had aimed only at a small, exclusive audience, "fit [. . .] though few" (7.31). Also, the text as originally published was quickly treated with familiar contempt: by the late seventeenth century, the texts of *Paradise Regain'd* and *Samson Agonistes* had both been published in what were degenerate transcriptions of the primary editions. Publishers added many errors through careless editing. At the same time that Milton's work was coming to be regarded as classic, Milton's texts were not being well preserved. The story of the perseverance of Milton's texts is as complex as the texts themselves.

An English Literary Criticism Begins

The last quarter of the seventeenth century saw the emergence of formal literary criticism in England, spearheaded by John Dryden, with much attention to genres such as heroic tragedy, the comedy of mode or the comedy of manners, and poetic satire. The leftover effects of the Protestant Reformation and what might be loosely called the Puritan movement had always encouraged close examination of texts (primarily the Bible) for etymologies, allusions, and cross-references. When Patrick Hume's 321-page folio *Annotations on Milton's* Paradise Lost appeared in 1695 as the first work of written critical commentary on Milton's poetry, it must have overwhelmed its readers by its erudition, its respect for the poet, and its thoroughness. Hume's breadth of knowledge and mastery of languages rivaled Milton's. Hume treated the epic as being as deserving of analysis as the Bible itself. His annotations take about as much space per line of poetry as a commentary on Genesis would take per line of biblical prose or poetry. Just as Michelangelo's Sistine Chapel might serve its viewers as an illustrated Bible, shorthand theology, Milton's epic, for some readers, began to take the place of the Bible as a source of sanctified information, especially with the story of the Fall in Genesis. Bunyan's *Pilgrim's Progress* and Milton's *Paradise Lost* both were seen throughout the eighteenth and nineteenth centuries as guides to Christian theology, dramatized.

In the early eighteenth century, in a series of essays first published in 1712 in *The Spectator* and widely reprinted afterwards, most notably in translations of Milton's works, Joseph Addison brought Milton into the English household through the London clubbiness of the first newspaper readers. Addison introduced generic terms like "Divine Poem" in his critique of Milton's epic, and he popularized the word "Fable" as meaning the plot, and sometimes the "moral," of an epic poem. Addison's 12 essays dealing with the 12 books were the first attempts at summary plus explication, and they are remarkable for their clarity and simple style as well as their good taste and sophistication. Addison set the tone and the standard for all subsequent criticism of Milton's epic.

Of course, as with all literary criticism, even early Milton editions confirmed the need for the caution "Reader, beware." In his declining years in 1732, Richard Bentley, an irascible classical scholar who picked nits and fought with his fellow dons at Cambridge over textual issues, produced a notorious edition of *Paradise Lost*, for which he invented a wicked publisher/editor/compositor who, according to Bentley, got the text all wrong. It was Bentley's self-appointed mission to get rid of lines or even lengthy passages that he did not like, and change others according to the neoclassical standards of his own era, using the invented rotten editor as an excuse. When Bentley did not like Milton's lines, he rewrote them, using the corrupt editor as his scapegoat. Bentley was immediately attacked by critics more sensitive than he to Milton's poetic style. David Mallet summed up what Bentley did to Milton in a poem addressed to Alexander Pope: "The *Roman Muse* [Bentley] arigns his mangling pen,/ And *Paradise*, by him, is *lost* agen" (Mallet 1733: 137–8). Most of Bentley's omissions and emendations seem ludicrous today, but some have been used by modern editors to examine the texts of 1667 and 1674 more closely, and a very few of Bentley's emended phrases have proved to be sensible improvements. For instance, at *Paradise Lost* 7.451, the first three editions have "Let th'Earth bring forth Foul living in her kinde," but Bentley argued for "Soul," and many sensible modern editors – like me, in *The Riverside Milton* – accept his emendation.

Throughout the eighteenth century, the best-respected editors of Milton, such as Bishop Thomas Newton, reacted to Bentley's scholarly hack-work. As Marcus Walsh puts it, "Precisely because Bentley's edition was so generally unacceptable it concentrated minds wonderfully" (Walsh 1997: 77). Bishop Newton created the first variorum edition, an attempt to collect all that was worthwhile from early commentary such as that of Patrick Hume. Unlike Bentley, Newton felt it necessary to look closely at Milton's biography and at his other works in prose and poetry for information that would help interpret the major poetry.

Beginning in the early nineteenth century, Henry John Todd (1763–1845) amassed huge stores of notes for all the poetry together with biographies for his very posthumously published *Some Account of the Life and Writings of John Milton* (1970). Cribbing from seventeenth- and eighteenth-century sources such as Hume, he produced his own variorum edition that again linked Milton's complex writings to his equally complex life. The poetic works of Milton, even more than the distant dramatic works of Shakespeare, lend themselves to annotation because they are full of literary allusions, biblical references, encapsulated world history, scientific knowledge, and what might be called deep etymology – the meanings of words traced through the many languages under Milton's command. Newton's leather-bound editions in the mid to late eighteenth century and Todd's gilt-edged editions at the beginning of the nineteenth century continued to dignify and canonize Milton's poetical works, as the interest in Milton's prose works grew outward from *Areopagitica* and *Of Education* to include the less well-known divorce tracts and the *History of Britain*. Newton's and Todd's commentary, fair and thorough, make their collections collectable rare books (a 2004 sale catalogue lists Newton's edition of the three major works at over $1,100), still valuable to editors and scholars.

Samuel Johnson's Brilliant Negatives and the Romantics' Dark Tributes

By the middle of the eighteenth century, the great biographer, critic, and lexicographer Samuel Johnson could react to Addison's praise of Milton in his own biased and heavily politicized biography and critical remarks on not only *Paradise Lost* but also many of the shorter works. Johnson set a kind of standard for cross or irritated remarks on Milton's life and work. Johnson seems to take Milton the regicide personally, as if Milton were still threatening to the existence of the British monarchy. From his Tory perspective, Johnson thought Milton's political career destructive of monarchy and domestic stability in England. Johnson certainly did not like Milton the man, but Johnson's brilliant phrasing made sure that each of his negative remarks would become the beginning of subsequent critical debates. For instance, is the genre of pastoral inevitably "easy, vulgar, and therefore disgusting" (Shawcross 1972: 293)? Johnson's brilliant phrasing in his often angry summaries cannot be ignored by later critics, nor can his accusations against Milton the man, the poet, or the dramatist. Even in this twenty-first century volume, Paul Alpers offers a fresh response (see chapter 6) to Milton's pastoral poetry, one that must necessarily refute Johnson's dismissal of the genre. Johnson described Milton as having a "Turkish contempt" for women (despite Milton's being married three times, writing memorial poems to women, and having close intellectual relationships with noblewomen). Later biographers have implicitly and explicitly answered Johnson's accusation of misogyny.

In general, the sophisticated poets and essayists of the late eighteenth and early nineteenth century saw Milton from a more international perspective than did Johnson. They read his life and works in light of the French Revolution. Milton was redefined as a revolutionary, a heroic Republican resisting the authority of an unjust and degenerate monarchy. They often made him into even more of a rebel than he was in real life, a free spirit, an artist, a prophet. When William Wordsworth rings out that memorable line, "Milton! thou should'st be living at this hour," in a section of his published sonnets devoted to liberty, he seems to be calling to an ancient spirit symbolizing freedom: "Oh! raise us up, return to us again;/ And give us manners, virtue, freedom, power./ Thy soul was like a Star and dwelt apart." Milton becomes a saintly revolutionary in the early Romantic period only to be converted, with the late Romantic William Blake, to one "of the Devil's party without knowing it." Throughout the Romantic period, however, Milton remains the "true Poet," as mystical as a medieval saint, as mysterious as a psychic or a medium, and a champion who was easily mythologized as a dark genius.

Perhaps not in a critical but in a worshipful mode, Wordsworth memorized sections of *Paradise Lost* and read others aloud to his friends and his sister (Wittreich 1970: 123). Keats and Shelley both made extensive notes in their copies of *Paradise Lost*, and their marginalia is preserved for its own sake in Miltonist Joseph Wittreich's collection. Milton was often read aloud or had his poetry recited from memory in the nineteenth century. Interestingly, though very few Milton scholars of the twentieth or twenty-first century have memorized long passages from *Paradise Lost* or from any of the poems longer than sonnets, there has been a growing recent interest in reading or performing his works, as with "Milton marathons," during which many people read all of *Paradise Lost* at sittings that last from 9 to 12 hours. These events possess a sense of veneration for the blind poet bard compelled to recite *Paradise Lost*, *Paradise Regained*, and *Samson Agonistes* to amanuenses.

With such keen attention, *Paradise Lost* became an elemental component of Romantic thought, shading and clarifying poetic expressions. Lord George Gordon Byron and Percy Bysshe Shelley were both in attendance at the ghost-story-telling session that prompted Mary Shelley to write *Frankenstein*, which is a dark Romantic answer to Milton's myth of Paradise and once-perfect people. Perhaps the most influential Romantic novel, Shelley's *Frankenstein*, first published in 1818, was built on the Prometheus myth and on the idea of a monstrous Adam, perhaps closer kin to Milton's Satan than to Aeschylus's Prometheus, subject of her husband Percy Shelley's "Prometheus Unbound." In fact, Percy Shelley added the quotation of *Paradise Lost* 10.743–5 to the first edition of his wife's novel: "Did I request thee, Maker, from my Clay/ To mould me Man, did I sollicit thee/ From darkness to promote me?" Byron's *Don Juan*, even as an extended mock epic in regular stanzas, has to measure up to *Paradise Lost*.

Romantic critique of Milton's works, however, was limited neither to *Paradise Lost* nor to literary tributes. The pastoral elegies written to the memory of dead poets – John Keats's "Endymion," Shelley's "Adonais," Alfred Tennyson's "In Memoriam," Matthew Arnold's "Thyrsis" – all trade on Milton's *Lycidas* as the model in the genre. The English Romantic painter Henry Fuseli created his 1799 Milton Gallery to depict the dark psychological sides of Milton's poetry, concentrating on un-settling and irrational dreams, nightmares, and on horrid imaginings visualized in terms of things that go bump in the night – bright things that come out of the darkness of one's unconscious brain. As Marcia Pointon describes in *Milton and English Art* (1970), Fuseli is often identified with the sublime, but he is also the artist of psychological terror. Less grotesque but just as dramatic is the illustrative work of John Martin, who in the first half of the nineteenth century mastered the art of etching in mezzotint the gradations between extreme light and darkness. Martin can show the extremes of Satan's glory and his desolation as well as any artist who has interpreted Milton.

Other Romantics also wrote critical essays. William Hazlitt and Samuel Taylor Coleridge both made their mark on Milton criticism (Wittreich 1970). Hazlitt noted Milton's excellent prose style in pamphlets as little known as the *Apology for Smectymnuus*. He could understand that Milton's being a good poet made him a better prose writer and that "this [grace in writing prose] probably arose from [his] just sense of metre." With equally subtle appreciation, Coleridge also noticed that, "Milton is not a picturesque, but a musical, poet." Coleridge commented on Milton's grandeur (as compared to the sublimity so often discussed in the eighteenth century) and the "delicate beauty of sound" in Milton's matching of words from line to line in *Lycidas* (Wittreich 1970: 230, 235, 245, 258). Coleridge, Shelley, and Keats were as much interested in the sound of Milton's verse as they were in the imagery.

The Romantic whose works provide us with the most extensive and generically diverse commentary on Milton is William Blake. His rela-tionship with Milton is more complex, more psychological, more sym-bolic, more confrontational, and perhaps more upsetting than that of any other Romantic poet or great essayist. Blake answered Milton's Christian theology even in a title like *The Marriage of Heaven and Hell*. (C. S. Lewis was to answer Blake in his own theological allegory, *The Great Divorce* [1944].) Blake investigated the attractiveness of Satan and was capable of seeing both Dante and Milton as atheists at one time or another in their poetical careers (Wittreich 1970: 96). Blake's long and complex poem *Milton* (1804) attempted to liberate Shake-speare and Milton, "both curb'd by the general malady & infection from the silly Greek & Latin slaves of the Sword" (38). The silly Greek and Latin slaves, according to Blake, were Homer and Virgil, from whom Shakespeare and Milton had to escape. In Blake's scheme, Milton subscribed to his own form of biblical inspiration and to his form of sexualized Christianity. Blake thought deeply about and interpreted Milton and criticized his works astutely, both by his poems in which Milton or his characters became Blake's characters, and through his graceful paintings. He illustrated his own poem *Milton* as well as editions of Milton's various poetic works, from "L'Allegro" through *Paradise Lost*. Blake sees himself as divine and prophetic interpreter of Milton, a kind of Milton medium – not logical or even rational, but inspired. It has fallen to subsequent critics to try to interpret what Blake meant in his reading of Milton the man and of Milton's poetic works.

Toward the Twentieth Century: Milton the Man

At close to the turn of the nineteenth century, David Masson finished his monumental biography of John Milton, "Narrated in Connexion with the Political, Ecclesiastical, and Literary History of his Time," and attitudes changed once again. Milton could no longer be the mythical figure constructed by William Blake. Masson's seven volumes of information, still unsurpassed in its collection of facts and contexts, was to Milton what the *Oxford English Dictionary* was to English lexicography: it collected all the significant data about the life of the poet, adding newly discovered information, newly perceived historical contexts, and a sweeping view of English literature in the seventeenth century. Masson's monument had to change critical perspectives toward the poet, because informed readers came to understand the poet and the poet's works better than they had ever been understood before.

How many literary critics of the early twentieth century actually read Masson is debatable, but Masson could not be ignored, nor could British history during the seventeenth century, after Masson covered it so thoroughly; nor could Milton's classmates at Cambridge; nor could obscure figures like Hermann Mylius, who had the chance to observe Milton from a foreigner's perspective, first-hand. Within the first three pages of the beginning of Masson's biography John Aubrey's sketches of the Milton family coat of arms are reproduced, in facsimile, so that the reader may examine primary evidence just as Masson saw it. Masson was an inspiration to later biographers in his use of primary materials.

The first great twentieth-century biography of Milton was the monumental Oxford University Press *Milton: A Biography* of William Riley Parker, first published in two thick and dense volumes in 1968. Parker used to joke that creating the wonderful index for that volume – just the index – nearly made him as blind as his subject. Parker himself drew from not only Masson but also J. Milton French's *Life Records of John Milton*, published by Rutgers University Press in 1949, but both biographers were hindered by the problems of collecting information in England during World War II. In 1996, Gordon Campbell corrected and augmented Parker's work, then in 2003 Barbara Lewalski issued her "critical" biography (the "critical" in this case means that literary works are analyzed as the biography proceeds) in its second, revised edition, in one volume, from Blackwell. Cedric Brown, Gordon Campbell, John Shawcross, and Edward Jones have also contributed significantly to the Milton chronology and to the adding of facts, plus the adding of the flesh of life to the bare bones of dry facts. Gordon Campbell's small but fully packed *Chronology* is especially noteworthy for getting all the facts right and setting them in proper order. Even I have tried my hand at biography, a slim, portable volume for everyday use, *John Milton: A Short Introduction* (Blackwell, 2002).

The Twentieth Century, Positive and Negative

As with Samuel Johnson's harsh criticism of Milton the man and poet, still being addressed in the twenty-first century, it was negative criticism in the early twentieth century that set critics to defending Milton the man and Milton the poet. Sir Walter Ralegh famously called *Paradise Lost* a "monument to dead ideas," which set several generations the task of validating seventeenth-century Puritan theology, social theory, divorce law, regicide, and incomplete notions of the freedom of the press. The modernist poet and critic Ezra Pound found the worship of what he considered the second-rate poet Milton deplorable. And T. S. Eliot, with his preference for the enigmatic wit, colloquialism, particularity, and rough metrics of John Donne, also famously accused Milton of representing a "dissociation of sensibility," a break between sincere emotion and poetry (Murray 1967: 3), which set other critics to defend the grand scope of Milton's theology as expressed in his epics and his tragedy. In reaction to Eliot and Pound, critics began seeking Milton's relevance to Eliot's jazz age, Picasso's powerful painting *Guernica*, or modernism in general. Milton was found anew to be a grand psychologist, sometimes following Freud (according to William Kerrigan) and sometimes Jung (according to John Shawcross). He was found to be doing much the same thing that James Joyce did in his epics *Ulysses* and *Finnegan's Wake*, in that he was building a coherent worldview out of the particular psychological state of Adam and Eve in Eden and out of it.

Milton was rediscovered as a grand Christian apologist by such critics and theologians as Owen Barfield and C. S. Lewis. His place in Christian theology was determined by "Christian tradition" studies, notably those by C. A. Patrides, F. Michael Krouse, and J. Martin Evans. In the 1940s, Milton's *De Doctrina Christiana* was examined under a critical microscope by Maurice Kelley in *This Great Argument* (1941), which attempted a point-by-point comparison between Milton's Latin treatise and *Paradise Lost*. Kelley's enormous labor of love has recently been called into question by a team of scholars from both sides of the Atlantic who have examined the provenance of the *De Doctrina Christiana*, all of them following William Hunter's question, first posed at the Fourth International Milton Symposium held at the University of Vancouver, British Columbia, "How do we know if Milton wrote this treatise?" The team of linguists, biographers, textual critics, and stylometricians, including John Hale, Gordon Campbell, Thomas Corns, David Holmes, and Fiona Tweedie, discussed the history, the translation, and the style of the treatise in a special issue of the *Milton Quarterly* in 1997, using computerized comparisons between Milton's Latin style in other published works and the style exhibited in different parts of the treatise. A major book on the subject is under contract at Oxford University Press.

Within just that one branch of scholarship are numerous fascinating cross-generational and cross-national discussions. The great British critic William Empson constructed a clever argument that Milton's God, and indeed the Christian God perceived from any perspective, is tyrannical, whimsical, abusive, sadistic, and unwholesome. In *Milton's God* (1961), Empson made Milton's God seem so bad that Canadian critic Dennis Danielson eventually had to answer with a book called *Milton's Good God* (1982).

The thumbnail sketch of just the line of investigation of Milton's Christianity reflects the collaborative nature, the conversation, in Milton studies. Scholars wrestle, agree with, and at times heatedly disagree not just with Milton but with each other. While nowhere approaching the quantity of Shakespeare studies, Milton studies in the twentieth century has been extensive enough for J. Martin Evans to be commissioned to produce his *John Milton: Twentieth Century Perspectives* (2003). At five volumes, it includes reprints of only the most influential and representative Milton scholarship.

My own role in Milton studies helps me show how individuals shape the field in collaborative, at times haphazard, and always serendipitous ways. In 1967, as a rash and unguided assistant professor, I began the first journal devoted to the study of Milton, the *Milton Newsletter*. The idea for the journal issued from my discussions with Merritt Y. Hughes at the Folger Library in Washington, DC, when I noticed that Hughes was in himself a clearinghouse of information because of all the scholars who wrote to him directly about their research, since his 1957 Odyssey Press edition of the poetry and selected prose had become the standard edition. In other words, people were telling only Hughes bits information that really needed to be distributed to the community of scholars all over the world who were working on Milton. Based in my home-state of Ohio, the journal began as a newsletter in order to solicit and collect all news fit to be distributed, but it quickly became the *Milton Quarterly* in 1970 as scholars in the rich and explosive sixties sought a place to publish rather than perish. At first, British scholars looked down their noses at the colonial effort, saying things like "In America, there is even a *Milton Newsletter*," or using terms like "the Milton industry," but eventually the journal, and then, beginning in 1969, its correlative hardbound, annual journal *Milton Studies*, began to publish substantive articles, useful abstracts, monographs, and even editions of the poet's work.

Those articles are often the eventual products of gatherings of scholarly friends, in the form of what are formally called academic conferences. The Milton Society of America has had meetings every year since the 1940s in conjunction with the annual Modern Language Association (MLA) meetings in late December: members describe the annual dinner as a quiet oasis away from the bustle and worry of the MLA convention. The first International Milton Symposium in July of 1981, organized by Ronald Shafer and Albert Labriola (who was to become the second editor, after James Simmonds, of *Milton Studies*), was the first attempt to honor Milton with a gathering on his home turf, in London and Chalfont St Giles. On three to four year intervals, there have been international symposia in cities across the world – at Cambridge, Florence, Bangor, Vancouver; in my newfound home Beaufort, South Carolina; and Grenoble. Not long after that first Symposium, in 1981, texts of Milton were flying across the Atlantic in the ozone, generated by the computer, and people were talking about computer-generated concordances to Milton (the poetry concordance at Oxford University Press, 1972, had been the first, followed by the Medieval and Renaissance Texts and Studies concordance to the prose in 1985). The global village envisioned by Marshall McLuhan was becoming a reality for the community of Milton scholars.

The computer had a long-range effect on creating and maintaining the community of Milton scholars that comprise Milton studies. In the early years of accessible internet, many of us investigated listservs such as Humanist, Ficino, and Shaksper, leading eventually to Kevin Creamer at the University of Richmond and myself founding Milton-L in 1991. The Milton-L home page (www.richmond.edu/~creamer/milton/about.html) describes the founding of the listserv and the present mission of the discussion group to keep members posted about current meetings, publications, and awards. For the sake of brevity, I have not even touched upon the growing interest and inclusion of Miltonists in non-Anglophone countries; but of course electronic media have certainly contributed to expanding the depth and breadth of Milton studies. The experience of the contributors of this volume is a model for the use of all available resources for cooperative work. The editor invited the international group of contributors based on her professional relationships with some and on her knowledge of their work in the forms of articles, chapters, and books. Then, in the midst of the volume's preparation, some of us had the good fortune of meeting each other at the International Milton Symposium in Grenoble. Also, contributors have emailed in chapters, easing editorial and publication tasks. And, finally, you might have noticed that I have often mentioned publishing houses, as I do here. I do so because I do not want to take for granted the many institutions that act as the nexuses for all these efforts.

What has happened since the explosion of research coming especially from North American universities from the 1960s to the present is that Milton scholars have explored in ever expanding formats every critical area that represents the fads and fascinations of the last third of the twentieth century: colonialism, postcolonialism, psychology, feminism, queer theory, structuralism, history of the book, computer-generated stylistics, ecological criticism, semiotics, multiculturalism, textual criticism, new historicism – you name it, Miltonists are there, and often in the lead. Milton biographer William Riley Parker was the sixty-ninth president of the MLA, with its 30,000 plus membership; was the editor of the MLA's influential journal *Publications of the*

Modern Language Association (*PMLA*); and is honored by the MLA's oldest prize, the William Riley Parker Prize for an Outstanding Article in *PMLA*. Miltonists have also been at the forefront on critical investigation. In 1963, Northrop Frye, the widely read University of Toronto mythographer, brought an archetypal perspective to the study of Milton with *The Return to Eden*, having provocative chapter titles like "The Story of All Things," for comments on Milton's version of the Eden myth, and "Revolt in the Desert," for the plot of *Paradise Regain'd*, in which Jesus resists the sterile temptations of Satan in a sterile environonment. And, in 1967, Stanley Fish began what was to become the reader-response school of criticism with *Surprised by Sin: The Reader in* Paradise Lost. Diane McColley's *Milton's Eve* (1983), though it was not intended to be a revolutionary manifesto at all, became a kind of Bible of feminist criticism to a generation of readers.

Into the Twenty-First Century, the World All Before Us

Milton research is still flourishing and still growing. At the turn of the twenty-first century, interest in Milton's science has increased and blended with an ecological perspective. Building on the past three hundred years of criticism, recent Milton criticism has seriously examined the natural world as recreated in Milton's poetry, from the early enthusiasm for daffodils and insect sounds of the twin poems "L'Allegro" and "Il Penseroso" and *Lycidas* to the maturity of Eden's walled garden or the sterile desert in *Paradise Regain'd*. Two of the more junior scholars in this volume, Juliet Cummins and Angelica Duran, are in careful conversation with their predecessors who have tried to determine Milton's role in the development of modern science. Their diverse backgrounds – the first, an Australian attorney; the second a first-generation Chicana – demonstrate the continued attraction that many feel to the long-dead male writer from England. In *Milton and the Natural World: Science and Poetry in* Paradise Lost (1999), Karen Edwards at the University of Exeter – also a contributor to this volume – combines the scientific experiments of the Royal Society with the discovery through optics of the microscopic life of plants, insects, and animals. Diane McColley shows how channels of study blend with one another within Milton studies but also within individual scholars' studies. In *Poetry and Music in Seventeenth-Century England* (1997), McColley, with as much finesse as she showed in *Milton's Eve*, traces the environmental movement back into the concerns of Milton's era for harmony in music as it was made parallel with harmony in the natural world and in seventeenth-century mathematics.

The torch of Milton studies is passing from generation to generation as I write. I recently turned over the reins of *Milton Quarterly* to Edward Jones, moving the seat of the journal from Ohio University to Oklahoma State University. At the same time the journal and *Milton Studies* have been increasing readership in places like Bulgaria and Taiwan. The world of Milton studies has been expanding from the Balkans to the Pacific Rim and Asia at large. Because of services such as Milton-L, college or high-school students who ask the list for help should be aware that, through the power of the computer and electronic mail, their questions may provoke or inspire future articles.

Just as Milton was uncertain in 1674 as to what would become of his works, at no time since could anyone have predicted where Milton studies would lead. In the same vein, I am uncertain about the future directions of Milton studies except to say that Milton's works continue to reward study and that past criticism provides a rich foundation. To be honest, there is a certain thrill in being ignorant of outcomes, or to invoke the amazing image that ends *Paradise Lost*, to be in a position where you can appreciate that the world is all before you, not just behind you.

References

Mallet, David (1733). *Of Verbal Criticism: An Epistle to Mr. Pope. Occasioned by* Theobald's Shakespeare *and* Bentley's Milton. London.

Milton, John (1998). *The Riverside Milton*. Edited by Roy Flannagan. Boston: Houghton Mifflin.

Murray, Patrick (1967). *Milton: The Modern Phase: A Study of Twentieth Century Criticism.* London: Longman.

Shawcross, John T. (ed.) (1972). *Milton 1732–1802: The Critical Heritage*. London: Routledge.

Walsh, Marcus (1997). *Shakespeare, Milton, and Eighteenth-Century Literary Editing: The Beginnings of Interpretative Scholarship*. Cambridge: Cambridge University Press.

Wittreich, Joseph Anthony, Jr (ed.) (1970). *The Romantics on Milton: Formal Essays and Critical Asides*. Cleveland: Case Western Reserve University Press.

Part II

Textual Sites

Chapter 4

First and Last Fruits of Education: The Companion Poems, Epistola, and Educational Prose Works

Angelica Duran

You cannot teach anyone anything: you can only help him to find it within himself.

Galileo Galilei

While Milton is rightly recognized as one of the most erudite poets of English literature, we would be mistaken to think that his learning came easily for him. He found himself regularly studying late into the night, indicating great interest but not precociousness; he entered Christ's College, Cambridge at the age of 16, "later than several of his schoolmates but better prepared than most" (Lewalski 2000: 13); he took seven years (1625–32) to earn his Baccalaureate and Master of Arts degrees but with no less than *cum laude*. The social aspects of his education were equally uneven. While he had warm relationships with his private tutor Thomas Young and master at St Paul's School Alexander Gil, he was rusticated (that is, suspended) after a still ambiguous altercation with his first Cambridge tutor, William Chappell; and, while he had a close friendship with Charles Diodati, he seems to have been a bit of an outsider with the general lot of students at

61

college, where by his own admission he found "almost no intellectual companions" (Milton 1953–82 [*CPW*] 1.314).

Such ambivalent experiences are articulated implicitly and explicitly in his writings. At times Milton locates the impediments to the productive use of his learning on himself and personal circumstances. In his early twenties, in "Sonnet 7: How soon hath time" (1632?), he laments that he has "no bud or blossom" to show for all his preparation (4); in his forties, in "Sonnet 16: When I consider" (1652?), he urgently seeks and finds "patience" in reconciling himself to his blindness, which will make applying his "one talent" even more difficult (8, 3); and even in his late blooming epic *Paradise Lost* (1667), he feels compelled to state that he is "not sedulous by nature" (9.27). Of course, he does not blame himself alone. Throughout his prose, he unleashes invectives toward pedagogues as the bane of his own education, his beloved nation, and humankind in general, men "who pollute all learning, divine and human, by their frivolous subtleties and barren disputations," "grievous Wolves," "unbending tutors," "babblers," "dancing divines," "hirelings," "driveling monks," and more. And, he does not gloss over the frustration that many earnest students and teachers feel about those who do not take education seriously, the "dullest and laziest youth, our stocks and stubbs" (*CPW* 2.376). In his earliest prose pieces, his *Prolusions* (assigned, intensive academic exercises), his frustrations with school bubble just under the surface. It is perhaps because of his own difficulties in education that he so vividly captures its varied aspects both in his earlier works with the experiences of being a student and a teacher fresh on his mind, and in works written near his death with equal vigor if different form.

We can look to Milton's works from a variety of genres and periods of his life to chronicle his enduring engagement with learning and education. We look first at Milton's poetic expressions of the youthful joys of learning, "L'Allegro" and "Il Penseroso" (1631–8?) – favorites of the Romantics, who also gloried in marrying erudition with personal passions. The playful tone of those companion poems is matched by the earnestness of his moving Latin epistola "Ad Patrem" (1631–8?) in which the young Milton gives thanks to his father for supporting his formal and informal education. From these poetic pieces, we turn to Milton's short educational tract *Of Education* (1644), published when he was a teacher in his own elite home-school; then to what essentially can be considered history and language textbooks published near the end of his lifetime, *Accedence Commenc't Grammar* (1669), *History of*

Britain (1670), *Art of Logic* (1672), and *A Brief History of Moscovia* (first published in 1682 but given to the publisher "sometime before his death" [*CPW* 8.475]).

Passion

Inviting beloveds to "come" to them primarily in octosyllabic couplets, the youthful and charmingly self-referential narrators of "L'Allegro" ["The Happy Man"] and "Il Penseroso" ["The Contemplative Man"] announce the poems' literary descent from Christopher Marlowe's famous seduction poem "Come live with me." L'Allegro invites personified Mirth to "come thou goddess fair and free,/ In Heav'n yclept Ephrosyne,/ And by men, heart-easing Mirth," while Il Penseroso prefers the very "goddess, sage and holy [. . .] divinest Melancholy" that L'Allegro rejects. He beckons, "Come pensive nun, devout and pure,/ Sober, steadfast, and demure." ("L'Allegro" 1–3; "Il Penseroso" 11, 31–2). The differences in Milton's mock seduction poems from the seduction poem genre highlight the educational modality of "L'Allegro" and "Il Penseroso."

Marlowe's poem is short, implying the narrator's passionate impatience for his beloved's consent. Also, its images are very accessible: valleys, groves, hills, and fields. These settings and others, like the "beds of Roses," comprise the secluded natural environment in which Marlowe's narrator offers his beloved gifts that ornament her eminently present body: the woolen "gown," the "Fair lined slippers" for her feet, the "belt of straw and ivy buds" for her waist (13, 15, 17). He takes nature into his hands to make items for an intimate, erotic relationship. "L'Allegro" and "Il Penseroso," on the other hand, saunter for 152 and 176 lines respectively, and allude to myths, urbane experiences, and books associated with higher learning. Correlatively, the companion poems are much more populated and are set in both natural and man-made settings. For example, L'Allegro instructs Mirth not to come empty-handed but instead to bring the personified "Jest and youthful Jollity,/ Quips and Cranks, and wanton Wiles,/ Nods, and Becks, and wreathèd Smiles" as well as "sweet Liberty" (27–9, 37). While Milton titillates readers by having the narrator suggestively ask Mirth and her companions to "admit me of thy crew/ To live with her, and live with thee,/ In unreprovèd pleasures free," he comically envisions quite moderated pleasures: "To hear the lark begin his flight" and listen to the bird all night long (38–40, 41). Il Penseroso woos Melancholy in similar fashion. She is to bring "calm Peace, and Quiet,/ Spare Fast" as well as "The Cherub Contemplation" (46–7, 54). Hardly the company for an exciting tryst. While the narrator cites his attraction to Melancholy's "holy passion," he teases her, suggesting that he seeks her only "'Less Philomel will deign a song" and goes so far as to shift his address from Melancholy to the mythological nightingale: "Thee chantress oft the woods among,/ I woo to hear thy even-song" (41, 56, 63–4). What does Il Penseroso ask from the potentially rebuffed beloved? Their nighttime activities would include having "gorgeous Tragedy/ In sceptred pall come sweeping by," or, in the day, walking the university's "studious cloister's pale," or hearing the church "organ" and "choir" (97–8, 156, 161, 162). Finally, the narrators end their respective poems specifying that the beloveds, not the narrators, are to give: "These delights, if thou canst give,/ Mirth with thee, I mean to live" and "These pleasures Melancholy give,/ And I with thee will choose to live" ("L'Allegro" 151–2; "Il Penseroso" 176–7).

Milton's companion poems actively and playfully refer to yet disengage from erotic relationships. The contrast to Marlowe's poem is again illuminating. Marlowe's narrator envisions an immediate, secluded companionship, where "*we* will sit upon the rocks,/ Seeing the shepherds feed their flocks" ("Come live with me" 5–6, emphasis added). Milton's L'Allegro, on the other hand, imagines only *his* leisurely viewing and, at one point, keeps his eyes off the beloved for ten lines before finally relegating her entirely: "Straight mine eye hath caught new pleasures/ While the landscape round it measures" (69–70). His lone eye is so distanced from the beloved that it allows him to imagine when he sees "Towers, and battlements" that "perhaps some beauty lies" therein (77, 79). Il Penseroso goes even further. He envisions no beauty in the "high lonely tow'r" but rather himself, alone, viewing the stars through a telescope, "Where I may oft outwatch the Bear" (86, 87).

What is the effect of the narrators' discomfited interactions with the personified passions Mirth and Melancholy? It creates what J. Martin Evans calls the "Miltonic moment," in his book of the same title (1998), a moment of transition from one stage to another. In this case, the moment is from educational preparation to application. The narrators are mentally organizing and safely responding to the academic subjects in the worlds of memory and futurity, the very same processes that graduating students experience when seeking to apply what they have learned. The sexual undertones indicate the passion and productivity with which they wish to imbue those applied endeavors, which stand in contradistinction to typical medieval and Renaissance characterizations of education. For example, in medieval characterizations, "Mother Grammar" leads young, male students to a firm understanding of the language arts, especially logic, through which they will communicate within the society in which they live. That formulation connotes a hierarchical relationship in which students feel deep honor and respect similar to that connoted in the again maternal term for one's formal institutions of learning, *alma mater*. Milton constructs distinct female personifications. Instead of a maternal figure associated primarily with the language arts to be used primarily within the human world, Milton constructs eroticized figures – potentially productive partners – associated with attitudes that can be applied to all studies in the human and natural worlds. That small but important modification reflects the historical moment in which humanism was converting through scientific revolution into modernity. As historian of science and education John Gascoigne reminds us of this period, "The universities had been founded to preserve and refine society's store of knowledge, and the idea of 'research' – of adding to rather than simply conserving what was known – only slowly took root in the universities, some of whose members felt [it was] no more their business to add to the existing body of knowledge than a librarian feels obligation to write new books" (1989: 392).

Both Milton's narrators unabashedly and repeatedly filter their world visions through the curriculum in which they have been so obviously instructed, the *trivium* of grammar, logic, and rhetoric, as well as the *quadrivium* of arithmetic, geometry, astronomy, and music. Significant to the reality of the curricular bifurcation of the arts and sciences during the period, L'Allegro envisions a primarily artistic vocation and Il Penseroso a primarily scientific one. Greg Zacharias notes in passing the key feature of L'Allegro's artistic imagination at lines 81–8, when he "places inside the picaresque cottage the typical pair from pastoral literature, Corydon and Thyrsis" (1988: 9). Through his learned pastoralism, L'Allegro imagines a typical English landscape filled with characters derived from classical and Continental literature rather than a rural setting comprised of bad odors, weather concerns, and other elements that preoccupy laborers and tradesmen. Moreover, his pastoralism focuses eminently on the ways in which imaginative fictions address people's fears and concerns about the imperfect world in which they live. He imagines that, rather than resting "On a sunshine holiday," the populace of "The upland hamlets" tell stories of the lurking dangers of "faery Mab," "friar's lantern," "drudging goblin," and "lubber fiend" ("L'Allegro" 98–110). As with his view of the tower, the cottage, and the hamlet, he fills and filters the court through poetry, with "a masque," other "Such sights as youthful poets dream," and the plays of Jonson and Shakespeare (128, 129). All these desired gifts that Mirth might provide contribute to the poem's final vision of the narrator's anticipated great mature poetry, so great that it will make "Orpheus' self [. . .] heave his head" (145).

It is through reading "L'Allegro" prior to "Il Penseroso" that we find the educational curriculum interacting as it did during this early period of the English scientific revolution, as complementary elements. While "L'Allegro" concludes with a vision of great poetry, "Il Penseroso" concludes with a vision of some form of natural study and writing. Like, "L'Allegro," "Il Penseroso" pays tribute to poetry (96–115). However, the longer "Il Penseroso" adds significantly placed passages that extol natural studies. When Il Penseroso envisions the sequestered tower, he does not, like L'Allegro, subsume it into literary pastoralism but rather pictures it as a site for the study of nature, where he might

> unsphere
> The spirit of Plato to unfold
> What worlds, or what vast regions hold
> The immortal mind that hath forsook
> Her mansion in this fleshly nook:
> And of those daemons that are found
> In fire, air, flood, or under ground.
> (88–94)

These astronomical observations and the contemplation of the philosophies he has learned in his youth would form the basis for the advanced natural studies of his "weary age" (167).

Both poems speak to and from youthful yearnings for future rather than present practice and fulfillment. Yet, while the first ends with the anticipation of poetic production, the latter ends with one of scientific production. The relationship, however, is not antagonistic. These deceptively simple poems mirror the complex relationship of individuals and their educations, and of the arts and sciences in a still unified "advancement of learning," to invoke Sir Francis Bacon's famous term.

Gratitude

As much as Milton's mock seduction poems capture the passion for productive learning, "Ad Patrem" ["To My Father"] expresses gratitude for the privilege of education, a feeling Milton voices elsewhere as well (see especially *CPW* 1.808). Roy Flannagan defines "Ad Patrem" as Milton's poem of thanks to "his father, John Milton Sr., for the extraordinary support he gave to the education of his eldest son" and his justification for choosing the rather questionable vocation of poet, rather than for example the more profitable career of lawyer, as had his brother Christopher. While English translations must leave behind the sonorous beauty of Milton's Latin, the images and meanings translate well as testaments to the love for father, learning, and poetry.

The primary audience of "Ad Patrem" is the provider of Milton's education, his father. Milton acknowledges the extraordinary privilege that his father has provided him by characterizing education as a gift. He values and therefore enumerates his studies in all fields: "the beauties of Latin," "the lofty speech of the sublime Greeks," French, and Italian, as well as nonlinguistic studies, "the air that flows between earth and sky, and whatever the water conceals, and the bright, tossing surface of the sea" (79–87). Further, he characterizes his education as comprised of not only his schooling at home with his private tutor, St Paul's, and Christ's College but also his "studious retirement" after graduation: "into deep seclusion and delightful leisure by the Aonian stream, and you allow me to walk by Apollo's side" (75–6). Milton's erudite reference to Apollo – reminiscent of the erudite namings in "L'Allegro" and "Il Penseroso" – recalls specifically the various studies with which Apollo is associated – poetry, music, and medicine – as well as the natural environment over which the sun god Apollo reigns and which Milton enjoyed at his father's suburban homes in Hammersmith and Horton.

He characterizes his passion for study even more strongly than he does in the companion poems, as an erotic relationship with a naked goddess: "Knowledge [*scientia*] comes into view from behind the parting cloud. Naked, she visibly bends her face to my kisses – if I choose not to run away, if I do not find her irksome" (90–3). But even such a glorious vision cannot distract *this* narrator from expressing his gratitude, unlike the easily sidetracked narrators of the companion poems. In the next lines, Milton pays wonderful homage to his father for providing him with the means for such passionate fulfillment, challenging "whoever has an insane preference for the ancient treasures of Austria or the realms of Peru. What greater gift could a father have given – or Jove himself – though he had given all things except heaven?" (94–7).

Milton directly addresses the difficult emotions that arise with great gratitude. (Milton later ascribes a misguided version of this feeling to Satan, who significantly addresses the Apollic sun in *Paradise Lost* [4.32–113].) While the companion poems play with the idea of uneven roles in the relationship between narrator and imagined addressees, where Mirth and Melancholy would bring dowries to wooers whose interests are at times elsewhere, "Ad Patrem" actively and anxiously seeks to create a mutual relationship. Throughout the poem, Milton aspires to balance the financial and emotional gifts that his father has given him (the means of his education) with his intellectual and poetic gifts (the products of that education). Early in the poem, Milton refers to the poem itself and admits that "this page shows all my possessions, and I have counted out on this paper all the wealth that I own, for I own nothing but what golden Clio has given me" (12–14). He devalues the poem to a certain extent by characterizing it as a twice-given gift, something he received from the muse of history and now gives to his father. Later, he takes more credit for this and anticipated works, and increases the value of poetry. Milton likens poetry to "divine song," which shows "our divine source, our heavenly seed; nothing better graces by its origin the human mind, for poetry retains some holy sparks of the Promethean fire" (17, 18–20). He also characterizes his chosen poetic discipline as valuable because it is a sister to music, thereby complimenting his father, who was a musical composer. Milton ends the poem personifying and addressing his "youthful poems and amusements," asking them to express gratitude in the future: "if dark oblivion does not carry you down to crowed Orcus, then perhaps these praises, and the name of the father celebrated in them, will be preserved as an example for future ages" (115, 118–20). At the time, Milton did not know if this or any of his poems would be strong enough to withstand the test of time. We know they were; and, in a lovely homology of fictional desire and fact, Milton Sr lived until 1647, having seen the publication of his son's first poetic collection, *Poems* (1645).

The self-referential and even egocentric "L'Allegro," "Il Penseroso," and "Ad Patrem" provide us with a broad and realistic sense of the many emotions that dedicated students feel toward their education. With "Ad Patrem" we get the added sense of the importance of education within society. It is not just about individual students: it is also about those who have provided education and those in society who will benefit from an educated citizenry. As we move to Milton's prose tract *Of Education*, the social aspects of education are much more foregrounded so that rather than having poetic descriptions of the hopes for the future success for individuals, we have a prose prescription of the hopes for the same level of success for the nation and even humankind. These three early poems help us appreciate the intimate components of individual emotions that need to be taken into account to create the vanguard of the advancement of learning that Milton imagines in *Of Education*.

Hope

Milton penned *Of Education* roughly 12 years after he had left Cambridge and while he was in his short tenure as private teacher (1640–6) in his elite home-school. At this juncture in his life, Milton was successfully applying the knowledge that he had gained in his own education to the education of others, and it seems he wanted to see successful education spread from what his pupil and nephew Edward Phillips lovingly called a "House of Muses" to the nation and humankind at large (Darbishire 1932: 67). Interesting to our understanding of the relationship of the arts and sciences during Milton's lifetime is the fact that another of Milton's students was Richard Jones, the nephew of the experimentalist and co-founder of the Royal Society Robert Boyle, most famous today for "Boyle's Law of Pressure and Volume."

In the conclusion of the tract, Milton most clearly expresses his hope that, with the right curriculum, teachers, and personal wherewithal, England could serve as a model so that "then other Nations will be glad to visit us for their breeding, or else imitate us in their own Country" (*CPW* 2.414). Such an England would be populated by educated leaders who "deserve the regard and honour of all men" as well as heroic teachers with "sinews almost equall to those which Homer gave Ulysses" (*CPW* 2.414, 415). The whole of humankind, then, might advance toward the end of learning, which "is to repair the ruins of our first parents by regaining to know God aright, and out of that knowledge to love him, to imitate him, to be like him" (*CPW* 2.366). But how to achieve such an ambitious goal? Milton provides some practical answers, now primarily from the perspective of a teacher and citizen rather than of a student.

In *Of Education*, Milton's addressee is not a female personification or his father but rather Samuel Hartlib. That addressee immediately designates Milton's larger concerns because it extends not only beyond erotic and familial relationships but also to the eminent Prussian reformist who worked with the leading circle of London intellectuals for social improvement. As historian of science Charles Webster records, "Hartlib and his associates completely dominated the educational literature of the puritan Revolution, being responsible for at least fifty educational works between 1640 and 1660" (1976: 112). Hartlib was successful during both the Interregnum and the Restoration in his newfound homeland of England: for his composition and advocacy of educational legislation with the Long Parliament, Oliver Cromwell awarded Hartlib an annual pension of £300, and Charles II supported the scientific Royal Society of London which Hartlib had worked so hard with others to create. While the exact nature of Hartlib and Milton's relationship is still debated, the fact remains that Milton wrote himself into the national conversation about educational reform by publishing the tract as a letter to Hartlib in 1644 and adding it to his collection of poems *Poems &c.* (1673) nearly 30 years later.

The tract's recommendation of, essentially, a national system of schools of academies each holding "a hundred fifty persons, whereof twenty or therabout may be attendants [. . .] as shall be needfull in every City throughout this land" participated in the emerging ideal of universal education (*CPW* 2.379). Approaches to methods and subjects for classrooms were being reconsidered in European countries not just in terms of the replication and standardization required within such a system but also in terms of the information explosion outside of educational institutions caused by the ongoing recovery of ancient and classical texts, explorations of the known world, and new observations of the cosmos and its microscopic elements through new scientific technologies. These factors created great pressures within a closed system of time and human capacity, pressures that face educators today in making decisions about textbook selection, degree requirements, classroom syllabuses, and more. For the most part, educational reformists of the seventeenth century clung to but altered the established *studia generalia* and sought to legitimize subjects formerly studied through private instruction or travel abroad, and to subsume subjects like engineering into familiar disciplines.

The important shift of authority from the advanced level *trivium* to the previously lower level *quadrivium* and, in advanced studies, from theology and law to natural philosophy and medicine that occurred during Milton's lifetime is reflected in *Of Education*. Those curricular shifts worked to include larger sections of the population as both beneficiaries and participants in the advancement of learning. As taught during Milton's time, language studies were particularly geared toward those who "speak in Parliament or counsell" and "appear in Pulpits," that is clergy, politicians, and lawyers (*CPW* 2.406). Perhaps the tract's most moving image of the importance of the shift to practical disciplines and practitioners in all social classes is in its justification for the (then) inferior study of physic, or applied medicine. Milton recommends that it be taught with the following aim:

> that they may know the tempers, the humors, the seasons, and how to manage the crudity: which he who can wisely and timely doe, is not onely a great Physician to himselfe, and to his friends, but also may at some time or other, save an Army by this frugall and expenseless meanes only; and not let the healthy and stout bodies of young men rot away under him for want of this discipline; which is a great pitty, and no lesse a shame to the commander. (*CPW* 2.392)

Milton eschews any false division between the arts and sciences, as did his scientific contemporaries Robert Boyle and Isaac Newton, whose verbal skills enabled them to communicate their important scientific theories and findings so successfully. He instead divides studies between those that are useful and those that are not. For example, understanding the dynamic of the writing process as one of learning, Milton recharacterizes the end result of languages studies to include the production of "writers and composers in every excellent matter, when they shall be thus fraught with an universall insight into things" (*CPW* 2.406).

In Milton's hypothetical academies, students would be constantly schooled to contextualize their studies as important components of society primarily by two methodological means. The first would be in Milton's suggestion to include guest speakers from the artisan classes. He recommends, "To set forward all these proceedings in nature & mathematicks, what hinders, but that they may procure, as oft as shall be needfull, the helpfull experiences of Hunters, fowlers, Fishermen, Shepherds, Gardeners, *Apothecaries*; and in the other sciences, *Architects*, Engineers, Mariners, *Anatomists*" (*CPW* 2.393). Such engagements would broaden students' understanding about the value of rustic life beyond the equally important but otherwise limited view to be gained by reading only pastoral poems – as with the narrator of

"L'Allegro." The second would be in Milton's equally homey yet revolutionary recommendation for field trips: "In those vernal seasons of the yeer, when the air is calm and pleasant, it were an injury and sullennesse against nature not to go out, and see her riches, and partake in her rejoycing with heaven and earth." Starting at about 15 years old, students would "ride out in companies with prudent and staid guides" and not just for daytrips or to nearby attractions but rather "to all the quarters of the land: learning and observing all places of strength, all commodities of building and of soil, for towns and tillage, harbours and Ports for trade. Somtimes taking sea as farre as to our Navy, to learn there also what they can in the practicall knowledge of sailing and sea fight" (*CPW* 2.412). While fostering the practical and active, these activities would also necessarily promote social interaction between the students and persons of various socio-economic classes.

Compassion

Anticipating the question with which Annabel Patterson introduces Milton's sonnets in the next chapter – "Why would a man [. . .] write a sonnet?" – I introduce the last set of texts to be considered by asking, why would Milton write and publish textbooks? While my answer, "compassion," may not be the answer that readily comes to mind when considering any textbook, it is one that often describes the primary motivation for writers of textbooks as they make their way through the difficult task of envisioning then eventually producing them – it is by and large a rather thankless job. Compassion implies an emphasis on the recipients, the readers of textbooks. We can locate compassion in the voices of Milton's textbooks, ones that are quite distinct from the poetic voices of the youthful "L'Allegro" and "Il Penseroso," and of the at times combative, often impatient tones of the speakers in Milton's other works. We might think in particular of the voice of the sonnet "On the late Massacher in Piemont," which the editor of *The Riverside Milton* correctly refers to as "the poet's scream of anger, breathless and intense" (Milton 2000: 254). In contrast, the speakers of Milton's textbooks are in the background.

Milton republished *Of Education* in *Poems, &c.* (1673) at about the same time he published works most likely penned much earlier for use in his home-school of the 1640s: *Accedence Commenc't Grammar, History of Britain, Art of Logic,* and *A Brief History of Moscovia.* Just as he articulates his fear that *Paradise Lost* might not "fit audience find" (7.31), he voices similar concerns about his textbooks. However, unlike the transhistoric popularity of his poetry and the limited but important attention to *Of Education*, these texts have not been widely read (*CPW* 8.34). Like Milton's more popular works, however, they reward careful reading; and, when read in light of the context Milton lays out, they emerge as compassionate expressions of his desire to make learning easier for earnest scholars at large, to whom he addresses those texts.

Indeed, Milton's "compassionate" voice participates in the long historical development of the "dispassionate" plain prose as the conventional discourse of modern textbooks, whose ideal is the foregrounding of subject-matter and audience. The primary audience of Milton's textbooks may have been the students of his home-school. As such, they are testaments to the dialectical rather than authoritarian pedagogy of Milton's home-school. After describing the somewhat daunting reading list Milton assigned his students, Edward Phillips writes that "by teaching he in some measure increased his own knowledge, having the reading of all these Authors as it were by Proxy" (Darbishire 1932: 60). This passage expresses the belief of one of Milton's students that students were active participants in the development of learning rather than simply passive receptacles of the teacher's knowledge. But, of course, as published works these texts take on another significance. As Milton had written in his defense of brave publication *Areopagitica* (1644), books "doe contain a potencie of life in them to be as active as that soule was whose progeny they are" (*CPW* 2.492). As such, his textbooks act in *locus personae* of the absent history- and language-teacher Milton to a nation of students at the end of his lifetime and any era thereafter.

With his studies and life's experiences, Milton meets the requirements of his own definition of a historian. In a letter to Henry de Brass, Milton writes that, "This then is my view: that he who would write of worthy deeds worthily must write with mental endowments and experience of affairs not less than were in the doer of the same [. . .] I want a Historian not an Orator" (*CPW* 5.1.xlv) – we would do well to remember this definition when reading the "divine/ Historian" Raphael in *Paradise Lost* (8.6–7). Through Milton's synthesis and interpretation of past histories, student-readers would learn to read critically and efficiently rather than wade through accounts in willy-nilly fashion. Milton provides historical data and ways of reading history from his informed personal perspective with the express aim to "best instruct and benefit them that read" (*CPW* 5.1.4). While the eventual benefits would extend to the nation, Milton acknowledges that he is addressing a limited audience. His aims are immediate, practical, and public, as he writes in his characterization of, for example, "The Third Book" of *History of Britain*, which he hopes will be a "benefit to them who can judiciously read: considering especially that the late civil broils had cast us into a condition not much unlike to what the *Britans* then were in" (*CPW* 5.1.129). Judicious readers would not simply memorize but rather activate history for present use. Taking the ancient, microcosmic directive towards individuals to "know thyself" to the macrocosmic public level, Milton writes that "it be a high point of wisdom in every private man, much more is it in a Nation to know it self" (*CPW* 5.1.130). Milton's history, therefore, purposefully contains both favorable and unfavorable tales of the nation rather than depicting a steady, progressive development of British civilization or glossing over setbacks.

The public role of his other "history," *A Brief History of Moscovia*, is not to be understood primarily in its content and method, as with *History of Britain*, but rather in its form and organization. The much shorter, posthumously published *Moscovia* is more rightly called a cultural geography; or, perhaps George B. Parks comes closest when he characterizes the work as "more akin to a foreign-office briefing than to a book" and "a brief extract of the English experience" (*CPW* 8.463, 469). Milton's own title was simply *Moscovia: Or, Relations of Moscovia, As far as hath been Discover'd by English Voyages*. While it was not addressed to Samuel Hartlib as was *Of Education*, the Hartlib circle was interested in this work (*CPW* 8.459). Indeed, *Moscovia* collects and organizes information in Baconian fashion: Milton's compilation first describes common travel routes, then peoples, lesser traveled routes, political history, and finally English missions to Moscow in previous centuries. While it may strike us as uneven in design – for example, chapter lengths – *Moscovia* reads very much like some of the most valued histories and geographies produced by the scientific Royal Society of London. And, when read alongside, for example, Marco Polo's much older, also seemingly haphazard account of the discovery of foreign lands, *Voyages* (thirteenth century), with its uni-visual perspective, it becomes clear that Milton's text is one of recovery that synthesizes various sources to encourage a global conversation that would expedite the second wave of scientific discovery in early modern England.

With *Accedence Commenc't Grammar* and *Art of Logic*, Milton turns to the first two disciplines of the *trivium*. Unfortunately for us, absent are books on rhetoric and poetry (Milton added poetry as a fourth language study in *Of Education*). There is a *caveat*, however, because in *Accedence* Milton defines grammar as "right understanding, speaking, or writing Latine" (*CPW* 8.47). For Milton, then, grammar includes the characteristics that traditionally had been attributed to all three topics of the *trivium*. As much as Milton levels the divisions between comprehension and production, his matter-of-fact grammar-book levels the divisions between elite institutions of learning and autodidactic training. For centuries, Latin had been the exclusive language of the elite, used primarily in colleges, the church, and law courts. The full title of Milton's short, 65-page text articulates a distinctly egalitarian view: "*Accedence Commenc't Grammar, Supply'd with sufficient Rules, For the use of such (Younger or Elder) as are desirous, without more trouble than needs to attain the Latin Tongue; the Elder sort especially, with little Teaching, and their own Industry.*" His grammar proposes that Latin is readily available to anyone with the wherewithal to learn it; and, indeed, *Accedence* is a very useful tool, akin to some of the best course readers that my own undergraduate instructors compiled or composed for student – that is, my – benefit.

Since *Accedence* is so helpful and its publication a compassionate act, as I argue, we might wonder why Milton delayed its publication perhaps 30 years from its original composition. In the preface to William Lily's *An Introduction of the Eyght Partes of Speech, and the Construction of the Same*, Henry VIII ordered that "this englysshe introduction here ensuing, and the latyne grammar annexed to the same, and none other" was to be used in all English schools. Although statutes well through the end of the seventeenth century continued to authorize only Lily's grammar, Milton's *Of Education* recommends that students "begin with the chief and necessary rules of some good Grammar, either that being now us'd, or any better" (*CPW* 2.382). Milton's suggestion of a possible substitution for Lily's grammar, then, may seem defiant, but it is not entirely so. Many schoolmasters wrote their own handbooks for student use. Additionally, while divergent from Lily's method, 60 percent of the examples from Milton's *Accedence* come directly from Lily (*CPW* 8.56). Milton's conversations with other specialists are always complex. We see this more so in *Art of Logic*.

Milton's *Logic* opens by establishing a conversation that includes the sixteenth-century poet, statesman, and literary critic Philip Sidney and the French philosopher Petrus Ramus. Milton issues a qualified praise of both in the preface: among those who carefully cultivate logic, "the most deserving in my opinion as in the opinion of our good Sidney, is Peter Ramus" (*CPW* 8.208). He speaks of the long-deceased Sidney and Ramus as if they were present, as he does with the authors he admires and names in the text – Aristotle, Bacon, Boethius, Cicero, Fabius, Hippocrates, Plato, Polus, Tully, Xenophon, and more, all coming together for the benefit of student-readers in his short book. When reading *Logic*, one gets a sense of them all in the same room as in Raphael Sanzio's famous painting *The School of Athens* (1510?), with renderings of intellectuals of different disciplines and epochs, Alcibiades, Aristotle, Diogenes, Euclid, Plato, Ptolemy, Pythagoras, Socrates, Zeno, Zoroaster, and even Raphael Sanzio himself. Milton gathers all these teachers in his *Logic* for the benefit of the student-readers who are also ever present in the pages of the book.

Milton's discussions are relentlessly directed toward student use, "for the sake of practice" (*CPW* 8.211). Milton offers his unusually concise textbook – perhaps not as lovingly as he offered "Ad Patrem" to his father but no less diligently – as an alternative to other methods, "which these others have themselves thrown onto the heap" and which "are either uncertain or useless and thus impede the learner and burden him instead of helping him" (*CPW* 8.211). When one recognizes the compassionate labor needed to create these textbooks – or almost any other textbook – their erudition ceases to be daunting and begins to be exemplary, instantiating the very hope Milton articulates in *Of Education* that any teacher of language studies be able "to catch them" – that is, intrigue and excite students – "chiefly by his own example" (*CPW* 2.385).

In outlining only some of the most crucial aspects of this handful of Milton's works, I have sought to emphasize the emotions that they evince in aiding readers in overcoming personal limitations for personal and social benefit. Hence, my section titles. In the works discussed, Milton challenges and encourages us to do what the best scholars have done with their *education* (whose suffix "-ion" means "action") and *learning* (with its progressive "-ing" ending), which is to understand that both words denote and demand active engagement. That engagement in turn enables us to understand the distinct ways in which various genres of Milton's writings fulfill distinct but equally important functions for personal, national, and global advancements of learning.

References

Darbishire, Helen (ed.) (1932). *Early Lives of Milton*. London: Constable.
Evans, J. Martin (1998). *The Miltonic Moment*. Lexington: University of Kentucky Press.

Gascoigne, John (1989). *Cambridge in the Age of the Enlightenment*. Cambridge: Cambridge University Press.

Lewalski, Barbara (2000). *The Life of Milton: A Critical Biography*. Malden: Blackwell.

Masson, David (1859). *The Life of Milton: Narrated in Connexion with the Political, Ecclesiastical, and Literary History of His Time*. 6 vols. London: Macmillan.

Milton, John (1953–82). *Complete Prose Works of John Milton* [*CPW*]. Edited by Don M. Wolfe. 8 vols. New Haven and London: Yale University Press.

Milton, John (1999). *John Milton, the Complete Poems*. Edited by John Leonard. New York: Penguin.

Milton, John (2000). *The Riverside Milton*. Edited by Roy Flannagan. Oxford: Blackwell.

Webster, Charles (1976). *The Great Instauration: Science, Medicine and Reform, 1626–1660*. New York: Holmes and Meier.

Zacharias, Greg (1988). "Young Milton's Equipment for Living." *Milton Studies* 24: 3–15.

Further Reading

Duran, Angelica (2006). *The Age of Milton and the Scientific Revolution*. Pittsburgh: Duquesne University Press.

DuRocher, Richard D. (2001). *Milton among the Romans: The Pedagogy and Influence of Milton's Latin Curriculum*. Pittsburgh: Duquesne University Press.

Fletcher, Harris Francis (1956). *The Intellectual Development of John Milton*. 2 vols. Urbana: University of Illinois Press.

Intrator, Sam M. and Scribner, Megan (eds) (2003). *Teaching with Fire: Poetry that Sustains the Courage to Teach*. Washington: Jossey-Bass.

McCulloch, Gary (1991). *Philosophers and Kings: Education for Leadership in Modern England*. Cambridge: Cambridge University Press.

Parker, William Riley (1962). "Education: Milton's Ideas and Ours." *College Teaching* 24: 1–13.

Chapter 5

Milton's Heroic Sonnets

Annabel Patterson

Why would a man (for it is almost always a man) write a sonnet, or sonnets? The answer in terms of literary history is inevitable: because of the cultural panache of Petrarch's sonnets, perhaps the most influential of all literary texts – with the exception of Homer's epics, or the tragedies of Sophocles and Euripides, or the odes of Pindar! One could add many instances of precedent-setting, culturally formidable models. If one wanted to be a poet in England in the seventeenth century, one looked for inspiration and guidance to the ways the great poets of the past had divided literature into kinds, or genres. It is interesting to note, however, that when Milton actually discussed the question of genre with his readers, in *The Reason of Church Government*, he says a good deal about his ambitions to write an epic, to write a tragedy, or to write a high ode in the mode of Pindar; but he never mentions the sonnet. Presumably this was because the genres he mentioned had once, and might conceivably have again, an important public and instructional role. He had already written, at the age of 21, one magnificent ode, "On the Morning of Christ's Nativity," suggesting that his future might include other grand fusions of the Pindaric with Christian history. The sonnet, on the contrary, was assumed to be part of a man's private life, communicated, if at all, as a bit of an open secret.

It is a rather important fact about Milton's career, however, that he wrote sonnets, sporadically, for a large part of his life, beginning at about the same time he wrote the Nativity Ode, and continuing until about 1658, after he was completely blind. He never articulated a theory of the sonnet and its role in poetics or in society, and indeed this would have been hard to do, for he must have been aware that the vogue for sonnets in England, as in Europe, seemed at the very least to be on the wane. It was simply too late to become a "sonnet-eer," to make one's mark in that form.

When Milton decided to start writing sonnets, he chose the Italian model. We know that he purchased a copy of the sonnets of Giovanni della Casa in 1629, put his name and the date on the title page, and annotated it copiously. At that time he was 21 and still an under-graduate at Cambridge (Smart 1966: 28–9). He chose the Petrarchan form of the sonnet, with a complicated rhyme scheme, *abba abba*, and six lines in some combination of *cde*. The Petrarchan sonnet had a conventional, but not undeniable, strong break between octave and sestet, whereas the Shakespearean, or English, sonnet with its rhyme scheme of *abab cdcd efef gg* had three quatrains and a final couplet, along with an easier and fixed rhyme scheme. But Petrarch had, of course, also patented the sonnet as a vehicle for idealized and eventu-ally sublimated love of a single woman. To the very end of his sonnet writing, Milton seems to have had Petrarch specifically, though per-haps ironically, in mind, for his last published sonnet, "Mee thought I saw my late espoused saint," begins with a quotation from Sir Walter Ralegh's sonnet in praise of Spenser's *Faerie Queene*: "Methought I saw the grave where Laura lay," a sonnet whose premise is that Spenser has outdone Petrarch and substituted for his Laura the ideal figure of Elizabeth I. The irony, if it's there, consists in substituting for the theme of lifelong fidelity to a single unconsummated passion the notion that the Petrarchan ideal could be embodied in a *wife* who died in childbirth and, if indeed Sonnet 19 was written about Katherine Woodcock, who so died in 1658, Milton's second wife at that.

We can be pretty sure, too, that Milton studied the model of Shake-speare, if not for its verse scheme, for its tone and themes. Milton's Sonnet 16, "When I consider how my light is spent," a tragic medita-tion on his blindness in his fifties, is manifestly an allusion to Shake-speare's Sonnet 15, typical in its emphasis on ageing and mortality: "When I consider everything that grows/ Holds in perfection but a little moment." These echoes suggest that Milton went on thinking about what a sonnet should do, and what its subject matter might be, from 1629 to 1658. But mere imitation was the last thing on his mind. For Milton, the sonnet was a marker in his personal develop-ment, in his life, in his career as a writer, and in the history of his time. And as the life was unconventional, so was the deployment of the sonnet.

The Subject Matter

One thing we can say for certain: Milton did not write a sonnet *sequence* in any normal sense of the term. In contrast, in the last decades of the sixteenth century, Shakespeare had composed a sequence of 154 sonnets, Philip Sidney 108 for his *Astrophil and Stella*, and Edmund Spenser 89 for his *Amoretti*. Milton wrote, in all, 23 sonnets, ten of which were published as a group in his first collected volume of poems, *The Poems of Mr. John Milton*, dated 1645. Five of this first decade were conventional love sonnets in Italian, addressed to an anonymous *donna*, but these were framed by two English sonnets (1 and 7) that signaled an autobiographical or self-analytical intention. The first (Sonnet 1) expresses the *desire* to be in love, rather than the experience thereof; the second (Sonnet 7) leads from the amorous to the vocational, the fear that his poetic talent will not bear fruit, the embarrassment of writer's block. Two of the last three sonnets in Milton's first volume (9 and 10) address a woman, but one is an unidentifiable, unapproachably virtuous person ("Lady that in the prime of earliest youth/ Wisely hath shunned the broad way and the green") and the other is a married woman, a learned friend, Margaret Ley, daughter of an earl; and the sonnet is mostly about her father. The other, Sonnet 8, a remarkable expression of Milton's confidence, real or assumed, in the power of literature to protect authors in wartime, is addressed to an unknown officer in the Royalist army.

Let us pause on Sonnet 8 for a moment, not least because it raises three important questions: what Milton thought the appropriate subject matter for sonnets might be in his belated age; the role of the famous Trinity College manuscript, in which Milton recorded most of his shorter poems, along with *A Mask* and *Lycidas*; and the question of dating. The last two issues are connected. Here is the poem, as it appears in Milton's manuscript (though in the case of this sonnet, in the hand of a scribe):

> Captaine, or Collonell, or Knight in armes
> Whose chance on these defenselesse dores may sease
> If ever deed of honour did thee please,
> Guard them, and him within protect from harmes.

> He can requite thee, for he knows the charmes
> That call Fame on such gentle acts as these
> And he can spread thy name or'e lands and seas,
> What ever clime the sun's bright image warmes.
> Lift not thy speare against the Muses bowre,
> The great Emathian conqueror bidd spare
> The house of Pindarus when temple and towre
> Went to the ground, and the repeated aire
> Of sad Electra's Poet had the powre
> To save th'Athenian Walls from ruine bare

Now it is fair to say that the theme of this sonnet is the power of poetry to bestow fame, not on its author but on its recipient. The poem claims that if the military leader spares the poet's house, as Alexander ("the great Emathian conqueror") did when he ordered his soldiers to spare the house of the great Greek lyric poet Pindar during the destruction of Thebes in 335 BC, he too will be recorded in history. There is some irony here too, in that the sonnet claims to be able to spread "thy name" over the world, whereas what remains is only a hypothetical tribute to an anonymous soldier, whose rank is indeterminate. Still, Sonnet 8 might be said to introduce the theme of the great Name as an appropriate subject matter for a sonnet, one which a neoclassical poet would more typically see as belonging to the Pindaric ode, with its serious tone and correspondingly complex stanzas; and it is no coincidence that the one historical name actually offered to the reader is that of Pindar himself.

The Trinity manuscript, however, gives us more information, not only about this sonnet but also about Milton's view of the sonnet in general. Above the poem are two titles, "On his dore when yᵉ City expected an assault," in the hand of a copyist, subsequently deleted, and below it in Milton's own hand, "When the assault was intended to yᵉ Citty." The difference seems slight, but the role of "when" is imperative. Both versions contain not just a sign of time but a sign of *the times*, the exciting times when Milton's house in London, he playfully imagined, might have been in danger from Royalist forces. The manuscript also contains a marginal date of 1642, thereby fixing the poem on a specific day, November 13, 1642, when London expected a Royalist assault. Someone, presumably Milton, later deleted the date. This means two things. First, that Milton saw the poem as created for, marking, a specific historical occasion; and second, that he later thought better of that specificity, and wished to publish the poem, as he did, without it.

When it appeared in the 1645 volume of his poems, Sonnet 8 carried *neither* title. Thus for readers in 1645–6, in the middle of the war, the sonnet appeared before them *almost* stripped of its uneasy ricochet between local wartime news and the claims, from time *almost* immemorial, for poetry's protective function. The result, as A. S. P. Woodhouse and Douglas Bush sensibly remark, in the *Milton Variorum*, is that the poem "uses the occasion for general reflections on the place and power of poetry in wartime," but transcendence (or privacy) is gained at the loss of the charming idea that Milton actually intended to nail the poem to his own front door. The change is compatible with the general effect of the 1645 volume as Thomas Corns has described it, as placing Milton in the gentlemanly and noncontroversial realm of the arts, even as his prose pamphlets on church government and divorce were establishing him as a controversial thinker and participant in the revolution.

I should add that when the poem reappeared in 1673 it might have acquired a newly topical resonance. In his late eighteenth-century edition of Milton's poetry, British poet laureate Thomas Warton not only supplied the information that helps us to understand the allusion to "the great Emathian conqueror" and "the house of Pindar," but also argued that Milton was making the poem seem pertinent to his post-Restoration predicament. Warton suggested that in reprinting the poem Milton appealed to Charles II for the same immunity as in 1642 he had asked from Charles I or his military agents: "As a poet, Milton had as good [a] right to expect this favour as Pindar. Nor was the English monarch less a protector of the arts, and a lover of poetry, than Alexander" (1785: 340). Warton's speculation may seem fanciful, but it is certainly the case that, denuded of its original historical markers in the two versions of the title, Sonnet 8 could have been a Restoration poem written by a defeated republican poet. *If* Milton saw it in this way, the original humor of the poem would by then have been inflected with a strong sense of the ironies of history.

Before we proceed, it is worth noticing that of the ten sonnets published in the 1645 volume, only 7, 8, 9, and 10 were recorded in the Trinity manuscript, and 7 ("How soone hath Time"), on his difficulties in producing poetry, only as an insert in a manuscript "Letter to a Friend." Thus the conventionally amorous sonnets were added to the published volume from another source, a point that will gather significance as we continue.

Between 1645 and 1657 Milton wrote 13 more sonnets in the Petrarchan form, and an Italian *sonneto caudato* in English. These later sonnets (with the exception of four to which we shall return) were published by Milton in the collected edition of his poems in 1673, 13 years into the reign of Charles II. Most of them had been motivated by a specific occasion in historical time, whether a massacre of Protestants in Europe or the hostile reaction to his divorce pamphlets (which Milton evidently thought was worth two sonnets). Three were personal, in the sense that the "occasion" was his blindness or the death of one of his wives. Four, which he chose not to publish in this volume, have become known as the "commonwealth" sonnets, because three are addressed to leaders of the English revolution, Sir Thomas Fairfax, Oliver Cromwell, and Henry Vane, and in the fourth, addressed to his friend Cyriack Skinner, Milton congratulates himself on having gone blind in the service of the new republic. One would have to work very hard to make a sequence, in the Petrarchan or Shakespearean sense, out of this.

Undeterred, Mary Ann Radzinowicz, in *Toward* Samson Agonistes (a book describing as teleological the trajectory of Milton's poetic career), decided that there was a shape in Milton's 23 sonnets as a group. Looking at the 1673 edition with its 19 sonnets, and, of course, at modern editions that include all 23, she proposed in 1978 that Milton, retroactively and quite deliberately (presumably in 1673), created a sonnet "sequence" composed of individual "clusters," whose interrelations can now be securely determined:

> Milton intended each sonnet to bear its individual meaning; he grouped the sonnets by interlinked cross-reference and wrote them at distinct periods, often several years apart, so that a thematic meaning emerges within subgroups. He then printed them retrospectively, breaking chronology for other effects, and brought them together so that a final polyphonic harmony would be apparent in them. (Radzinowicz 1978: 129)

Radzinowicz saw the final structure as a narrative of maturation: from Milton's "youthful confident sense of the irresistibility of virtue and the certainty of election" (Sonnets 1–7), to studies of the "ethics of purity" (8–10), to those of Milton's "most revolutionary period" that consider the consequences of writing the divorce tracts (11–14), to those in which "Milton labored to prevent the revolution from failure" (15–18), to the last and most purely autobiographical group, which "as a whole records calm of mind and assent to the temporal circumstances of the period."

The Names

This thesis suffers from several disabilities. The first is that only a very peculiar reading can extract from the five Italian love sonnets and their frame, Sonnets 1 and 7, which are fraught with anxiety, a "youthful confident sense of the irresistibility of virtue and the certainty of election." The second is that Milton clearly did *not* intend the sequence to include those in which he "labored to prevent the revolution from failure," that is, the sonnets to Fairfax, Cromwell, and Vane, since he omitted them from the 1673 edition. And the third is that it takes no account of what is probably the most striking and original aspect of Milton's second set of sonnets, a feature that is hinted at in Sonnet 8 and in the last words of Sonnet 10, "Honor'd Margaret," but which puts a special stamp on the later ones: the Names. Sonnet 10 ends with a name. In the later sonnets, seven open with a name, which gives them an immediacy that the conventional Petrarchan beginning of Sonnet 9, "Lady," cannot do. The Names are almost, but not quite, apostrophes. By the rule that allows an opening trochee, this line scans. Sonnet 13, which is about scanning, is addressed to "Harry, [of the] tuneful and well-measur'd song," that is to say, Henry Lawes, with whom Milton collaborated in the presentation of *A Mask*. Sonnets 15, 16, and 17 begin respectively, "Fairfax, whose name in arms through Europe rings," "Cromwell, our chief of men," "Vane, young in years, but in sage counsel old." Sonnet 22, which shares with these the distinction of authorial suppression, begins, "Cyriack," that is to say, it invokes Milton's close friend Skinner, although its true subject is Milton himself and his blindness. So does Sonnet 18, "Cyriack, whose grandsire on the Royal Bench [. . .] Pronounced and in his volumes taught our laws," thereby invoking also Sir Edward Coke, the most famous legal writer of the early seventeenth century and a jurist who eventually set himself against Charles I and on the side of the truculent parliamentarians. By similar token Sonnet 20, "Lawrence of virtuous Father virtuous Son," invokes not only Milton's friend Edward Lawrence, who shortly before he died became Member of Parliament for St Margaret in Hereford, but also his more famous father, Henry Lawrence, Lord President of the Council under Cromwell. These poems are a long, long way from the one that begins "O Nightingale" and that Milton decided should begin the "sequence."

As John S. Smart observed long ago, there were plenty of precedents for moving the sonnet as a canonical exercise beyond the territory of

Petrarchan *amor*. Sonnets of compliments to friends, or heralding books, or lamenting deaths, or even satirical sonnets, such as those of Petrarch against the Avignon papacy, were quite common in Europe. In particular, Milton would have known that Torquato Tasso, one of his most important models for the epic, had written no fewer than 486 "Heroical Sonnets," addressed to popes, kings, cardinals, princes and great ladies (Smart 1966: 34–6). But this was really not the case in England, even during the vogue for sonneteering in the 1590s. Milton, however, knew what he was doing. Sir Thomas Fairfax is praised as he "whose *name* in arms through Europe rings" (emphasis added), suggesting that Milton has now found the subject that he only toyed with in Sonnet 8. The epic quality of the great Name, when transferred to a tiny genre that might seem to have been epic's opposite, is here explicitly thematized, and the heroes of the revolution do not need a poet to make their names for them.

Not that Milton had lost his sense of humor. Sonnet 11, "A book was writ of late call'd *Tetrachordon*," is a mock-heroic poem on naming. His readers say they cannot pronounce the title of his pamphlet. "Why is it harder, Sirs, than Gordon [to rhyme with *Tetrachordon*],/ Colkitto, or Macdonnel, or Galasp?/ Those rugged *names* to our like mouths grow sleek,/ That would have made Quintilian stare and gasp" (emphasis added). Thus the Presbyterians who would suppress his reformist writings are associated with the unspeakable Scots, whom John Leonard, in his Penguin edition of the poems, has brilliantly identified as "real," historical persons: "*Galasp* is George Gillespie, a Covenanter and member of the Westminster Assembly. *Gordon, Macdonnel* (*Macdonald*), and *Colkitto* (a nickname for Coll Keitache) were officers in Montrose's Royalist army" (Milton 1998: 690).

When he was being serious, however, Milton's Names have a great deal of work to do, some of it ideological. With the exception of Henry Lawes, who remained a Royalist, all the Names that open and motivate a Miltonic sonnet would have been associated, clearly or indirectly, with the history of the Commonwealth and Protectorate. Though none were so obnoxious to Restoration ears as Cromwell, Vane, and Fairfax, a careful reading of the first sonnet to Skinner and that to Lawrence would indicate Milton's political loyalties, the very opposite of Tasso's. The formal impersonality of Milton's sonnets – that is, their nominal focus on other persons than himself – *was* observed by Anna Nardo, whose thoughtful study, *Milton's Sonnets and the Ideal Community*, appeared in the year following Radzinowicz's. Nardo did not, however, draw from it anything nearly as provocative as what I have implied was part of Milton's intention. For Nardo, the effect of Milton's Names was softened, if not muted, by the occasional address to someone anonymous, as in "Lady that in the prime of earliest youth" (Sonnet 9), or the sonnet to Mrs Catharine Thomason, wife of the great book and pamphlet collector George Thomason, from which Milton removed the manuscript heading that identified her. And the meaning of the Names, in Nardo's conception, was much less political, more transcendent. Nardo invented the idea of an "ideal community" to which Milton's sonnets paid tribute and which was effectually constituted by them. "[E]ach sonnet," wrote Nardo, "details a unique engagement with a person, event, or partisan issue of the day, but each also asked its readers to consider this one moment in the light of man's ongoing fight against barbarity":

> At the center of the ideal community is an individual – free and virtu-
> ous, with a calm and humble faith. Surrounding this "upright heart and
> pure" are the groups of significant "others" that form the society that
> Milton envisioned: a beloved woman, the home, friends male and female,
> the nation, and Protestant Europe. Embracing all, of course, is a totally
> provident and beneficent God. (Nardo 1979: 18)

"Of course." And in one of our moods we would all like to believe that that is what Milton intended, as we might also, in another mood, yearn for the comforting narrative of Mary Ann Radzinowicz. But the problem with *this* thesis is that it has to overlook the juvenile sexual frustration of Sonnet 1, "O Nightingale," the two (or three) exasperated sonnets on the reception of Milton's divorce pamphlets, the fact that "Protestant Europe" is represented primarily by the massacre of the Vaudois, and that the beloved woman who has died in childbirth is refused a name as much as she refuses to remain in the narrator's wake-time community. Nardo also does not deal with the fact that the three members of Milton's ideal community on whom he most relied in the "ongoing fight against barbarity," Cromwell, Vane, and Fairfax, were not only dead by 1673 but banished from the community by virtue of their exclusion from the volume. The story that Milton made his sonnets tell, then, was indeed of the importance of idealism and of the "ongoing fight against barbarity," but we learn of the defeats in that campaign as much or more than the victories. And one of the things Milton never does, unlike John Donne, whose religious sonnets he must have studied with as much care as those of Giovanni della Casa, is write a sonnet to, or about, a "totally provident and beneficent God."

"Late" as a Sign of Occasionality

Most Miltonists assume that Milton arranged his sonnets in roughly chronological order – chronology being that of their moments of composition. This premise explains why the four commonwealth sonnets are in most modern editions inserted into the "sequence" in what is inferred to be their chronological place, thereby defying Milton's evident intentions! The premise that Milton arranged the sonnets according to chronology might not itself have become canonical but for the amazing survival of the Trinity College manuscript, which has, paradoxically, enhanced the importance of chronology and occasionality even as Milton later denied them by crossing out of the manuscript the headers that placed the sonnets in their moment. Trinity gives (or originally gave) firm occasions for Sonnets 8, 11, 12, 13, 14, 15, and 16, a fact which has dangled before the eyes of editors the colorful lure of precise dating.

But it seems that Milton actually avoided the public presentation of his sonnets as a chronological record. Sonnet 12 (number 11 in the Trinity manuscript) included the sign of occasionalism in its first line: "A book was writ *of late* called *Tetrarchordon*" (emphasis added). It also carried in the manuscript an occasionalist title: "On the detraction which follow'd upon my writing certain treatises." But here the clear indication of sequentiality (the sonnet follows the detraction which followed the treatises) is accompanied by vagueness as to which treatises they were. Since Sonnet 11 (numbered 12 in the manuscript, and there carrying the title "On the same") mentions by name *Tetrachordon*, published on March 4, 1645, modern editors assume that "certain treatises" refers to the four divorce pamphlets as a group; but why was Milton not more helpful, and why was even that limited helpfulness reduced when Sonnet 12 appeared in the 1673 edition without the manuscript title? What we are apparently *not* being encouraged to do is to consider these two sonnets, along with the *sonetto caudato*, as temporal markers in the career of John Milton as radical pamphleteer, as proponent of "divorce at pleasure," as one of his enemies charged.

What we are left to consider is the deployment of sonnets for satirical purposes, and the state of the press in revolutionary England. Note how impersonally Sonnet 12 puts the problem of communication in a market flooded with pamphlets: "A book was writ of late called *Tetrachordon*." Not, the equally nice pentameter "Of late, I wrote the book *Tetrachordon*." Milton then describes "The subject new: *it* walked the town a while [. . .] now seldom pored on" (emphasis added). The vision of the pamphlet personified, cruising the bookstalls looking for properly educated readers, stands between us and the image of Milton doubly frustrated by his marital problems and the haste with which the Presbyterians, whose champion he had offered himself to be, discarded him. The problem in the poem seems to be *not* the detraction Milton personally experienced, but rather the short life of the radical proposal, the triviality of the objections (readers cannot pronounce the title), and the illiteracy of the audience. But that modest phrase "of late" will acquire infinitely greater resonance when this sonnet takes its middle place in the sequence that modern editors have reinstated. Note that the red flag of the word "divorce" never appears in either of these two sonnets. It is calmly replaced by "liberty." And as Milton aligned himself in Sonnet 8 with Pindar and Euripides, so here he aligns himself with the Roman rhetorician Quintilian and with Sir John Cheke, the early Tudor humanist, first professor of Greek at Cambridge, and tutor to the young Protestant king Edward VI. First-rate credentials, it would seem.

Sonnet 13, appearing first as a rough autograph draft in the Trinity manuscript, originally carried Milton's title, "To my friend Mr. Hen. Laws. Feb. 9. 1645," that is, 1646 by the Gregorian calendar. This gives a very different chronology from that implied by the second title added by an amanuensis to Milton's fair copy: "To Mr. Hen. Laws *on the publishing* of his Aires" (emphasis added), since Lawes' *Ayres and Dialogues* were not published until 1653, unless one posits, as does the *Milton Variorum*, that the poem was written in anticipation of a publishing event planned for 1646 but subsequently delayed (Woodhouse and Bush 1972: 399). But things get more complicated when one learns, from John Leonard, that Milton's poem was itself first published in Lawes' *Choice Psalmes* (1648), a self-evidently royalist volume dedicated to Charles I, then a prisoner of the revolutionary parliament, and commemorating Henry's brother William who had been killed fighting on the Royalist side (Milton 1998: 693). When the sonnet appeared in Milton's 1673 edition under the title "To Mr. H. Lawes, on his Airs," the intricacies of this textual history (and the high intellectual bipartisanship it may have signified) have disappeared, and only scholars could retrieve them. But the poem still appeared in its *proper* place as a testimony to what Milton was writing, and who his friends were, in early 1646.

The fact that all but one of the new sonnets (11 to 23) appear (or would have appeared, had not a page been lost) in the Trinity manuscript (following Milton's sketches for biblical or historical dramas) is testimony of their importance to him. Several appear in more than one draft. That they are numbered (erratically) suggests that Milton had printing in mind. So does the note before 11 ("I did but prompt the age"), which states "these sonnets follow the 10 in the printed booke" (i.e. 1645), which looks like a note to a fair copy maker. It is all the more significant, therefore, to find in Trinity the sonnets we now number 15, 16, and 17 in modern editions, those addressed to Fairfax, Cromwell, and Vane, numbered, surprise (!) 15, 16, and 17. These were, as already several times mentioned, omitted from the 1673 edition, for obviously prudential motives. They too carried in the Trinity manuscript specific autograph datings. "On ye Lord General Fairfax at ye seige of Colchester," that is to say, the summer of 1648; and "To the Lord General Cromwell May 1652/ On the proposalls of certaine ministers at y^r. Comm[it]tee for Propagation of the Gospell." Both titles were deleted in the manuscript, on the same principle as used in the case of Sonnet 8 ("Captain, or Colonell"), which supports the thesis of an original intention to publish, but in a less visibly occasionalist form. We have no way of knowing now at what point the self-censorship of these three sonnets would have occurred, along with that to Cyriack Skinner (now and in the manuscript Sonnet 22) which insisted that Milton did not regret his blindness, since he had lost his eyes "in libertyes defence, [my] noble task,/ Of which all Europe talks from side to side." In this remarkable poem, the thesis of fame, of a great Name, is transferred from the addressee (who must not have been easily slighted) to the poet himself, who thus becomes analogous to Fairfax, Cromwell, and Vane in terms of republican history.

It seems pretty clear that Milton or his printer decided that they could not risk the appearance of these sonnets in 1673, when Charles II was not only on the throne, but had recently abandoned his attempt to allow more liberty of conscience in England. The sonnets he did publish, to Lawes, Edward Lawrence, and the *other* sonnet to Skinner, might to Milton carry "commonwealth" implications, but they would have been inscrutable to any ordinary reader or licenser. The first of the "commonwealth sonnets" to see print, however, was in an unmistakably defiant and dangerous context. For in 1662, immediately following the execution of Sir Henry Vane by the Restoration government, there appeared *The Life and Death of Sir Henry Vane*, a set of documents collected by one George Sikes to honor the first of the Restoration "martyrs." Tucked away in the middle of the religious polemic which forms the bulk of this work is the first formal "reading" of a Milton sonnet, with Sikes's prefatory remarks:

> Would you know [Vane's] Title in reference to his countrey? He was *A Common-Wealths-Man.* That's a dangerous Name to the Peace and Interest of Tyranny [. . .] The Character of this deceased Statesman [. . .] I shall exhibit to you in a paper of Verses, composed by a learned Gentleman, and sent him, *July* 3 1652. (Sikes 1662: 93)

Thus Milton's sonnet to Vane (though fortunately for Milton in the early Restoration without Milton's name attached to it) appears with a date (now out of Milton's control) that matches *its* place in the Trinity manuscript sequence. What we also learn from this fortuitous accident of publishing is that Milton used to send the Names the sonnets he had written for them. Unsurprising, perhaps; but Sikes's inside knowledge pulls these occasionalist sonnets back into their time with a vengeance.

The Trinity manuscript, therefore, produced for modern editors the mainstay of the argument for a strictly chronological sequence in Milton's sonnets, while providing evidence of occasionalist motives that some modern editors wished to forget or reframe as a grander, more uplifting program. It looks as though Milton agreed with them. It is unfortunate, therefore, that the sonnet that strikes the most occasionalist pose in its title, *"On the late Massacher in* Piemont," is missing from the Trinity manuscript. There is no sonnet numbered 18 (or, for that matter, 19 and 20) and Sonnet 21, the first of the two to Skinner, appears in the manuscript without its first four lines. Evidently a page is missing. (This is a terrible loss in the case of what we now call Sonnet 19, "When I consider how my light is spent," since the manuscript might have left us a clue as to exactly when it was written, a matter which Milton's critics have debated incessantly.)

But Sonnet 18, "Avenge O Lord, thy slaughter'd Saints," does appear (as Sonnet 14) in the 1673 volume, under the title *"On the late Massacher in* Piemont." By this time, of course, the massacre of the Protestant Vaudois by the forces of the Duke of Savoy, which took place on April 24, 1655, was no longer "late" in the journalistic sense, but something, if you knew your history, from the Cromwellian past. It was also an exhilarating recall of Milton's service as Latin Secretary to Cromwell. In May 1655 Milton was required by Cromwell to write several letters to European rulers protesting the genocidal treatment of the Protestant sect, and his sonnet, as Merritt Hughes observed, opens in much the same way as his letter to the King of Sweden. Once again, however, an editor shrinks from the facts he himself must record. According to Hughes, "the sonnet rises above its topical subject to a vision of Truth triumphant" (Milton 1957: 167). It is indeed a great, a spectacular sonnet, more than rivaling Petrarch's Sonnet 108 from which it derives its honorable past, its horror of "the Babylonian woe." But what of its future? In 1673 it was far from clear that the Lord could or would avenge his saints in Piemont or elsewhere (if he even knew who his saints were). Our reading of its value to Milton in 1673 must therefore be plagued with the same doubts as that of *Samson Agonistes*, the play of vengeance against God's enemies which had appeared in 1671, and has ever since encouraged some to see it as resistance theory or political allegory, directed against the Restoration government and its "unjust tribunals, under change of times" (Milton 1998: 695–6).

Let us now look closely at one of Milton's most famous sonnets, but one that he chose not to publish, the sonnet to Oliver Cromwell. The sonnet was surely placed in Cromwell's hands in May 1652, because that is what its title in the Trinity manuscript says. The Trinity manuscript also shows it to have been written as an appeal against a new threat to freedom of speech emanating from the Committee chaired by John Owen, whose *Humble Proposals* [. . .] *for the furtherance and Propagation of the Gospel in this Nation* appeared, self-dated March 31, 1652. In the manuscript, the sonnet carried the title "On the Proposals of Certain Ministers of the Committee for Propagation of the Gospel." This manuscript title was subsequently struck through.

As Smart pointed out, it was probably the provision that no one should be permitted to speak in public on any religious question without a certificate as to his orthodoxy from two or more divines that particularly enflamed Milton (1966: 77). When his appeal to Cromwell was finally published, in 1694, by Milton's nephew John Phillips, it too was slipped in, as if accidentally, in Phillips's edition of the *Letters of State, Written by Mr. John Milton, To Most of the Sovereign Princes and Republicks of Europe*. A few years later John Toland republished the four "commonwealth" sonnets in his *Life of John Milton*. They are introduced separately, as biographical documents; first, the sonnets to Fairfax and Vane (Toland 1699: 72), and a few pages later, the defiant sonnet to Cyriack Skinner and that to Cromwell. Toland, however, introduced a *different* occasion for the sonnet to Cromwell (Toland 1699: 111, 112), as well he might, given the suppression of the original occasion:

> Our Author was now *Latin* Secretary to the Protector OLIVER CROMWEL, who, he confidently hop'd, would imploy his Trust and Power to extinguish the numerous Factions of the State, and to settle

such a perfect Form of Free Government, wherin no single Person should injoy any Power over or beside the Laws: but he particularly expected his establishing an impartial Liberty of Conscience, to which he incourages him by these lines, never printed among his Poems. (Toland 1699: 111)

Thus the sonnet became a Protectorate work, at least two years later than its actual composition, matching the address to the chief executive in Milton's *Second Defence* of 1654; a bigger, bolder statement, and one compatible with the profile of the Whig Milton that was now, in the 1690s, under construction; high-mindedness of a different kind.

If we read this sonnet solely as a *poem*, however, it becomes evident why Milton never, after his wonderful *On the Morning of Christ's Nativity*, attempted to write a high or Pindaric ode; he had in fact managed to emulate the Pindaric project in the smaller, more disciplined form of the sonnet. Look how its grandeur escapes the confines of 14 lines and a prescribed rhyme scheme:

> Cromwell, our cheif of men, who through a cloud
> Not of warr onely, but detractions rude,
> Guided by faith & matchless Fortitude
> To peace & truth thy glorious way hast plough'd,
> And on the neck of crowned Fortune proud
> Hast reard Gods Trophies & his work pursu'd,
> While Darwen stream w[it]h blood of Scotts imbru'd,
> And Dunbarr feild resounds thy praises loud,
> And Worcesters laureat wreath; yet more remaines
> To conquer still; peace hath her victories
> No less renownd then warr, new foes aries
> Threatning to bind our soules w[it]h secular chaines:
> Helpe us to save free Conscience from the paw
> Of hireling wolves whose Gospell is their maw.

What is always observed about this sonnet is the way that the octave triumphantly overflows into the sestet, thereby marking even more effectively the necessary turn to the different agenda of peace-making and church-settling. What is not usually mentioned is the way the great Names of Cromwellian victories, Darwen, Dunbar, and Worcester, take their proper place in the sonnets naming the great Names of Milton's experience, instantiating a language to which the sonnet had been unaccustomed, if not exactly inhospitable. Why would one need to write a Pindaric ode about the Civil War period, if this is what one could do with the sonnet?

But one can say more: for the manuscript shows us that "Worcesters laureat wreath," the reference to Cromwell's crushing defeat of the Scotch Covenanters, led by the temporarily returned Charles II, on September 3, 1651, was an afterthought. Originally the ninth line, the beginning of the sestet, read: "And twentie battles more." It is easy to see why the change was made (it seems to be in Milton's hand), since it increases the emphasis on resonant names (and Milton at first inserted the phrase, ametrically, in place of "Dunbarr feild," so anxious was he, we might infer, to insert the improvement). But of course the alteration increases the sonnet's overt hostility to Charles II, since the battle of Worcester was the great humiliation that laid to rest all Royalist hopes for an invasion and recapture of the country until after Cromwell's death, also on September 3, 1658.

A Last Word on Genre

This account of Milton's sonnets will seem to some a long way away from what they have been led to expect. It is not intended to cast aspersions on more high-minded or poignant approaches, such as those of Radzinowicz and Nardo, which should be read carefully, along with the more personal and elegiac sonnets, "O Nightingale," "How soone hath Time," "When I consider how my light is spent," and especially, perhaps, "Mee thought I saw my late espoused saint." It *is* intended to demonstrate how easily we may be misled if we bring to the term "sonnet" expectations derived exclusively from Petrarch, or Sidney, or Spenser, or Shakespeare. And perhaps some of my readers will be made happier by discovering that Milton's last sonnet was not Sonnet 23, "Mee thought I saw." We might see the final speech of Eve in *Paradise Lost* (12.610–23), consisting of 14 pentameter lines, as Sonnet 24. For this *is* a love sonnet, from the wife to the husband, and the fact that it is unrhymed can make Milton seem more modern, more adventurous, and, yes, more moving as a writer of sonnets and odes than anything in the preceding pages.

References and Further Reading

Abrams, M. H. (2005). *A Glossary of Literary Terms*. Boston: Thomson Wadsworth.
Goldberg, Jonathan (1990). "Dating Milton." In Elizabeth Harvey and Katharine Maus (eds), *Soliciting Interpretation*. Chicago: University of Chicago Press.

Milton, John (1694). *Letters of State Written by Mr. John Milton*. Edited by Edward Phillips. London.

Milton, John (1899). *Facsimile of the Manuscript of Milton's Minor Poems*. Edited by William Aldis Wright. Cambridge: Cambridge University Press.

Milton, John (1957). *John Milton, Complete Poems and Major Prose*. Edited by Merritt Hughes. New York: Odyssey Press.

Milton, John (1972). *John Milton Poems, Reproduced in Facsimile from the Manuscript in Trinity College Cambridge. With a Transcript*. Menston: Scolar.

Milton, John (1998). *Complete Poetry of John Milton*. Edited by John Leonard. New York: Penguin.

Nardo, Anna (1979). *Milton's Sonnets and the Ideal Community*. Lincoln: University of Nebraska Press.

Parker, William Riley (1958). "The Dates of Milton's Sonnets on Blindness," *Publications of the Modern Language Association* 73.3: 196–200.

Patterson, Annabel (1994). "'That old man eloquent.'" In Diana Trevino Benet and Michael Lieb (eds), *Literary Milton* (pp. 22–44). Pittsburgh: Duquesne University Press.

Patterson, Annabel (1997). "'Prejudice sways a world of people': Milton's Sonnets." In Annabel Patterson (ed.), *Early Modern Liberalism*. Cambridge: Cambridge University Press.

Radzinowicz, Mary Ann (1978). *Toward* Samson Agonistes. Princeton: Princeton University Press.

Sikes, George (1662). *The Life and Death of Sir Henry Vane*. London.

Smart, John S. (1966). *The Sonnets of Milton, with a Preface by B. A. Wright*. Oxford: Clarendon Press.

Toland, John (1699). *The Life of John Milton*. London: John Darby.

Warton, Thomas (1785). *Poems upon Several Occasions* [. . .] *by John Milton*. London: James Dodsley.

Woodhouse, A. S. P. and Bush, Douglas (eds) (1972). *A Variorum Commentary on the Poems of John Milton*, vol. 2. New York: Columbia University Press.

Chapter 6

The Lives of *Lycidas*

Paul Alpers

> *The philosopher's task consists in comprehending all of natural life through the more encompassing life of history. And indeed, is not the continued life of works of art far easier to recognize than the continual life of animal species? The history of the great works of art tells us about their antecedents, their realization in the age of the artist, their potentially eternal afterlife in succeeding generations. Where this last manifests itself, it is called fame.*
>
> Walter Benjamin, *Illuminations*

Lycidas is a famous poem, but it is also difficult and somewhat controversial. It is studded with learned allusions, mostly to classical poetry and mythology, and with challenging locutions. Beyond these difficulties, which can be addressed with the help of annotation, is a deeper one: though it is called a "monody" (i.e. an utterance by a single speaker), *Lycidas* does not "behave" like the usual lyric poem. It begins in the first person, but it ends by representing the poem's speaker in the third person, as an "uncouth swain"; in between, first person utterance is continually disrupted, often by words put in the mouths of speakers who seem to appear from nowhere. Yet though much of the poem seems challenging and elusive, it also has moments of deeply felt emotion, when the speaker expresses his own vulnerability to the fate of the young man he mourns and his dismay at the world in which he finds himself. Hence, *Lycidas* has seemed to many critics an intensely personal poem. To the famous complaint of Samuel

Johnson, in the eighteenth century – "where there is leisure for fiction [classical figures and pastoral conventions] there is little grief" (Patrides 1983: 60) – more than one modern critic has replied that the poem is less about the deceased Edward King than about Milton himself. Our consideration of *Lycidas* must therefore begin with a consideration of its place in Milton's life and in his career as a poet.

Lycidas in Milton's life

Lycidas was written at the end of the five-year period between Milton's departure from Cambridge (1632) and his travel to the cultural centers of Europe (1638–9). He spent these years in solitary study, as if to prepare himself for some great work. Sometime during them he decided to dedicate his life to poetry, rather than becoming a clergyman, as his father had intended and as would have been expected of a university graduate. We do not know when he made this decision. His most direct account of it is retrospective (in *The Reason of Church Government*, 1642), and we cannot definitively date the Latin poem to his father, "Ad Patrem," in which he speaks of the poet's calling in exalted terms. By the time of *Lycidas* itself, his choice seems clearly to have been made. The most famous passage in the poem, a scathing indictment of the English Church, is consistent with Milton's later statement that in his choice of career he had been "church-outed by the prelates" (i.e. the churchmen whose failures in Christian ministry made the poet feel he could not become one of them). Nevertheless, our understanding of the poem may depend on our view of Milton's internal development in these crucial five years. Does the poem mark "a decisive and un-ambiguous commitment" to a tradition of prophetic poetry or is its focus "not on King but on [Milton's] own anxieties about vocation, poetic and religious" (Norbrook 2002: 256, 266; Lewalski 2000: 71)? (For yet another view, cf. Evans 1983.)

The opening lines of *Lycidas* reveal another aspect of Milton's sense of himself and his vocation as a poet:

> Yet once more, O ye laurels, and once more
> Ye myrtles brown, with ivy never sere,
> I come to pluck your berries harsh and crude,
> And with forced fingers rude,
> Shatter your leaves before the mellowing year.
> Bitter constraint, and sad occasion dear,

Compels me to disturb your season due:
For Lycidas is dead, dead ere his prime.

(1–8)

In representing his poem as premature, the speaker suggests more
than the early death ("ere his prime") of the person he laments. The
language of unripeness refers to plants whose leaves traditionally
crowned poets (hence our phrase "poet laureate"). It is the poet or his
poetry, then, that is not yet ripe, and this is the way Milton regularly
speaks of himself during these years. Five years earlier, soon after he
left Cambridge, he used similar imagery of himself in Sonnet 7, "How
soon hath time": "My hasting days fly on with full career,/ But my late
spring no bud or blossom shew'th." He included this sonnet in a letter
to an unidentified friend, in which he speaks of his "tardy moving"
and acknowledges that his life is "as yet obscure and unserviceable to
mankind." At the same time, he defends the course of study on which
he has embarked as enabling him, in due course, to achieve "honour
and repute and immortal fame" and properly do God's work (Milton
1990: 1). This double way of representing himself – as not yet coming
to "inward ripeness" (Sonnet 7) and yet as knowing he has some
great work within him – explains a striking fact about Milton in the
1630s. Though dedicated to writing an English epic (as he tells us in
The Reason of Church Government), he wrote almost no poetry in English,
on his own initiative, in those years. The two great poems of that
decade, *Lycidas* and *A Maske* [*Comus*], are occasional poems, the first
prompted by a specific event, the second due to a specific commission.
Lycidas was written for a volume of poetry commemorating Edward
King, a Fellow of Christ's (Milton's college at Cambridge), who was
drowned in the Irish Sea in 1637, at the age of 25. *Justa* [funeral rites]
Edouardo King Naufrago, published the next year by King's Cambridge
associates, consists of two parts. The first contains poems in the classical
languages, 20 in Latin and three in Greek. The second, which has a
separate title page ("Obsequies to the memorie of Mr. Edward King"),
contains 13 English poems. *Lycidas* is the last poem in the volume. It
is also the only pastoral elegy, a form used throughout the European
Renaissance in emulation of ancient Greek poems (Theocritus, *Idyll* 1;
Moschus, *Lament for Bion*) and of the Latin Eclogues of Virgil, especially
Eclogues 5 and 10.

Many readers of *Lycidas* ask, like the students in John Berryman's
short story about teaching the poem ("Wash Far Away"), whether it
is about King or Milton. The answer, as Berryman's students help

Paul Alpers

their teacher realize, is not "either ... or" but "both ... and." One
purpose of pastoral conventions, according to which the dead Fellow
of Christ's is named "Lycidas" and the speaker is his fellow shepherd,
is to represent both the person commemorated and the commemorating poet as in the same situation. This is made explicit early in the
poem, in the pastoral passage beginning "Together both, ere the high
lawns appeared" (25–36). But the adequacy of the poem's fictions
and its various formal strengths may have led modern Miltonists to
downplay Milton's own presence in this highly conventional poem. The
argument that we should distinguish between the nominal subject,
Edward King, and the real subject, John Milton, was once felt to be
liberating (Tillyard 1930); but it was increasingly resisted on the
grounds that the poem's themes are "universal." (So that the answer to
the question raised in Berryman's classroom sometimes seemed to be
"neither ... nor.") Critics resisted saying that the poem is about Milton,
because modernist poetics were hostile to ideas of biographical motivation and unmediated self-expression in poetry. And yet the following
passage, though highly mediated by conventional usages, is also intensely
personal:

> Alas! What boots it with uncessant care
> To tend the homely slighted shepherd's trade,
> And strictly meditate the thankless muse,
> Were it not better done as others use,
> To sport with Amaryllis in the shade,
> Or with the tangles of Neaera's hair?
> Fame is the spur that the clear spirit doth raise
> (That last infirmity of noble mind)
> To scorn delights, and live laborious days;
> But the fair guerdon when we hope to find,
> And think to burst out into sudden blaze,
> Comes the blind Fury with th' abhorrèd shears,
> And slits the thin-spun life.
>
> (64–76)

Every element in these lines corresponds to the young Milton's choices
in life and his representation of them. Editors explain, as they should,
the references in Latin and neo-Latin poetry to Amaryllis and Neaera.
But not even the Variorum commentary notes that in presenting his
heroic ambition as a poet, Milton disparages "the writings and inter-
ludes of libidinous and ignorant poetasters" and "that which flows at
waste from the pen of some vulgar amorist" (Milton 1990: 171–2), or

98

that sometime in the 1630s he took a vow of chastity as an earnest of his high-minded ambitions. Nor do editors' notes tell us that Milton repeatedly speaks, as he puts it in a 1637 letter to his closest friend, Charles Diodati, of seeking "an immortality of fame" (Milton 1990: 718). (Milton was later to commemorate his friend in a Latin pastoral elegy, *Epitaphium Damonis*, in 1639.) In the letter that includes the sonnet "How soon hath time," he refers to "a desire of honour and repute and immortal fame seated in the breast of every true scholar" (Milton 1990: 1). Still later, justifying his decision to dedicate himself to poetry, he speaks of his "inward prompting" that "I might perhaps leave something so written to aftertimes as they should not willingly let it die" (*RCG* 169). The early death of a serious young cleric and poet – even one who had quite different views of church and state – must have made the poet who had chosen to "scorn delights, and live laborious days" question secular immortality and ask whether the God he meant to celebrate worthily would let him live to do so.

Edward King's death occurred at a critical moment in England's history. In July 1637, Charles I attempted to impose the Church of England's order of service on the Church of Scotland and provoked public resistance, including riots. The King's intervention in Scotland was of a piece with reforms introduced at home by William Laud, the Archbishop of Canterbury, whose anti-Calvinism, promotion of church ritual, and insistence on episcopal hierarchy made many suspect him of leading the country back to the Roman Catholic Church. To strengthen the Church's authority, Laud had tightened censorship. A month before ecclesiastical conflict began in Scotland, three notorious and outspoken opponents of his reforms were publicly mutilated and imprisoned. These events could hardly have been unknown or insignificant to Milton, and when he published his *Poems* in 1645, he introduced *Lycidas* with this head-note:

> In this monody the author bewails a learned friend, unfortunately drowned in
> his passage from Chester on the Irish Seas, 1637. And by occasion foretells the
> ruin of our corrupted clergy then in their height.

This retrospective claim about St Peter's speech (*Lycidas* 113–32) tells us a great deal about Milton's sense of himself in the 1640s, when a revolution had been effected in English political and church government. In these years, Milton put aside his poetic ambitions to participate in this revolution as a pamphleteer; the publication of his *Poems* may have been a way to remind the world that he was a poet (Lewalski

2000: 226–8). At this point, Milton claims that *Lycidas* bears witness to the powers he envisaged for poetry, that it should be "doctrinal and exemplary to a nation" (*RCG* 170). But we cannot be certain that this sense of himself as a national prophet can be read back into his intentions when he wrote the poem. Do the references to the miter and keys of St Peter (*Lycidas* 110–12), traditionally the original bishop of Rome, mean that in 1638 Milton was not unalterably opposed to episcopacy, as he was in the early 1640s? Or was he conscious of the vigilance and determination of Laud's censorship? Is it fear of censorship or quasi-prophetic style that makes for the degree of obscurity in the passage? (It ends with the most notorious puzzle in Milton's poetry – the reference to "that two-handed engine at the door" that "stands ready to smite once, and smite no more.") However we answer these questions, there is no denying the radical tone of the passage. The vehemence with which it appeals to the foundations of Christian ministry (the parable of the Good Shepherd, John 10) shows a readiness to participate in what came to be called a "root and branch" transformation of the Church, when, a few years later, the opportunity came.

The passages in which Milton's presence is most felt – St Peter's speech and the lines about poetry and fame which produce Phoebus's corrective intervention (76–84) – have at times been called "digressions." They seem to turn away from the expected progress of the poem, whether this is construed as the discourse of a lyric speaker or the conventions of pastoral elegy. If critics no longer speak of the "digressions" in *Lycidas*, it is because the term assumes that normal direction and development can be readily discerned in a poem that is full of disruptions and changes of direction. (It is true, however, that after each of these passages, the speaker of the poem calls for a return to its pastoral course [85–90, 132–5].) But even if the term is inadequate, its obvious pertinence and the questions it raises show that we must turn our attention from *Lycidas* as a "life document" and consider it as a poem.

Lycidas as a Pastoral Poem

Most readers and interpreters of *Lycidas* have thought it obvious that, as Samuel Johnson said, "its form is that of a pastoral." But identifying *Lycidas* as a pastoral raises more questions than it answers (though not for Johnson, who thought of it as a sort of automatic writing, "easy, vulgar, and therefore disgusting"). Almost all interesting interpretations of *Lycidas* involve one of two main ideas about pastoral. The first, deriving from eighteenth-century and Romantic poetics, takes an idealized relation between the human subject and nature to be the essence of pastoral expression and representation. This idea of pastoral emphasizes idyllic scenes of innocence and what John Ruskin called the pathetic fallacy, the fiction that external nature responds to human feelings and moods. Some key pastoral moments in *Lycidas*, according to this view, are the speaker's memory of a shared youth with the dead shepherd ("Together both [. . .]," 25–36), the mourning sounds of nature and its sympathetic manifestations of the pain of death (39–49), and the long catalogue of flowers (134–51), which is invoked "to strew the laureate hearse where Lycid lies" and which concludes by representing some flowers as sympathetically mourning. If these are the key pastoral passages, then the poem as a whole is seen as bringing the speaker to a fuller awareness of reality – the harshness of nature itself, the arbitrariness of death, the imperfections of the human world, the possibility of repose only in the Christian afterlife. The poem's chief means for educating the speaker in this way is to intervene in his idealizing desires and imaginings. This poetic action first occurs after he invokes the nymphs of mountain and stream and asks where they were "when the remorseless deep/ Closed o'er the head of your loved Lycidas?" (50–1). The terms in which Milton casts this conventional appeal suggest the speaker's naiveté: he imagines that the nymphs, fictional embodiments of the natural scene, also care for the shepherd and can protect him from the worst forces of nature in the raw. Five lines later, the speaker comes to his senses: "Ay me, I fondly dream!/ Had ye been there . . . for what could that have done?" This self-correction is recapitulated in two major interventions – first by Phoebus, correcting the plaintive speaker's idea of worldly fame, and then St Peter's invective against false pastors, which explodes any idealized account of shepherds and their lives. Perhaps enough has been said to indicate why these two passages are no longer called "digressions." Though they bring in speakers other than the lamenting, lyrical first person, they are essential to the work of the poem, which (in the view just sketched) is to bring the first-person speaker to a truer sense of the world and of human life in it.

Some such reading of *Lycidas* is still standard: it makes sense of the dynamics of the poem – the way the speaker's search for consolation and understanding is continually disrupted by sterner recognitions – and it is exemplified by some excellent essays (MacCaffrey 1965;

Friedman 1971; Fish 1981). Its limitation is its narrow idea of pastoral. It assumes that pastoral usages are inherently naive and weak, and that adequate representation and expression depend on stronger poetic modes, more grounded in vision and experience. This idea of the poem fails to recognize that some putatively unpastoral lines and episodes – "Phoebus replied and touched my trembling ear" (Virgil, Eclogue 6), "That strain I heard was of a higher mood" (Virgil, Eclogue 4), and the excoriation of false pastors – come from the repertory of classical and Renaissance pastoral. More importantly, it fails to explain why Milton would have undertaken a pastoral elegy in the first place or how he and his readers could take seriously the pastoral fictions that pervade and organize the poem. To take one specific example, if there is an inherent poetic weakness in the catalogue of flowers, it is difficult to see why, as the Trinity manuscript shows, Milton attentively revised and expanded it.

To understand *Lycidas*, we need to think of pastoral not as a form of lyrical wish-fulfillment, but as a specific mode of representation. Its founding fiction, as we see it in Virgil's Eclogues, is that herdsmen and their lives represent all human lives and situations. The underlying notion of this fiction is, in William Empson's words, that "you can say everything about complex people by a complete consideration of simple people": as Empson puts it, in a famous formulation, "the pastoral process" consists of "putting the complex into the simple" (Empson 1960: 131, 23). When we think of pastoral this way, we can understand why St Peter's speech is within its range. In accordance with the biblical metaphor, clergymen (sometimes called pastors) are represented as shepherds who are responsible for their flocks, those in their care. This pastoral equation provides all that is needed for the critique of ministers who deny their flocks' simplest, but most essential needs, nourishment and protection. This is not the only way in which *Lycidas* represents complex people – like the Cambridge graduates who put together the King volume – as simple herdsmen. (It has long been recognized that pastoral poetry is of the country, but by and for the court or city.) Poets, including the poem's speaker, are also represented as shepherds. This equation has always been part of pastoral poetry, with its singing contests and its figures of herdsmen as master-singers. What matters, of course, is not that *Lycidas* employs this convention, which in other hands can be as thin and tiresome as Johnson thought; it is that the convention is a source of poetic life and meaning. In two of his most vivid lines, St Peter says: "And when they list, their lean and flashy songs/ Grate on their scrannel pipes of wretched straw" (123–4). (This second line translates a piece of rustic abuse in Virgil, Eclogue 3.) What sense does it make to attack bad ministers as bad singers? These lines suggest that the whole character of one's life has the quality of a poem, good or bad. As Milton later said, defending his own character, one who seeks "to write well here-after in laudable things, ought himself to be a true poem" (*Smectymnuus* 180). The point and energy of these lines is only one way in which the pastoral fictions of *Lycidas* raise the question – central to the poem and central to Milton himself – of whether "the faithful herdman's art" (121) is most importantly that of the clergyman or of the poet.

This second model of pastoral underlies the conventions of pastoral elegy. We need to understand these conventions in their usual form, in order to see how Milton draws on and transforms them, questioning them and pushing them to their limits. Pastoral is a consciously post-heroic mode of poetry, originally defined by its distance from Homeric epic. For the Hellenistic poet Theocritus (3rd century BCE) and his imitator Virgil, the figure of the herdsman was a conscious reduction, in power and individuality, of the warriors and rulers who define human nature and experience in epic and tragedy. The representative herdsmen of ancient pastoral encounter death in a correspondingly distinct way – not as fulfilling the individual destiny or career of a hero, who is imagined as able to meet death "on his own," but as an abrupt disruption of the world shared by mutually dependent people. (The inexplicability of Lycidas's death is not only true to the facts about Edward King, but also in character for a literary pastoral.) As a poetic form, pastoral elegy represents the way a human community deals with death that is experienced in this way. In a typical pastoral elegy, two or more herdsmen come together to sing about their dead companion. These gatherings take place neither at nor immediately after the fatal event, but at a certain distance in time from it. The herdsmen's songs are formal compositions; they both register the shock of death and celebrate the dead person, so as to keep a representation of his or her value present in their world. Their function is to sustain the pastoral world in the face of its loss. Some of these poems explicitly promise commemorative ceremonies, to which the highly formalized elegy offers itself as an analogy.

From beginning to end, *Lycidas* deploys the usages and fulfills the purposes of the pastoral elegies that preceded it. It begins with the disruption of the harmonious shepherds' world ("But O the heavy change, now thou art gone [. . .]!"), and brings on figures from the afflicted world (the so-called "procession of mourners," 88–131, ending with St Peter) who express their puzzlement and dismay. It envisages bringing flowers "to strew the laureate hearse where Lycid lies"; when that ceremony is dismissed as a "false surmise" (153), for the corpse is absent, the poet's imagination pursues it to the bottom of the deep, so that the speaker can say (in a traditional gesture) "Weep no more, woeful shepherds weep no more" and reconstitute the pastoral community in heaven, where their lamented companion now dwells. Nor does the poem turn away from the community of shepherds on earth:

> Now Lycidas the shepherds weep no more;
> Henceforth thou art the genius of the shore,
> In thy large recompense, and shalt be good
> To all that wander in that perilous flood.
> (182–5)

Milton surely did not believe that the dead Edward King would become a local deity who would protect those who crossed the sea in which he drowned. But by suspending disbelief in this piece of paganism (which appears, most notably, in Virgil, Eclogue 5), he brings out its metaphoric significance. The phrase which explains why Lycidas will be "the genius of the shore" – "thy large recompense" – has a double meaning. It refers both to the dead person's salvation in heaven, which compensates him for his early death, and to the way he compensates his dead companions for their loss of him. Indeed, these two meanings are inseparable. In this Christian elegy, recognition of the dead person's salvation *is* the compensation for his loss, and thus helps sustain us as we "wander in that perilous flood," life itself. Thus *Lycidas* performs the work of the traditional pastoral elegy: by mourning their lost companion, the herdsmen can carry on their lives, "tomorrow to fresh woods, and pastures new."

Yet *Lycidas* is unlike any previous pastoral elegy. This can be seen most readily in the effect of its ending. There is a sudden distancing effect when the vulnerable and impassioned speaker is represented in the third person: "Thus sang the uncouth swain to th' oaks and rills" (186). These final lines supply a setting and a frame which are usually present from the beginning, either in a brief narration (e.g. Virgil, Eclogue 10, cf. *Shepheardes Calender*, "January") or, more usually, by dialogue between two herdsmen (e.g. Virgil, Eclogue 5; *Shepheardes Calender*, "November"). *Lycidas* recalls past scenes in which the speaker and his lost companion tended sheep and sang together; but until the end, it does not fully represent a pastoral world as the setting in which the present complaint is uttered. Hence the shifts and turns of the poem are more abrupt and unsettling than in other pastoral eclogues. Again St Peter's speech provides the clearest example. One can point to the "September" eclogue in Spenser's *Shepheardes Calender* as a pastoral precedent for ecclesiastical satire: there too a harsh style, conceived to be rustic and plain-spoken, is used to attack false churchmen. But in Spenser's poem, this critique is put in the mouth of an ordinary shepherd, who is speaking to one of his fellows. Even though Milton's "pilot of the Galilean lake" is ushered in by a conventional procession of mourners, he seems to appear from nowhere, as if from a different world from the figures who precede him (the god of winds Aeolus and the river Cam, representing Cambridge). Similarly, the vehemence of Spenser's satiric speaker is countered by his fellow shepherd, who urges him to speak more discreetly. The response to St Peter's speech is uttered by a recognizably pastoral speaker, who invokes the river-god Alpheus and the "Sicilian [i.e. Theocritean] muse." But this speaker does not address St Peter or otherwise seem to inhabit the same world: rather he shrinks from "the dread voice" as if it had invaded his world. This effect feels unpastoral, though it can be represented in pastoral terms. One could say that Milton has taken his two speakers from two different pastoral worlds – harsh rural actuality and idyllic scenes responsive to human feeling – which Spenser kept apart in his calendar scheme, by assigning them to different months of the year.

We can see how *Lycidas* is both traditional and profoundly innovative by asking a simple question: who or where are the "woeful shepherds" whom the speaker addresses in the final passages of the poem and who in any other eclogue would appear as singers and auditors? Milton's shepherds are not in the poem, and yet their identity seems clear. The speaker's fellow mourners are the other Cambridge graduates who contributed elegies to the King volume. Some of them were clergymen, all of them wrote poems, so they can fittingly be represented as shepherds, the more so as Milton's pastoral elegy concludes the volume and brings the contributors together in their common endeavor. But to identify the pastoral community with the writers and readers of the printed volume and to displace it from a world represented in the poem – one in which each speaker is like his fellows and each utterance is coherently motivated – is also to unsettle the nature of the one shepherd left in the poem, the speaker himself. Again putting it in pastoral terms, the effect is that the speaker performs a wide range of pastoral singing roles, without the frame or social ritual that gives them a stable relation to each other, and even suggests that some are interchangeable. But one can go further than this. The poem's opening lines do not establish the speaker's pastoral identity. Despite their imagery, the poet seems to speak in his own voice, like the other poets in the volume. Like them he dwells on the manner of King's death, and in offering "some melodious tear," he uses a familiar conceit, playing on the fact that funeral elegies were often called *Lachrymae* or "Tears." Hence some readers and critics think of *Lycidas* as an unusually wide-ranging first-person lyric. But this does not resolve all problems, because the question remains whether the intervening voices, notably those of Phoebus and St Peter, are those of separate dramatic characters or whether, in the course of the poem, they are assimilated to the speaker: after all, Milton called the poem a "monody." The speaker certainly becomes more capable and authoritative as the poem proceeds, as when he summons his fellows and their commemorative tributes in the flower passage. The turning point consists of three consecutive strong utterances: "Look home- ward angel now, and melt with ruth./ And, O ye dolphins, waft the hapless youth./ Weep no more, woeful shepherds weep no more" (163–5). These urgings and commands are a far cry from "Ay me, I fondly dream!" and "Return Alpheus, the dread voice is past." Yet in their strength and disparity, they strain the lyric speaker and the coherence we attribute to him as we reperform his utterance in read- ing. Some critics, indeed, want to attribute the last of these lines and the passage it initiates to another speaker altogether. (St Michael, "the great vision of the guarded mount" [161] is the favorite candidate; others are the soul of Lycidas and a chorus of souls in heaven.) At every point at which we feel the energy and power of *Lycidas*, it seems to open up fundamental questions.

The Afterlives of *Lycidas*

Over the centuries, *Lycidas* has been something of a benchmark for English poetry. "He who wishes to know whether he has a true taste for Poetry or not, should consider, whether he is highly delighted or not with [. . .] 'Lycidas,'" said an eighteenth-century critic (Shawcross 1972: 317). These words were echoed in the Victorian era – "Lycidas is a good test of a real feeling for what is peculiarly called poetry" (Elledge 1966: 235) – and when Yeats asked Virginia Woolf whether there was any poem to which she could come back unsated, her answer was *Lycidas* (Low 2003: 221). At the same time, it has always been a controversial poem. We have already noted Samuel Johnson's mocking the inauthenticity of its pastoral fictions, but the criticism that counted most with his contemporaries was a graver charge: "With these trifling fictions are mingled the most awful and sacred truths, such as ought never to be polluted with such irreverend combinations" (Patrides 1983: 61). A century later this sense of a poem divided against itself became central to the Victorian understanding of Milton. Where Johnson and his contemporaries discussed the propriety of the poem's fictions and usages themselves, Victorian critics, the heirs of Romanticism, viewed them as expressing conflicts within the poet. "Poet versus Puritan" became the key to understanding Milton and his poems – the disparity between St Peter's speech and the catalogue of flowers in *Lycidas* no less than the difference between the Garden of Eden and the severities of life after the Fall in *Paradise Lost*.

Much of twentieth-century interpretation of *Lycidas* has been devoted to justifying the integrity of both the poem and its author's sensibility. The fundamental point of view is that rightly understanding the purposes of the poem enables us to understand its aesthetic life and coherence. Similarly, Milton's seventeenth-century Protestantism has been seen as in a vital relationship with his humanism and commitment to poetry. Nevertheless, there are still some unresolved divisions in our idea of *Lycidas*. In a once famous essay, John Crowe Ransom, the intellectual leader of American New Criticism, called *Lycidas* "a poem nearly anonymous." The best known and most challenging postmodern essay is Stanley Fish's "*Lycidas*: A Poem Finally Anonymous." In the handful of unrhymed lines in *Lycidas*, Ransom discerned a conflict between the artist and the (rebellious) man, so that the poem, in his view, fails to achieve an ideal impersonality. Fish augmented this modernist aesthetic bias with a view of seventeenth-century theology in which God is all and the human subject nothing. But in the 1645 headnote, which begins the afterlife of the poem, Milton draws atten-tion to himself as a prophetic poet. And the historicism that has been a main current in literary studies in recent decades has led to accounts of *Lycidas* that put Milton, the man and citizen, back at the center of the poem (Norbrook 2002; Kendrick 1997; Lipking 1996).

An equally important question about *Lycidas* recapitulates the earlier contrasts of pagan and Christian, poet and Puritan. Indeed, it brings us back to Milton himself and his choosing to become a poet, not a clergyman. In the eyes of most Miltonists, there is no conflict between

Paul Alpers

these two roles, because for Milton himself both entailed service to God. By the same token, most interpretations of *Lycidas* appeal to a bedrock of reality, the truth at which the poem arrives about the fate of Lycidas's body and the Christian promise of his immortality. But we have already noted the final turn to poetic fiction in calling Lycidas "the genius of the shore." And the priority of poetry is evident in one of the greatest passages in the poem:

> Ay me! Whilst thee the shores, and sounding seas
> Wash far away, where'er thy bones are hurled,
> Whether beyond the stormy Hebrides
> Where thou perhaps under the whelming tide
> Visit'st the bottom of the monstrous world;
> Or whether thou to our moist vows denied,
> Sleep'st by the fable of Bellerus old,
> Where the great vision of the guarded mount
> Looks toward Namancos and Bayona's hold.
>
> (154–62)

T. S. Eliot said of these lines that "for the single effect of grandeur of sound, there is nothing finer in poetry" (Eliot 1957: 145), and they provide the title of John Berryman's great story. Because they follow the speaker's recognition that the catalogue of flowers is a "false surmise," their power has usually been taken to inhere in the brute facts about Edward King's drowning. But a better lead was provided by Thomas Warton in 1785. The flower passage, he says, is "a pleasing deception [. . .] natural and pathetic"; but then "the real catastrophe recurs [. . . and] opens a new vein of imagination" (Shawcross 1972: 319). Imaginative endeavor is the hallmark of this passage. As the speaker seeks Lycidas's body in the deep, one speculation follows another, and the firmness of utterance, with a memorable locution in each line, is free of any grammatical mooring, for the sentence has no main verb. As the passage proceeds, its noun phrases become more artful and opaque (compare "the whelming tide" with "the fable of Bellerus old," which is not only elliptical but draws attention to poetic fiction). The alternative to "false surmise" is not the truth *tout court* but what poets have always claimed to provide – true surmise. When Sir Philip Sidney said, in *A Defense of Poetry*, that "the poet nothing affirmeth, and therefore never lieth," he was speaking of actions and characters, the main constituents of epic and tragedy. In an unusually bold (but characteristically Miltonic) way, the visionary and vocalizing energies of *Lycidas* give lyric form to this claim for the poet's authority.

108

Though we cannot know precisely when Milton decided to be a poet, *Lycidas* itself makes clear what he intended to make of his life when he set out to "fresh woods, and pastures new" – even though, in 1638, he could not know what the world held in store for him.

References and Further Reading

Alpers, Paul (1996). *What Is Pastoral?* Chicago: University of Chicago Press.

Benjamin, Walter (1968). *Illuminations.* Edited by Hannah Arendt, trans. Harry Zohn. New York: Harcourt, Brace and World.

Berryman, John (1976). "Wash Far Away." In John Berryman, *The Freedom of the Poet.* New York: Farrar, Straus and Giroux.

Eliot, T. S. (1957). *On Poetry and Poets.* New York: Farrar, Straus and Cudahy.

Elledge, Scott (1966). *Milton's "Lycidas": Edited to Serve as an Introduction to Criticism.* New York: Harper and Row.

Empson, William (1960). *Some Versions of Pastoral.* Norfolk, CT: New Directions.

Evans, J. Martin (1983). *The Road from Horton: Looking Backwards in "Lycidas."* Victoria, Canada: English Literary Studies.

Fish, Stanley E. (1981). "*Lycidas*: A Poem Finally Anonymous." *Glyph* 8: 1–18. Repr. in C. A. Patrides (ed.), *Milton's "Lycidas": The Tradition and the Poem.* Rev. edn. Columbia: University of Missouri Press, 1983.

Friedman, Donald M. (1971). "*Lycidas*: The Swain's Paideia." *Milton Studies* 3: 3–34. Repr. in C. A. Patrides (ed.), *Milton's "Lycidas": The Tradition and the Poem.* Rev. edn. Columbia: University of Missouri Press, 1983.

Johnson, Samuel (1779). "Life of Milton." Repr. in C. A. Patrides (ed.), *Milton's "Lycidas": The Tradition and the Poem.* Rev. edn. Columbia: University of Missouri Press, 1983.

Kendrick, Christopher (1997). "Anachronism in *Lycidas*." *English Literary History* 64.1: 1–40.

LeComte, Edward (ed.) (2001). Special Issue: *Justa Edovardo King* [Full Reproduction] with Introduction, Translations, and Notes. *Milton Quarterly* 35.3.

Lewalski, Barbara K. (2000). *The Life of John Milton: A Critical Biography.* Oxford: Blackwell.

Lipking, Lawrence (1996). "The Genius of the Shore: Lycidas, Adamastor, and the Poetics of Nationalism." *Publications of the Modern Language Association* 111.2: 205–21.

Low, Lisa (2003). "Feminist Elegy/Feminist Prophecy: *Lycidas, The Waves*, Kristeva, Cixous." *Woolf Studies Annual* 9: 221–42.

MacCaffrey, Isabel G. (1965). "*Lycidas*: The Poet in a Landscape." In Joseph Summers (ed.), *The Lyric and Dramatic Milton: Selected Papers from the English Institute* (pp. 65–92). New York: Columbia University Press. Repr. in C. A. Patrides (ed.), *Milton's "Lycidas": The Tradition and the Poem.* Rev. edn. Columbia: University of Missouri Press, 1983.

Milton, John (1990). *John Milton*. Edited by Stephen Orgel and Jonathan Goldberg. Oxford: Oxford University Press.

Norbrook, David (2002). *Poetry and Politics in the English Renaissance*. Rev. edn. New York: Oxford University Press.

Patrides, C. A. (ed.) (1983). *Milton's "Lycidas": The Tradition and the Poem*. Rev. edn. Columbia: University of Missouri Press.

Ransom, John Crowe (1938). "A Poem Nearly Anonymous." In John Crowe Ransom, *The World's Body* (pp. 1–28). New York: Charles Scribner's Sons. Repr. in C. A. Patrides (ed.), *Milton's "Lycidas": The Tradition and the Poem*. Rev. edn. Columbia: University of Missouri Press, 1983.

Shawcross, John T. (1972). *Milton 1732–1801: The Critical Heritage*. London: Routledge and Kegan Paul.

Tillyard, E. M. W. (1930). *Milton*. London: Chatto and Windus. Repr. in C. A. Patrides (ed.), *Milton's "Lycidas": The Tradition and the Poem* (pp. 79–85). Rev. edn. Columbia: University of Missouri Press, 1983.

Tuve, Rosemond (1957). "Theme, Pattern, and Imagery in *Lycidas*." In Rosemond Tuve, *Images and Themes in Five Poems by Milton* (pp. 73–111). Cambridge, MA: Harvard University Press.

Chapter 7

A *Mask*: Tradition and Innovation

Katsuhiro Engetsu

From *Comus* to *A Mask*

We would be as naive as the young, tragic Romeo if we were to ask, "what's in a name?" with *A Mask Presented at Ludlow Castle*. John Toland's biography of Milton in 1699 renamed the masque *Comus* (Darbishire 1932: 114), which has been its most popular name since the early eighteenth century. While "On the Morning of Christs Nativity" has come to be known as "The Nativity Ode," and Sonnet 16 ("When I consider how my light is spent") as "On his Blindness," *Comus* is more misleading than helpful because, centralizing the antimasque villain, it fails to spell out the occasional quality of the aristocratic entertainment. The generic nature of the masque suggests that any single character can never be more significant than the occasion of the whole event. The work's original full title in the first collection of Milton's poems in 1645 reads as follows: *A / MASK / Of the same / AUTHOR / PRESENTED / At LUDLOW-Castle, / 1634. / Before / The Earl of BRIDGEWATER / Then President of Wales*. Milton simply summarized the place, year, and audience of the performance – without mentioning any specific character – when he gave a title to the masque in his own publication. As Cedric Brown and Leah Marcus have noted in their recent discussions of this text, doing so guides Milton's *readers* to appreciate what the piece's *audience* would have readily noted: its occasional nature (Brown 1985; Marcus 2003). The unique aim of this essay is to examine this occasional piece as a historical and cultural collaboration in order to interrogate the modern Western concept of authorial identity and verbal priority by demonstrating how contemporary critical approaches, such as New Historicism and Post-colonialism, provide a basis for the advancement of multicultural and multimedia studies of performance art in seventeenth-century England.

As the original full title in 1645 *Poems* shows clearly, the masque was an aristocratic entertainment for John Egerton, the Earl of Bridgewater, in 1634. The title page of the first print edition of *A Mask* published by Henry Lawes in 1637 is even more specific about details of the occasion: *A MASKE / PRESENTED At Ludlow Castle, / 1634: / On Michaelmasse night, before the / RIGHT HONORABLE, IOHN Earle of Bridgewater, Vicount BRACKLEY, Lord President of Wales, And one of His MAIESTIES most honorable Privie Counsell*. The date itself provides important clues to the cultural components dictating the masque. There were strong associations between holidays and court revels (Welsford 1928: 3–18). Michaelmas, September 29, was traditionally the holiday reserved for the inauguration of new officials, and the holiday night at Ludlow Castle in 1634 celebrated the Earl of Bridgewater's formal installation as Lord President of Wales and the border counties. *A Mask* was, then, a theatrical ceremony to praise the public glory of the aristocrat who occupied the important office in Wales under the reign of Charles I.

The aristocratic entertainment was primarily designed to give leading roles to the three young members of the Egerton family. The family was more important than each individual in early modern aristocratic society. This particular aristocratic household entrusted Milton to create appropriate roles for its members because the young poet seems to have already done a good job on a previous occasion. Although the beginning of the connection between Milton and the Egerton family remains speculative, the first hard evidence is found in the poet's *Arcades*, which, as its headnote states, was "Part of an entertainment presented to the Countess Dowager of Derby at Harefield, by some noble persons of her family, who appears on the scene in pastoral habit, moving toward the seat of state, with this song." The arrangement of the 1645 *Poems* suggests that, although undated, *Arcades* must have been written before *A Mask*. Alice, the Dowager Countess of Derby, was famous as a patroness of poets like Edmund Spenser, whom the young Milton admired greatly. She was also the stepmother of John Egerton, who became the Earl of Bridgewater in 1617. The imbricated relationship of these pieces reminds us that the cultural network within the English aristocracy was of special significance in aristocratic entertainments.

Like *Arcades*, *A Mask* was a family entertainment in which "noble persons" appeared "on the stage" in special costumes, like "pastoral habit." The text of *A Mask* is preceded in 1645 *Poems* by the following description of the characters and performers:

> The Persons.
> The attendant Spirit, afterwards in the habit of *Thyrsis*.
> *Comus* with his crew.
> The Lady.
> 1. Brother.
> 2. Brother.
> *Sabrina* the Nymph.
>
> ---
>
> The cheif persons which presented,
>   were
> The Lord *Bracly*,
> Mr. *Thomas Egerton* his Brother,
> The Lady *Alice Egerton*.

We do not know who played Comus and Sabrina. The "chief" performers were the unmarried children of the Earl of Bridgewater. His youngest daughter, Alice, then aged fifteen, played the Lady while his only surviving sons, John (Lord Brackley), aged eleven, and Thomas, aged nine, portrayed the Elder and Younger Brothers respectively.

The Attendant Spirit or Thyrsis was played by Henry Lawes, the Egerton children's musical tutor as well as the musical composer of the aristocratic entertainment. The musician penned an epistle to the eldest son of the Earl of Bridgewater and printed it in his 1637 edition. I quote the intriguing letter in full because it is often omitted from current editions of Milton's poetry:

> MY LORD,
> *THis Poem, which receiv'd its first occasion of birth from your self, and others of your noble familie, and much honour from your own Person in the performance, now returns again to make a finall dedication of it selfe to you. Although not openly acknowledg'd by the Author, yet it is a legitimate off-spring, so lovely, and so much desired, that the often copying of it hath tir'd my pen to give my severall friends satisfaction, and brought me to a necessitie of producing it to the publick view; and now to offer it up in all rightfull devotion to those fair hopes, and rare Endowments of your much-promising Youth, which give a full assurance, to all that know you, of a future excellence. Live sweet Lord to be the honour of your Name, and receive this as your owne, from the hands of him, who hath*

> *by many favours beene long oblig'd to your most honour'd Parents, and as in*
> *this representation your attendant* Thyrsis, *so now in all reall expression*
>
> Your faithfull, and most
> *humble Servant,*
> H. Lawes.

Lawes underscores the significance of the occasional quality of the work with special gratitude to John's participation in "the perform-ance." *A Mask* was a collaborative performance art in which the com-poser, actors, and audience were as important as the characters and authors. This Stuart masque accordingly asks readers to reassess some central assumptions of current literary criticism: the supremacy of verbal text over nonverbal elements, the distinction between the author and audience or between the audience and performers, and the concept of inalienable authorship as the privileged single source of the meaning of a literary work. This masque, in which Milton joined others as "the Author" of the text, is a multimedia product of aristocratic society in seventeenth-century England where Lawes played as important a role culturally as he did theatrically at Ludlow Castle in 1634.

Music and Costume

Lawes's epistle suggests that he contributed no less than Milton to the production and publication of *A Mask*. He first duplicated and circu-lated manuscripts of the masque and then decided to put the text into print in 1637 before Milton "openly acknowledg'd" his authorship in 1645. It was Lawes rather than Milton who controlled the text's early circulation and first print publication. Milton presumably agreed to the print publication, as he prefixed the letter to *A Mask* in his 1645 *Poems*. The text of the masque in 1645 *Poems* also carries a letter from Sir Henry Wotton, the famous former English ambassador to the court of Venice, to Milton in 1638 immediately before the young poet's departure for Italy. Wotton's letter tells us that he did not realize the identity of the author of the masque until he received a presentation copy of the 1637 edition from Milton himself. Wotton first found it bound with the poems of Thomas Randolph, Milton's contemporary at Cambridge, who enjoyed a short but great reputation as a promis-ing member of Ben Jonson's literary circle. The association between the successful cavalier poet and Lawes's publication of *A Mask* was justifiable because the composer, a member of the King's Private Musick since 1630, represented the Stuart court.

The eminent court musician's strong presence in the performance gives us several clues to what the aristocratic entertainment was like at Ludlow Castle in 1634. First of all, *A Mask* was a kind of musical drama (Finney 1962: 175–94). Lawes's manuscript in the British Library preserves five songs from his collaboration with Milton. One song, "To the ocean [Bridgewater: "From Heav'ns"] now I fly" – inserted at the beginning of Bridgewater MS but at the end of Milton's 1645 *Poems* – was probably sung by Lawes as the Attendant Spirit to open the masque. The second song was composed for Alice as the Lady lost in darkness: "Sweet Echo, sweetest nymph that liv'st unseen." The third was sung by Lawes "in the habit of Thyrsis" to invoke Sabrina: "Sabrina fair." The fourth and fifth songs were also prepared for Lawes "in the habit of Thyrsis" when he brings the Lady and Brothers to their father and mother: "Back, shepherds, back, enough your play" and "Noble Lord, and Lady bright." While Alice's youthful voice is properly highlighted, Lawes's professional skills in singing performance as well as in musical composition are predominant from the opening to the ending. *A Mask* is Lawes's work rather than Milton's if it is considered primarily as a musical drama.

A Mask was, however, visual art, too. Lawes had had much experience in court spectacles. In January 1630, when he was appointed to the King's Private Musick, *Love's Triumph through Callipolis*, a masque by Jonson in collaboration with Inigo Jones, was performed as the main feature of the Twelfth Night Revels on January 9 at Whitehall. Jonson was the greatest authority for the genre of the Stuart masque (Orgel 1967). It is often pointed out that *A Mask* was influenced, for example, by Jonson's *Pleasure Reconciled to Virtue* (1618) since both masques share the similar topic of the moral relationship between pleasure and virtue as well as the antimasque figure of the same name, "Comus, the god of cheer, or the belly" (Jonson 1969: 263). Although we do not know how Milton familiarized himself with Jonson's unpublished masque, performed at court when he was only ten years old, we are sure that Lawes had something to do with the production of Jonson's *Love's Triumph* in 1630 at Whitehall. Its stage direction to the last scene reads as follows: "Which ended, the scene changeth to a garden, and heavens opening, there appear four new persons in form of a constellation sitting" (Jonson 1969: 460). Although Lawes's name was not mentioned in Jonson's text, there is good reason to guess that the newly appointed King's musician played one of the "four new persons in form of constellation" because the members of the King's Private Musick were expected not only to set lyrics to music but also to plan and join aristocratic entertainments. Lawes knew from his immediate experience at court that spectacular costumes and scenes were as necessary as good poetry for the successful performance of an aristocratic entertainment (see Creaser 1984).

Costumes, which add visual effects to a theatrical performance, deserve special critical attention (Nicoll 1938: 161–2). When he appeared on the stage as the Attendant Spirit in *A Mask* at Ludlow Castle, Lawes wore a spectacular costume that might have been very similar to those worn by the "four new persons in form of constellation" in *Love's Triumph* at Whitehall. The text of *A Mask* defines him as a descending star at the beginning of the masque: "Before the starry threshold of Jove's court/ My mansion is" (1–2). His opening speech then refers twice to his own costume before he exits. First, he draws attention to the fact that his costume is too celestial to be used on earth: "I would not soil these pure ambrosial weeds,/ With the rank vapours of this sin-worn mould" (16–17). Second, he declares that he will change the clothes: "but first I must put off/ These my sky-robes spun out of Iris' woof,/ And take the weeds and likeness of a swain,/ That to the service of this house belongs" (82–5). The Attendant Spirit in the opening scene puts on robes whose texture or shape reminds the spectators of a rainbow. The repeated references to the "sky-robes" suggest that Lawes's costly costume and his quick disguise into a shepherd were among the main attractions of *A Mask* at Ludlow Castle.

The "sky-robes" Lawes wore in the opening scene locate *A Mask* in the tradition of the Stuart court masque. Lawes joined the production of Aurelian Townshend's *Albion's Triumph*, which was acted for the Twelfth Night Revels at Whitehall in 1632. Townshend puts the following stage direction after the dance of the main masque:

> The Scene is varied into a Landscipt, in which was a prospect of the Kings Pallace of *Whitehall*, and part of the Citie of *London*, seene a farre off, and presently the whole heauen opened, and in a bright cloud were seene sitting fiue persons, representing *Innocency, Iustice, Religion, Affection to the Countrey, & Concord*, being all Companions of Peace, and thus attired. *Innocency*, a woman in a pure white robe, with a garland of flowers on her head [. . .] *Concord* a man in a skie coloured Robe, and a yellow Mantle. (Townshend 1912: 73)

Like Jonson's *Love's Triumph* of 1630, Townshend's court entertainment for the Twelfth Night Revels at Whitehall of 1632 shows new persons from the opening of "the whole heauen" with a quick change of scenes. Townshend's detailed description of the costumes clearly tells us that the Stuart court masque is a highly costume-conscious genre. Concord's "skie coloured Robe" with "a yellow Mantle" anticipates the Attendant Spirit's "sky-robes" in *A Mask* at Ludlow Castle. The tradition of the Stuart court masque was partly transmitted by costumes.

As a professionally trained musician, Lawes composed music for *Coelum Britannicum*, Thomas Carew's magnificent entertainment at Whitehall for Shrove Tuesday in 1634. When we consider Milton's masque in the tradition of the Stuart masque, Carew's example deserves special attention because it also featured the sons of the Earl of Bridgewater, John and Thomas, who were to appear as the Elder and Younger Brothers in *A Mask* the same year (Carew 1949: 185). The performance of *Coelum Britannicum* at Whitehall was a shared memory between the eminent court musician and his aristocratic pupils. Drawing on highly elaborate machines designed by Jones, Carew gives the following stage direction to the fabulous spectacle of "a great Cloud [. . .] of severall colours" in the last scene: "in the Ayre, sate Eternity on a Globe, his Garment was long of a light blue, wrought all over with Stars of gold" (Carew 1949: 182). Eternity's "Garment" in Carew's *Coelum Britannicum* in 1634 reminds us of Concord's "skie coloured Robe" with "a yellow Mantle" in Townshend's *Albion's Triumph* in 1632 and the Attendant Spirit of *A Mask* in 1634. The costume was a combination of a long robe of light blue and a mantle spangled with gold, representing a constellation in the sky. The Attendant Spirit's "sky-robes" were an imitation of the costume in the Jonsonian masques after 1630 at Whitehall.

Spectacle and Dance

Dazzling costumes complemented the sumptuous and ingenious stage devices of Stuart court theater (see Campbell 1923 and Southern 1952). At the opening scene of Carew's *Coelum Britannicum*, for example, the very curtain that rises to start the Whitehall masque is described as follows: "[t]he Curtaine was watchet and a pale yellow in paines, which flying up on the sudden, discovered the Scaene" (Carew 1949: 154). The stage directions to *A Mask* suggest that the stage at Ludlow Castle also made use of devices designed for quick changes of scenes: "The first scene discovers a wild wood" at the beginning of the masque while "[t]he scene changes, presenting Ludlow Town and the President's Castle," at the festive ending of the performance

117

(957–1022). In *Coelum Britannicum*, there was also a machine to lift the performers up and down on the stage: "At that instant the Rocke with the three kingdoms on it sinkes, and is hidden in the earth. This strange spectacle gave great cause of admiration, but especially how so huge a machine, and of that great height could come from under the Stage" (Carew 1949: 179). *A Mask* at Ludlow Castle reproduced some of the applauded visual effects of the Whitehall masque: "Sabrina rises, attended by water nymphs" when the Attendant Spirit invokes her and "Sabrina descends" when she finishes disenchanting the Lady from Comus's magic (907–20).

The stage devices, however, do not seem to have been as elaborate at Ludlow Castle as at Whitehall. The stage direction for the opening of the Ludlow masque is ambiguously simple: "The Attendant Spirit descends or enters." Since the Attendant Spirit identifies himself as a star by putting on the "sky-robe," it would be the most effective for him to descend from the ceiling down to the stage, as the performers did at Whitehall on the last Shrove Tuesday. Its stage directions, however, are much briefer than those of Jonson's *Love's Triumph*, Townshend's *Albion's Triumph*, or Carew's *Coelum Britannicum* at Whitehall. The paucity of textual references to any spectacular effects of *A Mask* is evident especially when we compare the aristocratic entertainment at Ludlow Castle in 1634 with James Shirley's *Triumph of Peace* at Whitehall in the same year. Shirley's masque overshadowed all its predecessors' by its gaudy spectacular effects, starting with a sumptuous procession from Holborn to Whitehall; there was a rumor that it cost £20,000 (Carew 1949: 273). Lawes and Milton could not expect great stage effects from the Great Hall ("Comus Hall") at Ludlow Castle because it was a simple local edifice lacking an ingenious stage designer like Jones.

Dances and poetry were enhanced to make up for the relative paucity of spectacular effects at Ludlow Castle. While the Whitehall masques displayed wonderful spectacles to enhance the sense of triumph, *A Mask* at Ludlow Castle introduced "Country Dancers" on the stage "To triumph in victorious dance/ O'er sensual folly and intemperance" (973–4). The Stuart court masque derived as much from the tradition of the formal court dance (*ballet de cour*) in France as from that of the musical drama (*drama per musica*) in Florence (Demaray 1968: 10–30; Strong 1984: 63–170). But we should be cautious of oversimplifying the genre of the Stuart court masque as a precursor of modern ballet or opera because, as we have seen, each piece was a unique theatrical mixture of poetry, music, and dance.

Sexual and Textual Harassment

The most impressive scene of Milton's masque is primarily neither visual nor musical but rather poetical: the extended rhetorical debate over the "serious doctrine of virginity" (786) between the Lady and Comus. It deserves special critical consideration in its own historical context. Indeed, the most heated critical issue in historical studies of *A Mask* of the past 30 years is the "Castlehaven scandal," the notorious case of the domestic sex crimes committed by a member of the Egerton family (see Breasted 1971 and Herrup 1991). Fact is sometimes stranger than fiction. The Dowager Countess of Derby, for whom Milton wrote *Arcades*, had three daughters by her first marriage with the Earl of Derby: Anne, Frances, and Elizabeth. While her second daughter, Frances, was married to the Earl of Bridgewater, for whom Milton wrote *A Mask*, her eldest daughter, Anne, was married in 1624 to Grey Brydges, Lord Chandos, and, after his death, to Mervin Touchet, 2nd Earl of Castlehaven. Unfortunately, Anne's second marriage was, simply put, abusive; the Earl of Castlehaven was said not only to have committed sodomy repeatedly with his male servants but also to have encouraged them to rape his wife Anne. The Earl of Castlehaven's behaviors extended beyond his wife and servants to his son by his first marriage, James Touchet, and his stepdaughter by his second marriage, Elizabeth Brydges. Elizabeth was married to James, the only heir of the Touchet family. In order to disinherit and ruin his own son by producing a bastard as a legitimate heir, the Earl of Castlehaven solicited his favorite male servant to ravish Elizabeth. The Earl of Castlehaven was eventually accused by his estranged son James, and was beheaded in 1631 for the criminal charges of sodomy and rape. In seventeenth-century England, it was extremely unusual for an aristocrat to be condemned to death for sexual offences.

How did the 1631 Castlehaven scandal affect the original production of the 1634 family entertainment? Although the Earl of Bridgewater and his family were not directly involved in the domestic crime, there are some hints to suggest that the Egerton family were embarrassed by the 1631 scandal. For example, although the Earl of Bridgewater was appointed as President of Wales in 1631, he did not move into the official mansion until 1634. It was impossible for the Earl and Countess of Bridgewater to dismiss the family dishonor completely. It was equally impossible for Milton and Lawes to be unaware of the scandal. We should not forget, however, that there is no explicit reference to the scandal in the text of *A Mask*. Nevertheless, the main action of *A Mask* concerns the sexual harassment of the Lady by Comus. We could easily find some similarities as well as differences between the dramatic situation of the family entertainment and the Castlehaven scandal. Comus is a debauched son "in a sensual sty," like the Earl of Castlehaven in a disordered household. Comus's "ugly-headed monsters" who offend the Lady "with grim aspects" might have reminded the most sensitive audience of the Earl's male servants who humiliated the noble ladies. The Lady is "all chained up" in "a stately palace" just as the victims of the Castlehaven domestic crime were shut in the aristocratic residence (77, 693–4, 659, 658 stage direction). The pitiful image of the Lady would have seemed almost identical with Elizabeth's; at the trial of 1631, she was the same age as Alice at the original production of *A Mask* in 1634. But, of course, there are as many important differences. Whereas the Lady is unmarried, deceived by the strange god in the disguise of a "gentle villager," and rescued by her brothers to go back securely to her happy "father and mother, " Elizabeth was married, deceived by her titled family member, and liberated by her husband's legal action only to see her parents dishonorably ruined (303, 965 stage direction).

Significantly, textual variations of the masque center on sections related to sexual matters. The text of *A Mask* has the most complicated history among Milton's works. We possess (1) the Trinity Manuscript, which was a kind of working copy for Milton, (2) the Bridgewater Manuscript, which is thought to have been a presentation copy for the Egerton family after the original production, (3) the print version Lawes published in 1637, and (4) the print version Milton included in his *Poems* of 1645 and reprinted with minor revisions in 1673. Most modern scholars do not regard the Bridgewater Manuscript as a faithful representation of the original performance since the presentation copy shows several major textual variants that may suggest the sensitive situation of the Egerton family in the 1630s. Comus's much-quoted speech in the printed editions ("List Lady be not coy [. . .] Think what, and be advised, you are but young yet" [736–54]) is, for example, absent from the Bridgewater Manuscript. The motif of the passage is the classical convention of *carpe diem*; Milton's phrase "a neglected rose" is particularly reminiscent of Robert Herrick's "Gather ye rosebuds, while ye may." In a sense, Comus is at his most touchy about the aristocratic family's sex scandal not only because he makes fun of the virtue of "virginity" but also because his sexual aggression is based on his distorted pride in aristocratic privileges; he despises the "homely" with a cynical glance at "courts." There are unusually careful revisions in the relevant passage in the Trinity Manuscript, too; Milton was highly cautious about the characterization of Comus in his climactic speech, as is apparent in his working copy.

Scholars are now divided roughly into two groups about the relationship between the original performance of *A Mask* and the Castlehaven scandal. One group points out the "irrelevance" of any effort to detect possible topical allusions to the Castlehaven scandal in the aristocratic entertainment (Brown 1985; Creaser 1984). Both occasional and generic qualities of *A Mask* strictly define the purpose of the performance as a celebration of the inauguration of the Earl of Bridgewater as President of Wales. Neither the young poet nor the court musician was expected to criticize the corruption of aristocracy. As such, Comus's speech against "virginity" was omitted simply because it was irrelevant to the ceremonious occasion. The other group is interested, on the other hand, in elucidating the insidious politics of the aristocratic entertainment. Although it is true that *A Mask* was performed to aid the Egerton family in forgetting the scandal, the act of forgetting presupposes an awareness of the problem. Additionally, the Earl of Bridgewater knew about not only the Castlehaven scandal but also, for example, the case of Margery Evans, a serving maid who, raped and robbed near the Welsh border, was unfairly imprisoned in 1631, and appealed to him for her redress (Marcus 1983). Appointed as President of Wales, the Earl of Bridgewater was responsible in part for upholding local and social order. New Historicism of the 1980s was willing to see the cultural conflicts of English society before the Civil War in the omission of Comus's speech against "virginity" from the Bridgewater Manuscript and Milton's nervously repeated revisions of the passage in the Trinity Manuscript.

The Theater State Reconsidered

Seventeenth-century England anticipates what Clifford Geertz, the modern anthropologist so influential to New Historicism, defines as "the theater state" in his study of nineteenth-century Bali. The young Milton's contribution to the Stuart court masque makes the place of *A Mask* uneasy in his whole life and work. The happy ending of the masque in 1634 was, for example, represented by "Country dancers" who embodied the local unity of the Earl of Bridgewater's new estate in Wales. They dance on the stage until the Attendant Spirit starts to sing the last couple of songs as follows: "Back, shepherds, back, enough your play,/ Till next sunshine holiday" (957–8). *A Mask* supports the traditional pastimes of dance and music. But these very holiday pastimes were a nationwide political issue about which Puritans attacked the Anglican Church. The year before the performance of *A Mask*, in 1633, Charles I reissued James I's *Book of Sports* of 1618 which tactfully encouraged traditional pastimes on Sundays and holidays in order to restrain the strict observance of the Puritan doctrine of sabbatarianism (Marcus 1986). Charles I's reissue of the anti-Puritan proclamation enraged Puritans. Dance and music on holidays became highly politicized activities in the 1630s. *A Mask* supports Anglican policy rather the Puritan position, inflecting what it means to call Milton a Puritan poet.

It was not only in terms of the political issue of holidays that Milton stood against Puritanism in *A Mask*. Its genre and production could offend Puritans in the 1630s. Puritan hostility to dramatic performance resulted in the closure of London theaters in 1642, immediately after the outbreak of the Civil War. Among the flood of Puritan pamphlets against theater, the most famous is William Prynne's *Histrio-Mastix* (1633). His laborious criticism of theater was rewarded by the loss of his ears because his outright definition of "Women-Actors" as "notorious whores" in the index was interpreted as a seditious libel of Queen Henrietta Maria, who often appeared on the court stage. In his bulky pamphlet attacking the sensual qualities of theatrical performances, Prynne was especially critical of "women-Actors" in "Masques" (Prynne 1972: 214). Prynne would have raised a strong objection to the appearance of Alice in the sexual harassment scene on the stage at Ludlow Castle.

After the outbreak of the Civil War, Milton's own references to court masques are all critical, too. In *Eikonoklastes* (1649), for example, Milton justifies the execution of Charles I by disputing *Eikon Basilike* (1649), a collection of essays and meditations allegedly written by the condemned king, which aroused great sympathy for the royal martyr among the populous. Milton criticizes the frontispiece of *Eikon Basilike* by pointing out that "the conceited portraiture before his Book" is "drawn out to full measure of a Masking scene, and sett there to catch fools and silly gazers" (*CPW* 3.342). Milton here repudiates the theatrical spectacle of the court masque as a dishonest device to please and deceive gullible spectators. Defending republicanism in *The Readie and Easie Way* (1660), he then warns his readers against the ongoing

Restoration because "a king must be ador'd like a Demigod, with a dissolute and haughtie court about him, of vast expence and luxurie, masks and revels" (*CPW* 7.425). For the republican Milton, "masks and revels" are reminders of the corruption of the Stuart court. His republican discourse puts a special emphasis on the folly of the waste of wealth for aristocratic entertainments, as is poetically rendered for full effect in *Paradise Lost* (1667). He makes a sharp contrast between the ideal of love in Paradise and its degeneration at court:

> Here Love his golden shafts employs, here lights
> His constant lamp, and waves his purple wings,
> Reigns here and revels; not in the ought smile
> Of harlots, loveless, joyless, unendeared,
> Casual fruition, nor in court amours,
> Mixed dance, or wanton masque, or midnight ball.
> (4.763–8)

Denouncing court entertainments in his great epic, Milton is especially critical of "mixed dance," which comprised the happy ending of *A Mask*.

Milton's growing ideological commitment to republicanism, however, does not translate into a strict break from all courtly or Royalist ties. John Shawcross has amply demonstrated Milton's enduring relationships with persons of various political, religious, and socioeconomic groups (Shawcross 2003). Most pertinent to this discussion, Milton did not terminate his friendship with Lawes. Milton was proud of his collaboration with the eminent court musician even after the outbreak of the Civil War. "Sonnet 13" (1646) still praises Lawes as "Harry whose tuneful and well-measured song/ First taught our English music how to span/ Words with just note and accent" (1–3). Perhaps surprisingly, the sonnet was first printed in *Choice Psalmes* dedicated to Charles I in 1648. Henry Lawes published the book to commemorate his younger brother, William, another talented court musician, who was killed while fighting for the King's cause in the battle at Chester in 1645. Milton's connection with the Royalist publication reminds us that the first collection of Milton's poems in 1645 carried the following description in the title page: "The SONGS were set in Musick by / Mr. HENRY LAWES Gentleman of / the KINGS Chappel, and one / of His MAIESTIES / Private Musick." "The SONGS" are undoubtedly the five songs in *A Mask*. The collaboration with the Royalist musician was a great sales point in the first publication of his poems during the

Civil War. Interestingly, the last collection of his poems in 1673, well into the Restoration, deletes the description above from the title page.

One of the concerns that runs through Milton's whole canon – from *A Mask* to *Paradise Lost* – is a nationalist glance to the world outside Britain. The Attendant Spirit's opening speech lets the audience know that Comus roved "the Celtic, and Iberian fields" before he settled down in the "ominous wood" (60–1). The transcendental voice of the celestial messenger initially defines the antagonist's origin as non-British, suggesting the "Celtic" otherness of the Welsh culture. Comus's "Celtic" origin anticipates the locale of the fallen angels in *Paradise Lost* who "o'er the Celtic roamed the utmost isles" (1.521). Like the devils in the epic, Comus in the masque is a disturbing non-British creature within the British nation. Early modern British nationalism, which was represented by the Stuart masque like Townshend's *Albion's Triumph* or Carew's *Coelum Britannicum*, constitutes the geographical and racial framework of *A Mask* and *Paradise Lost*, multiplying the imaginary figure of the non-British antagonist, such as Comus and the fallen angels. And, what are we to make of those "Iberian fields" of Spain and Portugal?

Nationalism is closely connected with colonialism in early modern England. The Elder Brother develops the Attendant Spirit's rhetoric of nationalism by conjuring up the non-Western monstrous image of Comus as follows: "let him be girt/ With all the grisly legions that troop/ Under the sooty flag of Acheron,/ Harpies and hydras, or all the monstrous forms/ 'Twixt Africa and Ind, I'll find him out" (601–5). The allusion to Acheron, one of the rivers of Hades, adds an infernal association to Comus among the "monstrous forms" between Africa and India. The reference to "Ind" in the representation of the infernal antagonist is an early version of the oriental image of Satan in Pandemonium in *Paradise Lost*:

> High on a throne of royal state, which far
> Outshone the wealth of Ormus and of Ind,
> Or where the gorgeous East with richest hand
> Showers on her kings barbaric and gold,
> Satan exalted sat.
>
> (2.1–5)

Although the explicit connection of the infernal figure with "royal" culture contradicts the ideology of the young Milton's commitment to the Stuart court masque, the association between the antagonist and

Indian or oriental riches is consistent from *A Mask* to *Paradise Lost*. Both Comus and Satan are represented as rich, formidable enemies to be conquered and contained by Christian people. The cultural location of Comus is as uneasy in early modern British nationalism as the place of *A Mask* is in Miltonic canon. We should not forget that the politics of the seventeenth-century aristocratic entertainment in Wales matters not only in the context of seventeenth-century British history but also in terms of postcolonial and comparative literary criticism which seeks to enrich our understanding of the influence of the national and international on the personal and familial, elucidating the innovative uses of tradition within varied contexts.

A Mask has perhaps become an even more important work for contemporary literary critics than for their predecessors because its framework contains so many elements that contradict established critical frameworks about Milton's life and works, and by extension of literary works in general. It is true that Milton was a great poet who decidedly committed himself to Puritanism and republicanism in the English Civil Wars. But *A Mask* reminds us that he escapes any of our modern generalizations about any univocal ideology and aesthetic of literature. Occasionally independent of religious and political conflicts around him in London, he could enjoy his friendship with a court musician in order to expand the possibilities of dramatic poetry, taking the greatest advantage of the opportunity for an aristocratic entertainment in Wales. *A Mask* is charming evidence that Milton's whole achievement has yet to be sufficiently appreciated. It leaves ample room for study by a new generation sensitive to the dynamic and self-contradictory qualities of the politics of theater both historically and in the twenty-first century's newly emerging multicultural and multimedia society.

References and Further Reading

Bevington, David and Holbrook, Peter (eds) (1998). *The Politics of the Stuart Court Masque.* Cambridge: Cambridge University Press.

Breasted, Barbara (1971). "*Comus* and the Castlehaven Scandal." *Milton Studies* 3: 201–24.

Brown, Cedric (1985). *John Milton's Aristocratic Entertainments.* Cambridge: Cambridge University Press.

Brown, Cedric (1999). "Milton's Ludlow Masque." In Dennis Danielson (ed.), *A Cambridge Companion to Milton* (pp. 25–38). New York: Cambridge University Press.

Campbell, Lily B. (1923). *Scenes and Machines on the English Stage during the Renaissance*. Cambridge: Cambridge University Press.

Carew, Thomas (1949). *The Poems of Thomas Carew: With his Masque* Coelum Britannicum. Edited by Rhodes Dunlop. Oxford: Clarendon Press.

Creaser, John (1984). "Milton's *Comus*: The Irrelevance of the Castlehaven Scandal." *Notes and Queries* 31 (229) 3: 307–17.

Creaser, John (1984). "'The Present Aid of This Occasion': The Setting of *Comus*." In David Lindley (ed.), *The Court Masque* (pp. 111–34). Manchester: Manchester University Press.

Culler, Jonathan (2000). *Literary Theory: A Very Short Introduction*. Oxford: Oxford University Press.

Darbishire, Helen (ed.) (1932). *The Early Lives of Milton*. London: Constable.

Demaray, John G. (1968). *Milton and the Masque Tradition: The Early Poems, "Arcades," and* Comus. Cambridge, MA: Harvard University Press.

Diekhoff, John S. (ed.) (1968). A Maske at Ludlow*: Essays on Milton's* Comus. Cleveland: Case Western Reserve University Press.

Evans, Willa McClung (1941). *Henry Lawes: Musician and Friend of Poets*. New York: MLA.

Finney, Gretchen Ludke (1962). *Musical Backgrounds for English Literature: 1580– 1650*. New Brunswick: Rutgers University Press.

Fletcher, Angus (1971). *The Transcendental Masque: An Essay on Milton's* Comus. Ithaca: Cornell University Press.

Geertz, Clifford (1980). *Negara: The Theatre State in Nineteenth-Century Bali*. Princeton: Princeton University Press.

Herrup, Cynthia B. (1991) *A House in Gross Disorder: Sex, Law, and the 2nd Earl of Castlehaven*. New York: Oxford University Press.

Hunter, William B. (1983). *Milton's* Comus*: Family Piece*. Troy, NY: Whitston.

Jonson, Ben (1969). *The Complete Masques*. Edited by Stephen Orgel. New Haven: Yale University Press.

Lindley, David (ed.) (1984). *The Court Masque*. Manchester: Manchester University Press.

Marcus, Leah S. (1983). "The Milieu of Milton's *Comus*: Judicial Reform at Ludlow and the Problem of Sexual Assault." *Criticism* 25: 293–327.

Marcus, Leah S. (1986). *The Politics of Mirth: Jonson, Herrick, Milton, Marvell, and the Defense of Old Holiday Pastimes*. Chicago: University of Chicago Press.

Marcus, Leah S. (2003). "John Milton's *Comus*." In Thomas Corns (ed.), *A Companion to Milton* (pp. 232–45). Malden: Blackwell.

McGuire, Maryann Cale (1982). *Milton's Puritan Masque*. Athens: University of Georgia Press.

Milton, John (1953–82). *Complete Prose Works of John Milton* [*CPW*]. Edited by Don M. Wolfe. 8 vols. New Haven and London: Yale University Press.

Milton, John (1997). *Milton: Complete Shorter Poems*. Edited by John Carey. 2nd edn. London: Longman.

Nicoll, Allardyce (1938). *Stuart Masques and the Renaissance Stage*. London: G. Harrap.

Orgel, Stephen (1967). *The Jonsonian Masque*. New York: Columbia University Press.

Orgel, Stephen and Strong, Roy (1973). *Inigo Jones: The Theatre of the Stuart Court*. 2 vols. Berkeley: University of California Press.

Prynne, William (1972). *Histrio-Mastix: The Player's Scourge or, Actor's Tragedy*. [London, 1633.] Reprint. New York: Johnson Reprint.

Shawcross, John T. (2003). *The Arms of the Family: The Significance of John Milton's Relatives and Associates*. Lexington: University of Kentucky.

Southern, Richard (1952). *Changeable Scenery: Its Origin and Development in the British Theatre*. London: Faber and Faber.

Spink, Ian (2000). *Henry Lawes: Cavalier Songwriter*. Oxford: Oxford University Press.

Sprott, S. E. (ed.) (1973). *John Milton:* A Maske*: The Earlier Versions*. Toronto: University of Toronto Press.

Strong, Roy (1984). *Art and Power: Renaissance Festivals 1450–1650*. Berkeley: University of California Press.

Townshend, Aurelian (1912). *Aurelian Townshend's Poems and Masks*. Edited by E. K. Chambers. Oxford: Clarendon Press.

Welsford, Enid (1928). *The Court Masque: A Study in the Relationship between Poetry and the Revels*. Cambridge: Cambridge University Press.

Chapter 8

The Bible, Religion, and Spirituality in *Paradise Lost*

Achsah Guibbory

Milton's epic about the "Fall" of Adam and Eve is the most famous biblically based Christian poem in English literature. Milton's narrative, with its powerful description of Satan's rebellion and the fall of the angels, is probably the version most widely known in the Western part of the world – known even to those who have never read the Bible, for Milton's epic account has over the centuries become part of the culture's DNA. Indeed, the narrative of *Paradise Lost* is often confused in the popular imagination with the biblical version, which is, in fact, quite stark and brief. The whole account of Creation, Adam and Eve's eating the fruit of the Tree of Knowledge, God's judgment of them, and their expulsion from the Garden of Eden takes up only the first three chapters of Genesis. But Milton's poem goes well beyond the Bible. He draws on material from later Christian and rabbinic traditions and commentaries, and from Greek and Roman mythologies and literature (Evans 1968; Patrides 1966; Rosenblatt 1994; Revard 1980; Shoulson 2001; Sims 1962; Turner 1987). His poem attempts to incorporate the whole sweep of human history and culture as it was known in Milton's day – as if he is out not just to "justify the ways of God to men" (as he says in his opening invocation, 1.26) but also to explain the order, nature, and meaning of the world.

One could say that that impulse to explain the universe, to figure everything out, makes Milton one of the most rational of religious poets. Rather than attempting some sort of mystical transcendence, he is always seeking reasons, explanations, trying to make sense of

128

the world. But this impulse can also be the deep well of spirituality, which I understand as the effort to seek the largest meanings, to "connect the dots" of experience, as it were, to try to see in the apparent chaos of the world a deeper order.

Reading the Bible

In certain ways, *Paradise Lost* sticks closely to the account in the Bible. When we speak of "the Bible" we need to recognize that there is more than one, and to recognize which one Milton would have considered his (Pelikan). The Hebrew Bible, in which Genesis (or *Beresheet*, its Hebrew name) tells the story of the world's beginning and is the first book, was incorporated by Christians as the "Old Testament," and followed by the "New Testament." Although Milton knew Hebrew as well as Greek (and Latin), and was familiar with the Hebrew language version of Genesis, as a Christian he read Genesis as part of the "Christian" Bible. That is, he read the Hebrew account through a distinctly Christian lens. Thus, Raphael's account to Adam (Book 7) of the creation of the world follows the order and detail of Genesis 1 and 2, but Milton has the Son do the actual creating, indeed with "golden Compasses" (7.225) that are an anachronism from a later age.

Biblical scholars speak of two versions of the creation of "man" in Genesis. One version stresses their equality: "Let us make man in our image [. . .] so God created man in his own image, in the image of God created he him; male and female created he them" (Gen. 1:26–7); the other, their disparity and Eve's derivative, secondary nature: "And the Lord God caused a deep sleep to fall upon Adam and he slept; and he took one of his ribs [. . .] And the rib, which the Lord God had taken from man, made he a woman, and brought her unto the man" (Gen. 2:21–2). Milton's initial description of Adam and Eve in Book 4 incorporates both versions of their creation. In Milton's descriptive passage, we move from emphasis on their similarity to their difference.

> Two of far nobler shape erect and tall,
> Godlike erect, with native Honor clad
> In naked Majesty seem'd Lords of all,
> And worthy seem'd, for in thir looks Divine
> The image of thir glorious Maker shone,
> Truth, Wisdom, Sanctitude severe and pure,

> Severe, but in true filial freedom plac't;
> Whence true autority in men; though both
> Not equal, as thir sex not equal seem'd;
> For contemplation he and valor form'd,
> For softness shee and sweet attractive Grace.
> Hee for God only, shee for God in him:
> His fair large Front and Eye sublime declar'd
> Absolute rule; and Hyacinthine Locks
> Round from his parted forelock manly hung
> Clust'ring, but not beneath his shoulders broad:
> Shee as a veil down to the slender waist
> Her unadorned golden tresses wore
> Dishevell'd, but in wanton ringlets wav'd
> As the Vine curls her tendrils, which impli'd
> Subjection, but requir'd with gentle sway.
>
> (4.288–308)

The tension between the two biblical versions of Eve's creation is evident throughout *Paradise Lost*, though the second carries greater weight in Milton's stress on Adam's need to retain supremacy. This emphasis on Adam's superiority not only reflects the dominant patriarchal values of seventeenth-century English society; we might also see it as the consequence of the fact that Milton's interpretation of the Genesis account is shaped by the New Testament. The details of his description of this first couple – details not there in the plain Hebrew text of Genesis – echo repeated comments in the Pauline epistles about the wife's proper "subordination" to her husband as her "head" (cf. Ephesians 5:22–4; 1 Cor. 11:3). Paul had said that women should be "covered" (1 Cor. 11:4–15). Milton's Eve is created already "veil[ed]."

Milton's version of the Genesis story, that is, is subtly Christianized. But there is also much that Milton adds to the Bible. Although he follows the Bible in having Adam name all the creatures, Milton gives Eve the surprising role of naming the flowers (*Paradise Lost* 11.273–9). Another change is more radical. The Bible explicitly says nothing about the sexual relations of Adam and Eve before the Fall, despite the blessing to "be fruitful and multiply." In sharp departure from Christian tradition, Milton has Adam and Eve consummate their marriage before the Fall, perhaps echoing a rabbinic tradition. Whereas Christian tradition had long associated human sexuality with sin, in Book 4 we see Adam and Eve enjoying a kind of holy sex that is framed by prayer. They pray before entering their nuptial "bower"

(4.738) and again when they rise in the morning. Milton's narrator comments, "nor turn'd I ween *Adam* from his fair Spouse, nor Eve the Rites/Mysterious of connubial Love refus'd" (4.741–3), and even inserts a defense of their sexuality as pure and unshameful in his own hymn, "Hail wedded Love" (4.750) (Guibbory 1995; Turner 1987).

The biblical account of the temptation and Fall is minimalist; motivations or explanations are lacking. In Milton's poem, the narrative is fleshed out. Christian traditions about Satan's temptation are brought to bear on the brief Genesis script. Satan assumes a role so enormous and powerful that some readers have felt him to have heroic proportions. Milton frames and explains Satan's temptation of Adam and Eve by describing Satan's earlier rebellion against God in Heaven, his being cast down into Hell with the other rebel angels, and their subsequent plot for revenge. Invoking but going beyond traditions, many of Milton's creative additions in the poem humanize the story and develop the characters, making them believable, recognizable. One might say he makes the Bible his – and our – own. Milton invents a powerful scene in Pandemonium (the theatrical congress in Hell), in which Satan indirectly masterminds the plot. We see Satan in these early books as proud, disdaining "Submission" (1.661) or "subjection" (4.50), envious, sometimes despairing. Later, when Raphael explains to Adam the details of the rebellion in Heaven, we see that Satan's rebellion was triggered by what might seem the arbitrary preferment and exaltation of God the Father's "only Son" (5.604, more generally 600–15) – an act that produces the first case of sibling rivalry. Milton seemingly feels impelled to fill in the lacunae in the biblical story not just to enrich his poetry or to give range to his imagination, but also so that the Fall can make better sense, so there is a logic, a reason, and psychological plausibility.

Let's take another example. In Genesis 3, when the serpent speaks to "the woman" (3:1) it is not clear where Adam is – if he is there and silent, or if the woman is alone. This is a problem in the text. If Adam is there, why doesn't he stop Eve? The Bible says that "she took of the fruit thereof, and did eat, and gave also unto her husband with her; and he did eat" (3:6). Was he standing there? Did she have to travel a distance? Milton addresses these questions, filling in what is not in the Bible (without adding anything that actually conflicts with it) by having Adam and Eve separate at the beginning of Book 9. Eve here wants a certain freedom, and Adam like God must allow her to go rather than compel her love. Milton invests this powerful, ominous scene with theological meaning (the issue of free will, and Milton's commitment to a God who allows choice rather than predetermining everything) but also with psychological truth, for Eve as Adam's child as well as wife has reached the point where she must separate from the parent in order to develop her own identity. Each of my interpretative statements here is, of course, open to disagreement – Milton does not avoid the complexity of Eve's desire to leave or of Adam's granting her permission, or fail to suggest alternative explanations or even the impossibility of a "right" answer. Nevertheless, in the various narratives that Milton spins onto and out of the Bible, one could say that Milton's poem becomes a meditation or *midrash* on the Bible, for, much like the earlier rabbis in their commentaries and stories, Milton tries to explain enigmatic passages, fill in gaps, and grapple with the biblical text in the belief that he's doing God's work, pursuing truth.

Adding to the Bible: Protestantism and the Problem of Invention

Milton's additions to the biblical text are numerous and significant. He imagines Satan's speeches in Hell: his conversation with Beelzebub, his inspiring speeches to his troops. He imagines Satan's feelings of desolation when he enters Eden and sees its beauty and that of the first human couple. Before the Fall, Milton has God the Father send Raphael to "converse with Adam" (5.230), to educate Adam (and Eve indirectly) so that their choice will be an educated one – to "render Man inexcusable" (as "The Argument" to Book 5 puts it), to make sure that God cannot be blamed for their sin. Raphael communicates the vivid details of what Milton imagines the war in Heaven was like. After the judgment but before the final expulsion from the Garden, Milton has God the Father send Michael to instruct Adam in the history of the world, not neglecting to give him hope and an understanding of Christ, thus turning the Adam of Genesis into the first Christian (see Rosenblatt 1994: 204–34).

Milton, as a Christian following a tradition of Christian interpretation of the "Old Testament," would say that Christ and the Gospel were already in some sense "in" the Hebrew scriptures, understood as "shadowy Types" (12.303) intimating "Truth" that would be finally revealed in the Gospel and with the coming of Christ. But so much of what Milton adds is not simply a Christianization of the Hebrew Bible's account. Too much is invented. Milton even invents speeches for God the Father and the Son in Heaven, putting words in God's mouth, as it were. Raphael's explanation before he tells Adam about the revolt in Heaven seems to provide also Milton's rationale for the liberties he takes in retelling the story of the Fall in this poem:

> Sad task and hard, for how shall I relate
> To human sense th'invisible exploits
> Of warring Spirits; [. . .
>
> . . . .
> . . .] how last unfold
> The secrets of another World, perhaps
> Not lawful to reveal? yet for thy good
> This is dispens't, and what surmounts the reach
> Of human sense, I shall delineate so,
> By lik'ning spiritual to corporal forms,
> As may express them best, though what if Earth
> Be but the shadow of Heav'n, and things therein
> Each to other like, more than on Earth is thought?
> (5.564–66, 568–76)

He is "accommodating" a higher reality to human understanding, trying to put into material, corporeal words a spiritual truth that surpasses language. In this way Raphael – and Milton – can invent their stories.

Yet, for Protestants the word of God, the Bible (not human invention) was supposedly the supreme authority. Reformers had attacked the Roman Catholic Church for, among other things, exalting human (i.e. church) tradition above the Bible, or for making it an alternative source of truth. For Protestants, at least theoretically, it was *sola scriptura*, the Bible alone. Milton was clearly taking risks in "adding" to the biblical account in his poetic creation. Yet how could he write an epic poem without taking liberties? Milton's solution to the dilemma was to invoke, from the beginning, the holy muse, to call on God as his inspiration – the being who would authorize and legitimate his poem.

Milton's invocations of his divine muse suggest a passionate desire and an urgent need to authorize his poetic invention, to legitimize his poem as sacred. In the first, at the opening of the poem, he invokes the

> Heav'nly Muse, that on the secret top
> Of *Oreb*, or of *Sinai*, didst inspire
> That Shepherd, who first taught the chosen Seed,
> In the Beginning how the Heav'ns and Earth
> Rose out of *Chaos*.
> (1.6–10)

Milton needs the muse that inspired Moses as he undertakes his "advent'rous Song," pursuing "Things unattempted yet in Prose or Rhyme" (1.13–16). His divine muse was "present" at the very beginning of things, at the creation of the world, when it "Dove-like satst brooding on the vast Abyss,/ And mad'st it pregnant" (20–2). This invocation, and the others at the beginning of Books 3 and 7, are, significantly, prayers, and in this sense the poem (if we are to consider that the prayer for divine inspiration has been granted) becomes itself a kind of inspired prayer directed to God as well as to a human audience that Milton hopes to instruct (Lieb 1981; Guibbory 1998; Schwartz 1988). Milton also implies in these invocations that revelation did not cease with the Bible, that God continues to speak to select human beings. "Nightly" Milton "visit[s]" Sion's hill (3.32); and his muse "Visit'st my slumbers Nightly, or when Morn/ Purples the East" (7.29–30). So, in *Paradise Lost*, Milton presents himself as one of these "chosen of peculiar grace/ Elect above the rest" (3.183–4), not only one of the redeemed but a divinely ordained poet, minister of God, and prophet. God, he suggests, continues to speak to him and has authorized his ambitious poem, with all its additions to the Bible, allowing him even to speak for God, as the ancient Israelite prophets did in the Old Testament and as St John did in the book of Revelation of the New Testament.

Milton knows he is treading on risky ground, that a suspicious reader could see a similarity between Milton's poetic aspirations to achieve something unique with his poem and Satan's desire for glory and adventure. Yet Milton insists, throughout *Paradise Lost*, that there is a difference between his inspired creation and satanic "inventions." The opening of Book 1 allies his poetic creation, his inspiration, with the creation of the world, as he invokes the spirit who hovered over the waters and made them pregnant. Milton insists on the vital, creative aspect of his work and contrasts it to the destructive "inventions" of Satan and the fallen angels, which invariably turn out to be glorious but idolatrous or instruments of death. In the revolt in Heaven, they invent gunpowder and canons, the first instruments of mass destruction. It is an "invention" all of the rebel angels "admired" (6.498), and the narrator predicts that "in future days" someone will "devise/ Like instrument to plague the sons of men" (6.502–5). Sin and Death build a "Bridge of wondrous length" (2.1028) so that they can travel and spread their poison more easily to the new world once it is conquered by Satan. Pandemonium is built by disemboweling creation. It is a glorious building, but a place where death and destruction is plotted.

> Anon out of the earth a Fabric huge
> Rose like an Exhalation, with the sound
> Of Dulcet Symphonies and voices sweet,
> Built like a Temple, where *Pilasters* round
> Were set, and Doric pillars overlaid
> With Golden Architrave; nor did there want
> Cornice or Frieze, with bossy Sculptures grav'n.
>
> (1.710–16)

Milton's description of Pandemonium recalls not only the "magnificence" (718) of Babylon, but also St Peter's in Rome, and Solomon's Temple, with all its gold. It has been argued that behind Milton's account of the architecture of Pandemonium stands Vitruvius, the influential ancient Roman author, and that Milton's rhetorical strategy in this passage involves both celebration and criticism of this glorious structure (DuRocher 2001). However, even as Milton's poetry suggests admiration for this wondrous building, he makes it clear that Pandemonium is a place of idolatry. After the devils conclude their conference and Satan offers to go to the new world to seduce the new creation "to our party," the fallen angels bow down and worship him: "Towards him they bend/ With awful reverence prone; and as a God/ Extol him equal to the highest in Heav'n" (2.477–9).

Milton shares the Protestant obsession with idolatry, and the impulse towards iconoclasm (or the destruction of idols) that might be seen to exist in tension with his creative impulse (Gilman 1986; Cable 1995). Indeed, just as Milton is concerned to distinguish between his divinely inspired creation and satanic "invention," so throughout the poem he attempts to distinguish sharply between true worship and idolatry, between true and false religion (Guibbory 1998). Even if some readers think the distinction artificial, Milton insists on its legitimacy and necessity. He represents and indicts in his poem a world that has difficulty making the distinction, that is repeatedly drawn into false worship, into idolatry. We see this in the first books with Satan and the fallen angels. As the beginning of the second book shows Satan "exalted" "High on a Throne of Royal State" (2.5,1), we see that, despite his protests in Book 1, Satan does not want to "be free" (1.259). He wants to be God. The other rebel angels become guilty of idolatry, as they bow to him, offering him the servitude they refuse to God and the Son, whom we learn in Book 3 God has chosen to reign (3.313–17).

The unfallen Adam and Eve in Paradise engage in true worship. Adam and Eve spend their days pruning the garden and acknowledging their creator and his goodness. They pray to God together before retiring to their nuptial bower where they will enjoy "the Rites/ Mysterious of connubial Love" (4.742–3) which themselves seem a form of prayer. They pray when they wake in the morning:

> Lowly they bow'd adoring, and began
> Thir Orisons, each Morning duly paid
> In various style, for neither various style
> Nor holy rapture wanted they to praise
> Thir Maker, in fit strains pronounct or sung
> Unmeditated such prompt eloquence
> Flow'd from thir lips, in Prose or numerous Verse.
> (5.145–50)

Unfallen, true prayer is spontaneous, inspired, from the heart, a debt of gratitude cheerfully paid. It is not, Milton implies, like the formal prayers of the Church of England, or Jewish or Catholic liturgies. Milton had in his earlier prose voiced his opposition to the formal or "set prayers" of the English Church, which he felt constrained the free spirit and were in fact not much different from the Roman Catholic liturgy (e.g. *Of Reformation* and *Eikonoklastes*). But in *Paradise Lost*, Milton is able to imagine what unfallen prayer would have been like, natural, instinctive, attuned to the cycles of the day. Prayer is also an activity Adam and Eve share.

This prelapsarian worship contrasts with Eve's actions when she succumbs to temptation and eats the fruit. Immediately after eating,

> Thus to herself she pleasingly began.
> O Sovran, virtuous, precious of all Trees
> In Paradise, of operation blest
> To Sapience, hitherto obscur'd, infam'd,
> [. . . . .
> . . .] but henceforth my early care,
> Not without Song, each Morning, and due praise
> Shall tend thee.
> (9.794–7, 799–801)

That her speech is at once a soliloquy and an address to a tree expresses Milton's view that idolatry is ultimately self-worship. Eve bows "lowly" to the tree (rather than God), and promises to tend the tree with praise every morning, replacing her morning prayers to God with a kind of nature-worship that Milton associates with the diabolic.

True and False Worship, Spirituality and Religion

Milton is at pains to articulate what true worship is in his poem. It seems embodied in the Son's perfect obedience to his father in Heaven; in Milton's prayerful invocations to the divine, creative spirit; in the heavenly angels' hymns of praise; in Adam and Eve's thankful prayers to God before the Fall; and maybe even in Eve's unfallen (but learned) reverential expressions of love for Adam: "O thou for whom/ And from whom I was form'd flesh of thy flesh,/ And without whom am to no end, my Guide/ And Head" (4.440–3). Although most are offended by the gender hierarchy here and by Eve's subjection, what she says to Adam here is an image of the relation of humans to the God in whose image they are formed, who is the "end" and source of their being. True worship is an acknowledgment of dependency on the divine source of life, the Author, the Creator, in whose image the poet (as well as Adam and Eve) is made. It is notable that Satan in his conversation with Abdiel refuses to acknowledge his Creator: "We know no time when we were not as now;/ Know none before us, self-begot, self-rais'd/ By our own quick'ning power" (5.859–61).

Examples of false worship in *Paradise Lost* are rife, and complex. Most problematic is the fact that idolatry seems latent in Adam and Eve, part of their very nature. Adam's first impulse after being created is to worship God: he instinctively knows there is a "great Maker [. . .] In goodness and power preeminent" (8.278–9), and he asks the creatures to tell him who his author is so he may "adore" him (8.280). But that impulse is complicated as soon as Eve is created, and he feels from the first an inadequacy, a lack. (We might note that the word *Eros*, which in Christianity is often distinguished from *Agape* or love of God, denotes "lack," suggesting that some sort of lack or absence is essential to erotic desire.) Adam's reaction at her disappearance – "she disappear'd and left me dark" (8.478) – is ominous. Even before Adam succumbs to Eve's temptation, he admits to Raphael that he is prone to idolize her, to make her "his god":

> when I approach
> Her loveliness, so absolute she seems
> And in herself complete, so well to know
> Her own, that what she wills to do or say,
> Seems wisest, virtuousest, discreetest, best.
> (8.546–50)

And thus the Son, when he comes to judge Adam and Eve after the Fall, says to him, "Was she thy God, that her thou didst obey/ Before his voice[?]" (10.145–6). Eve, for her part, prefers the image of herself reflected in the water (she thought Adam "less fair [. . .] than that smooth wat'ry image" [4.478, 480]) and needs to be taught to revere Adam as her superior, to address him as her "Author and Disposer" (4.635) – which implies that woman has less of an immediate, instinctive connection with God. Although she feels intimately connected to the natural world (she names and tends the flowers, lies down "on the green bank, to look into the clear/ Smooth Lake" [4.458–9]), she doesn't instinctively look up to God as Adam does at his birth ("straight toward Heav'n my wondring Eyes I turn'd" [8.257]). Still, both have their weaknesses, the things that dispose them to idolatry.

But as we have seen, idolatry and rejection of God go back before the creation of the "world" to the time in Heaven. Indeed, Milton's poem might well be seen as a meditation on the varieties, prevalence, and persistence of idolatry and false worship, which Milton characteristically associates with material buildings, formal ritual, and institutions. In the early 1640s, in such tracts as *Of Reformation* and *The Reason of Church Government*, Milton allied himself with the Presbyterians as he criticized the institution of the Church of England, its rites, ceremonies, and episcopal structure of power, with priests, bishops, and archbishops. These aspects of England's Church suggested to Milton that it was insufficiently reformed from the supposed Roman Catholic corruptions, and that England was sliding back toward what was labeled "popery." In the 1640s, at the beginning of the English Civil Wars, Parliament, dominated by Presbyterians, outlawed episcopacy and the use of the *Book of Common Prayer*, essentially dismantling the Church of England. Debates ensued about how to restructure the church. The issues were never resolved, and various religious sects proliferated throughout the 1640s and 1650s. Fearing "heresy" and anarchy, the Presbyterians favored a national church but wanted to replace an Episcopal with a simpler Presbyterian structure of ministers and deacons. Milton soon moved away from the Presbyterians, concluding that the Presbyterians, too, would constrain the free spirit. As he said in his sonnet "On the New Forcers of Conscience under the Long Parliament," "*New Presbyter* is but *Old Priest* writ large" (14). For Milton, the Roman Catholic, English, and Presbyterian clergy were all after power, glory; all sought to restrict the spirit of God and restrain the conscience. Milton's commitment to following the light of conscience led him, like other religious radicals during the time, to separate from all religious institutions. As far as we know, Milton never belonged to or attended any church after the Restoration in 1660 reconstituted the monarchy and the national English Church. Milton's essentially anti-institutional stance is evident in *Paradise Lost*, where Milton expresses skepticism about ritualized, organized religion and locates worship in the spirit, particularly in the postlapsarian world.

Book 1 invokes a God who prefers the "upright heart" to any "Temples" (1.17–18) built with hands – and we should recall this image when we see the building of Pandemonium at the end of that Book. The narrator's roll call of the fallen angels in Book 1, which mentions the various guises the angels would later take and the "religious" places they would inhabit, emphasizes the connection of the demonic with institutions.

> wand'ring o'er the Earth,
> Through God's high sufferance for the trial of man,
> By falsities and lies the greatest part
> Of Mankind they corrupted to forsake
> God thir Creator, and th'invisible
> Glory of him that made them, to transform
> Of to the Image of a Brute, adorn'd
> With gay Religions full of Pomp and Gold,
> And Devils to adore for Deities:
> Then were they known to men by various Names,
> And various Idols through the Heathen World.
> (1.365–75)

The devils inhabit the temples of the pagan world, but also the holy sites of the Israelites (1.382–90). Infiltrating "his Sanctuary itself" (388), building their temples "right against the Temple of God" (1.402), the satanic presence has been always "bold" against the house of God (1.470), which has not been able to escape "Th'infection" (1.483).

The last two books of the poem – with their overview of human history – show the centrality of religion to human experience, but also the persistence of idolatry and the concomitant persecution of the godly. Michael shows Adam that the first murder (of Abel by Cain) took place over a disagreement about worship. Milton's retelling of the biblical incident emphasizes the distinction between true and false worship. When God accepts Abel's but not Cain's offering, we see God's clear preference for the "meek" (1.437) person, for the "sincere" (11.443) offering of the heart, and God's dislike of careless or feigned worship. Later in Michael's history we see "fair Atheists"

(11.625); we hear that the Jewish Temple will be polluted by "foul Idolatries" (12.337). Even after the coming of the Messiah, the Son, idolatry will persist. "Wolves shall succeed" the apostles "for Teachers" (12.508) and the godly will be persecuted:

> heavy persecution shall arise
> On all who in the worship persevere
> Of Spirit and Truth; the rest, far greater part,
> Will deem in outward Rites and specious forms
> Religion satisfi'd; Truth shall retire
> Bestuck with sland'rous darts, and works of Faith
> Rarely be found; so shall the World go on,
> To good malignant, to bad men benign,
> Under her own weight groaning, till the day
> Appear of respiration to the just,
> And vengeance to the wicked.
>
> (12.531–41)

There will be no justice, no triumph of the true worship until that Second Coming. Milton's history of the Christian church makes no reference to the Reformation – there is no idealization of the early institution of the church, no reference to the sixteenth-century effort to reform religion and return to primitive piety. For Milton, it seems, true religion has never dwelled in institutions.

When Milton's poem was published in 1667, the Church of England which Milton regarded as idolatrous had been restored along with the institution of monarchy, which Milton considered equally idolatrous and which was at the time bound up with the national church since the king was nominally its head. There had been no effort to accommodate within the church those who had wanted some reform. Legislation was enacted against "dissenters" from the official state church. There was no policy of toleration. But we must not forget that many radical Protestants like Milton actually opposed toleration because it would extend to Roman Catholics, whom they did not consider to be truly Christians.

Perhaps we might say that, as "religious" a poem as *Paradise Lost* is, it also expresses a deep suspicion of religion, indeed an incipient distinction between "spirituality" (spiritual devotion and a sense of connection to God, to the divine) and "religion" (as something more formally constituted, characterized by dogma and an institution). For Milton, once devotion takes on outward, public forms, becomes regularized and regimented, it tends to lose the spirit or soul. It is significant that

Milton's examples of good "men" of God in this poem – people who show proper devotion to God – are always "single" or alone, surrounded by an idolatrous or hostile mass. There is the exemplary Abdiel – the one who stands up to the peer pressure of Satan and the rebel angels and declares his allegiance to God. Milton the poet feels alone, beset by foes, and his visitation by God is private, unobserved, and takes place at night. Enoch is the one person in his time to speak of "Right and Wrong,/ Of Justice, of Religion, Truth and Peace" (11.666–7). Noah preaches "Conversion and Repentance" to a corrupt world (11.723–4); he and his family are the only humans to be saved. Abraham, the "one faithful man" (12.113), though "Bred up in Idolworship" (12.115), "leaves his Gods, his Friends, and native Soil" (11.129), following only God. The Son, too, is alone, and his crucifixion does not change the world, which is still unjust to the few good men, who will continue to be persecuted.

Milton leaves us at the end of the poem with the feeling that true devotion resides only in a personal relation with God that may not be visible to others but is threatening to the surrounding idolaters. The indwelling spirit is the "Comforter" (12.486) as the individual faces a hostile, ungodly world that threatens to return everything to the primordial state of chaos, with warring factions. That spiritual relation will not necessarily protect the good person from the evil that surrounds him or her. There is little comfort from community. Yet, there is some hope for company, as Milton by the end of the poem has allowed the relation of Adam and Eve (by the grace of God) to be in part repaired. If the prelapsarian harmony between Adam and Eve expressed the harmony between humans and God, then a restored relation between husband and wife who leave paradise "hand in hand" (12.648) – in Milton's addition to the Bible – gives hope of humanity's reconnection with the divine. This image of an imperfect but loving marriage finally tempers the loneliness that otherwise might be felt in this world, and perhaps may still be the best image of the relation between human and divine in the fallen world.

References and Further Reading

Achinstein, Sharon (2003). *Literature and Dissent in Milton's England.* Cambridge: Cambridge University Press.

Berry, Boyd (1976). *Process of Speech: Puritan Religious Writing and* Paradise Lost. Baltimore: Johns Hopkins University Press.

Cable, Lana (1995). *Carnal Rhetoric: Milton's Iconoclasm and the Poetics of Desire.* Durham, NC: Duke University Press.

Christopher, Georgia (1982). *Milton and the Science of the Saints.* Princeton: Princeton University Press.

Dobranski, Stephen B. and Rumrich, John P. (eds) (1998). *Milton and Heresy.* Cambridge: Cambridge University Press.

DuRocher, Richard J. (2001). *Milton among the Romans: The Pedagogy and Influence of Milton's Latin Curriculum.* Pittsburgh: Duquesne University Press.

Entzminger, Robert (1985). *Divine Word: Milton and the Redemption of Language.* Pittsburgh: University of Pittsburgh Press.

Evans, J. Martin (1968). Paradise Lost *and the Genesis Tradition.* Oxford: Clarendon Press.

Gilman, Ernest B. (1986). *Iconoclasm and Poetry in the English Reformation: Down Went Dagon.* Chicago: University of Chicago Press.

Gregerson, Linda (1995). *The Reformation of the Subject: Spenser, Milton, and the English Protestant Epic.* Cambridge: Cambridge University Press.

Guibbory, Achsah (1995). "Donne, Milton, and Holy Sex." *Milton Studies* 32: 3–23.

Guibbory, Achsah (1998). *Ceremony and Community from Herbert to Milton: Literature, Religion, and Cultural Conflict in Seventeenth-Century England.* Cambridge: Cambridge University Press.

Haskin, Dayton (1994). *Milton's Burden of Interpretation.* Philadelphia: University of Pennsylvania Press.

Keeble, N. H. (1987). *The Literary Culture of Nonconformity in Later Seventeenth-Century England.* Athens: University of Georgia Press.

Lieb, Michael (1981). *The Poetics of the Holy: A Reading of* Paradise Lost. Chapel Hill: University of North Carolina Press.

Loewenstein, David (1990). *Milton and the Drama of History: Historical Vision, Iconoclasm, and the Literary Imagination.* Cambridge: Cambridge University Press.

Milton, John (1953–82). *Complete Prose Works of John Milton* [*CPW*]. Edited by Don M. Wolfe. 8 vols. New Haven and London: Yale University Press.

Milton, John (1957). *Complete Poetry and Major Prose.* Edited by Merritt Y. Hughes. New York: Odyssey Press.

Patrides, C. A. (1966). *Milton and the Christian Tradition.* Oxford: Clarendon Press.

Pelikan, Jaroslav (2005). *Whose Bible Is It? A History of the Scriptures Through the Ages.* New York: Viking.

Revard, Stella (1980). *The War in Heaven:* Paradise Lost *and the Tradition of Satan's Rebellion.* Ithaca: Cornell University Press.

Rosenblatt, Jason (1994). *Torah and Law in* Paradise Lost. Princeton: Princeton University Press.

Schwartz, Regina M. (1988). *Remembering and Repeating: Biblical Creation in* Paradise Lost. Cambridge: Cambridge University Press.

Shoulson, Jeffrey S. (2001). *Milton and the Rabbis: Hebraism, Hellenism, and Christianity*. New York: Columbia University Press.

Sims, James H. (1962). *The Bible in Milton's Epics*. Gainesville: University of Florida Press.

Sims, James H. and Ryken, Leland (eds) (1984). *Milton and the Scriptural Tradition*. Columbia: University of Missouri Press.

Turner, James Grantham (1987). *One Flesh: Paradisal Marriage and Sexual Relations in the Age of Milton*. Oxford: Clarendon Press.

Werman, Golda (1995). *Milton and Midrash*. Washington, DC: Catholic University of America Press.

Chapter 9

Gender, Sex, and Marriage in Paradise

Karen L. Edwards

Among the most troubling lines of *Paradise Lost* are those in which Adam and Eve are first described:

> Two of far nobler shape erect and tall,
> Godlike erect, with native Honour clad
> In naked Majestie seemd Lords of all,
> And worthie seemd, for in thir looks Divine
> The image of thir glorious Maker shon,
> Truth, wisdome, Sanctitude severe and pure,
> Severe but in true filial freedom plac't;
> Whence true autoritie in men; though both
> Not equal, as thir sex not equal seemd;
> For contemplation hee and valour formd,
> For softness shee and sweet attractive Grace,
> Hee for God only, shee for God in him.
> (Paradise Lost 4.288–99)

In the first annotations to *Paradise Lost*, in 1695, Patrick Hume rather uneasily justifies "Hee for God only, shee for God in him" by referring to the Bible: "The Asseveration of our Author seems maintainable from St. *Paul's* Doctrine" (1695: 144). In 1732, editor Richard Bentley seeks (or pretends to seek) to distance Milton from the phrase by calling it a "shameful Error to have pass'd through all the Editions. The Author gave it, *He for God only, She for God* AND *Him*" (Milton 1732: 117).

Lines 296–9 still give us pause. They invite two main interpretive strategies. Either readers can at once declare Milton misogynistic, or they can assess his representation of Adam and Eve in light of a very complex seventeenth-century historical and cultural context. Milton *has* been called a misogynist, the "inhibiting Father – the Patriarch of patriarchs" (Gilbert 1978: 370); he has also been charged with mistreating Eve in his "silencing and voiding of female creativity" (Froula 1983: 338). To place Milton's portrait of the first human couple in its historical context leads to a different and more sophisticated engagement with *Paradise Lost*. It is an approach that has produced defenses of Milton every bit as impassioned, forceful, and eloquent as the attacks upon him (see Bennett 1983; McColley 1989; Webber 1980). But its chief benefit is to enable readers to respond with all of their intellectual and imaginative powers – and to keep responding – to an inexhaustible poem. The excitement and challenge of reading *Paradise Lost* in this way accompanies one for life. And it *is* a challenge. The fact that the passage quoted above occurs within Satan's first survey of the Garden of Eden (4.205–357) hints at the nature of the challenge. Readers must ask from whose perspective it is that "thir sex not equal seemd." *Seem* and *seeming* are words that in *Paradise Lost* typically signal satanic duality and a creature's failure to understand the loving bond between Creator and Creation. But we cannot simply read lines 288–9 as registering Satan's (as opposed to Milton's) point of view (see Aers and Hodge 1979: 22). An interpretive strategy that finds Milton to be a modern feminist is as inadequate as a strategy that finds him to be a misogynist. Satan is not invariably mistaken, or at least not always wholly so. Adam and Eve, for instance, not only *seem* "worthie" to him (*PL* 4.292); they *are* "worthie," a term having a much stronger sense of excellence and value than it has today. There is no single key to interpreting Milton's portrait of Adam and Eve's relationship. Instead, interpreting it requires taking into account and carefully weighing a number of factors, one of the most important of which is Milton's understanding of marriage. That understanding, grounded both in Reformation and seventeenth-century Puritan teachings and in Milton's extensive reading of classical, medieval, and Renaissance poetry and philosophy (see Haller 1946), is explicitly laid out in Milton's works.

Marriage

In Book 8 of *Paradise Lost* Adam narrates for Raphael his own and Eve's first moments of life and their subsequent union. His narrative closely follows the account in Genesis, when the biblical Adam says of the first woman: "This *is* now bone of my bones, and flesh of my flesh: she shall be called Woman, because she was taken out of Man. Therefore shall a man leave his father and his mother, and shall cleave unto his wife: and they shall be one flesh" (Gen. 2:23–4).

When Milton's Adam first sees Eve, he exclaims:

> I now see
> Bone of my Bone, Flesh of my Flesh, my Self
> Before me; Woman is her Name, of Man
> Extracted; for this cause he shall forgoe
> Father and Mother, and to his Wife adhere;
> And they shall be one Flesh, one Heart, one Soule.
> (*Paradise Lost* 8.494–9)

Twice in the passage Milton amplifies "my Flesh": in line 495, "my Flesh" is immediately followed by "my Self," and in line 499, by "one Heart, one Soule." The first addition, "my Self," relates to the particular circumstances of Eve's creation. Unlike other women, Milton notes elsewhere, she is "moulded out of her husbands rib," so that the first human couple have "a neerer alliance" than any couple since (*CPW* 2.601). In this sense, Eve is part of Adam's body, hence his "Self." (It may be that in *Paradise Lost* we need to think of Adam and Eve not as entirely separate characters but as composing, in their union, a single character.) But "Self" encompasses much more than the body, of course. Milton makes a crucial point about the nature of Adam's marriage to Eve when he adds "one Heart, one Soul" to "one Flesh" at *Paradise Lost* 8.499. Because sexual intercourse by itself cannot produce the intimate union between a man and a woman that marriage is intended to be, Milton reasons, the Bible's "one flesh" must encompass emotional ("Heart") and spiritual ("Soul") compatibility. Indeed, Milton elsewhere coins the term "no-mariage" for a marriage *without* "love and solace and meet help" (*CPW* 2.605, 603).

The "elsewhere" in which Milton reflects on the nature of marriage is *Tetrachordon*, one of the four tracts advocating a liberalization of the law on divorce that he wrote over twenty years before the publication of *Paradise Lost*. Perhaps ironically, we can best approach Milton's views on marriage by way of his views on divorce (Patterson 2001: 279). It is true that his own experience of marriage did not begin well, and no doubt that experience led him to confront his culture's rigid enforcement of lifelong marriage in a way that a happy experience of marriage may not have. But to say that Milton advocated divorce "just" because he was unhappily married (at least for a time) is to miss a vital preoccupation of the mid-seventeenth century: to continue the spiritual Reformation begun by Luther. Milton connects marriage law and Reformation. An unhappy marriage without hope of release, he argues, causes disease, melancholy, and despair and so is detrimental to spiritual health. Therefore, reforming marriage law must be part of the ongoing Reformation, a Reformation unfinished in England (so Milton and many others believed). The fundamental point of his divorce tracts is that a marriage in which there is no intimacy of heart and mind as well as of body frustrates the purpose of marriage and so should be dissolved. When Adam says in *Paradise Lost* that he and Eve are "one Flesh, one Heart, one Soule," Milton is poetically rendering in his epic the convictions about marriage that he had expressed in the divorce tracts. In other words, marriage as Milton portrays it in the Garden of Eden, a setting ostensibly far removed from ordinary human history, is conditioned by opinions formed in the controversies of the 1640s.

The phrase, "Hee for God only, shee for God in him," is also illuminated by arguments made in the divorce tracts, particularly about the image of God. Milton notes in *Tetrachordon* that Adam, who had the wisdom to know the nature of all the animals that passed before him and so could name them (Gen. 2:20), must also have had the wisdom to know that Eve was created by God to be his perfect mate. Therefore, declares Milton, when Adam says that Eve is bone of his bones, and flesh of his flesh, he means that "this is she who was made my image, ev'n as I the Image of God: not so much in body, as in unity of mind and heart" (*CPW* 2.602). We see here the familiar expansion of flesh to include mind and heart; we *also* see mind and heart identified with the image of God. The word "image" appears crucially in Genesis 1:27: "So God created man in his *own* image, in the image of God created he him; male and female created he them." Milton argues that "him" in this verse must mean Adam, since "them" in the next clause clearly means Adam and Eve. That is, Adam's mind and heart were created in the image of God, to permit unity with God; so, Milton concludes, Eve's mind and heart were created in the image of Adam, to permit unity with him. Here Milton cites weighty evidence from the New Testament to support his reading of Genesis:

St. Paul ends the controversie by explaining that the woman is not primarily and immediatly the image of God, but in reference to the

> man. *The head of the woman*, saith he, I *Cor.* 11. *is the man: he the image and glory of God, she the glory of the man*: he not for her, but she for him. Therefore his precept is, *Wives be subject to your husbands as is fit in the Lord, Coloss.* 3:18. (*CPW* 2.589)

Milton is claiming, in other words, that I Corinthians 11 teaches Christians how to read Genesis 1:27, and that Colossians 3:18 (that wives should be subject to their husbands) is a corollary that *may* be drawn from the reading. Milton adds this qualification: "Neverthelesse man is not to hold her as a servant, but receives her into a part of that empire which God proclaims him to, though not equally, yet largely, as his own image and glory: for it is no small glory to him, that a creature so like him, should be made subject to him" (*CPW* 2.589). The standard qualification of the injunction that wives ought to obey their husbands is provided by Paul himself at Colossians 3:19: "Husbands, love *your* wives." It is of course made abundantly clear in *Paradise Lost* that Adam loves Eve. Here, in the divorce tracts, Milton adds a different kind of qualification: sometimes a woman may "exceed her husband in prudence and dexterity," in which case he should "contentedly yeeld," for "the wiser should govern the lesse wise, whether male or female" (*CPW* 2.589). Wisdom, that is, outranks masculinity.

The discussion of marriage in the divorce tracts is not a blueprint for the representation of Adam and Eve's marriage in *Paradise Lost*. Milton's target in the divorce tracts is the debased concept of marriage current in his own day; he is measuring the distance between the glory God had ordained for marriage and the diminished thing his contemporaries accepted (no doubt reluctantly) in its place. *Paradise Lost* is not a tract or a theoretical analysis of marriage, but a poem in which the relationship – the *unique* relationship – between Adam and Eve is realized imaginatively. Theirs is a marriage in which the phrase "made for each other" has literal and unrepeatable significance. *Paradise Lost* was written, moreover, after two decades in which the author's lived experience undoubtedly tested the theory about which he had written in the divorce tracts. How the imaginative rendering of a marriage escapes the rigidity of argumentative exposition will become clearer when we turn to *Paradise Lost*, Book 9. For the present, it should be noted that in the poem fallen creatures possess a preoccupation with hierarchy, rank, and relative status. In Hell, comparative and superlative forms of adjectives (e.g. *higher* and *highest*) are in constant use, whereas in Heaven, each creature is praised for a peculiar and distinctive excellence without implicit comparisons to other creatures.

Yet a preoccupation with hierarchy seems to underlie *Paradise Lost* 4.295–6: "though both/ Not equal, as thir sex not equal seemd." The observation accords with Satan's usual concerns about rank and status. But neither does it contradict Paul's statement that the man is the head of the woman, a statement (as we have seen) that Milton carefully weighs and shapes in the divorce tracts: woman shares man's glory "not equally, yet largely." *Paradise Lost* 4.295–6 is as carefully weighed and shaped. The peculiar grammatical construction, "both/ Not equal," insists upon the sameness of Adam and Eve even as it admits some unspecified degree of difference. Later, when Eve calls Adam "my Guide/ And Head," the address occurs in response to Adam's calling *her* "Sole partner and sole part of all these joyes" (4.442–3, 411). That is, the context of their loving union emphasizes near-equality rather than slight inequality (a fact that bears significantly upon the argument at the beginning of Book 9). William Haller points out that Milton's delicate way with Paul's injunctions is typical of Protestant theologians and ministers of his day, who "seem to have felt less need for telling their hearers that men were superior to women [. . .] than for insisting how nearly women might be expected through love and marriage to approach their husbands' level" (1946: 84).

"Not equal" may instead (or also) mean that Adam and Eve are not identical, just as their sexual attributes ("thir sex") are not identical. This meaning is reinforced by the lines that follow, in which Adam's particular strengths of character ("contemplation [. . .] and valour") are contrasted with Eve's ("softness [. . .] and sweet attractive Grace"). These virtues have differential values in Milton's culture, contemplation and valor being more highly esteemed (and hence traditionally considered masculine) than softness and attractive grace (traditionally considered feminine). Nonetheless, both sets of virtues are necessary for productive human existence, Milton believed. Adam's virtues are those fostering independent individuality and philosophical speculation; Eve's are virtues enabling human relations, those that nourish communion and communication

Their different virtues manifest themselves in Adam and Eve's accounts of their first moments of life. In his narrative of awakening into consciousness, recalled for the archangel Raphael, Adam represents himself as taking a philosophically distanced view of himself and his surroundings (8.250–99). When Eve wakes into life, as she recalls for her husband, she immediately defines herself in relation to her surroundings (4.449–91). Their different ways of thinking about and conducting themselves in their first moments of life demonstrate both the strength and the potential weakness of their individual characteristics. Adam's philosophical independence allows him to deduce that a Maker is responsible for his existence, but it also leads him to seize Eve's hand (a detail that she, not he, mentions), thus threatening to override her wishes. The threat is unrealized, for these are unfallen creatures; Adam's hand is "gentle" as it seizes Eve's, and she willingly accompanies him to the bower (4.488). For her part, Eve is immediately alert to the possibility of communicating with others; hearing "a murmuring sound," she moves toward it (4.453). But she also mistakes what she sees in the lake, the "Shape within the watry gleam," for another being (4.461). Even after having been corrected by the warning voice and brought to Adam, she turns back to the watery image. The threat of narcissism passes, however, as she yields to Adam's hand and words. In both cases, what is significant is that a mistaken mode of behavior is rectified before it becomes a confirmed way of acting. Adam's seizure of Eve's hand is swiftly followed by his use of persuasive words (i.e. he eschews self-assertion for negotiation with another); Eve's staring at her image is swiftly followed by her valuing of Adam's character (i.e. she relinquishes a superficial notion of the self for a more profound one).

With the dream that Satan induces in Book 4, Eve's development swerves away from the parallel with Adam's. The dream incident has usually been read either as "a stage towards [Eve's] fall, forging several illusions that remain with her," or as a "good temptation" (Fowler 1998: 283; McColley 1983: 89), providing another occasion for reevaluation and growth, as when she encounters her image in the lake. Each of those readings can be used to argue that Milton has reduced Eve's culpability for the Fall; each can *also* be used to argue that he has increased it. It may well be more productive to consider instead why Eve is dismayed rather than attracted by the dream, which she describes to Adam as a dream "of offence and trouble" (5.34). If the temptation in Book 9 is Satan's masterpiece, the dream is his apprentice work. At its core are literary traditions of sexual seduction, in which witty lovers try to persuade coy mistresses into bed. Eve, of course, is already in bed with her husband. Milton departs from convention in making it clear, first in the narrative and then in an authorial aside, that Adam and Eve have a fully sexual, satisfying, mutual relationship *before the Fall* (see Kerrigan and Braden 1986; Turner 1987: 230–87). The poem's narrator avows that "God declares/ Pure" the sexual relationship of husband and wife (4.746–7): there is accordingly no reason that unfallen Adam and Eve should *not* perform "the Rites/ Mysterious of connubial Love" (4.742–3). When Satan creeps into the bower, Adam and Eve are asleep after their "rites." Their "blissful Bower" is a space sacred to their love, their lovemaking an act of worship (*Paradise Lost* 4.691; Turner 1987: 236–7). No other creature, "Beast, Bird, Insect, or Worm," dare enter the bower, which turns Satan's trespass into a voyeuristic profanation (4.704).

The contrast between Adam and Eve's mutual, pure, and blissful "wedded Love" and the nighttime "ravishment" promised in the satanic dream is startling (4.750, 5.46). In two direct addresses to the reader, the narrator defends the love of Adam and Eve from hypocritical refusal of bodily union and distinguishes it from promiscuous license (4.744–5, 765–70). (The description of their lovemaking occurs literally between these passages.) Satan's induced dream draws on the extremes of refusal and license. Its language of ardent, near-idolatrous, eye-worship of the mistress derives from the Petrarchan tradition, in which union between lover and beloved is never achieved; its representation of sensual "tasting" derives from Cavalier and courtly traditions, in which union occurs without commitment. In the sterility of the former and the licentiousness of the latter, male and female are pitted against each other. *This* prospect is what Satan's induced dream holds out to Eve in exchange for her physically and emotionally fulfilling, mutual, and dynamic relationship with Adam (see Kerrigan and Braden 1986).

Satan is too subtle simply to cast the dream-speaker, a version of himself, in the role of Eve's wooer, either Petrarchan or Cavalier (although in Book 9, it becomes clear that he feels lustful desire for her). Instead, he makes desire for her universal: "Heav'n wakes with all his eyes,/ Whom to behold but thee, Natures desire,/ In whose sight all things joy, with ravishment/ Attracted by thy beauty still to gaze" (5.44–7). Having thus established desire as the ruling passion of the dream world, he forces Eve to watch him as he gazes at *another* fair creature: the tree of forbidden knowledge. The language in which he addresses the tree is that of a seducer. "O fair Plant [. . .] with fruit surcharg'd,/ Deigns none to ease thy load and taste thy sweet" (5.58–9), he asks, as one might offer to "taste the lips" of a mistress. It is not surprising that Eve is chilled with "damp horror" when she sees him "pluck" and "taste" the fruit (5.65). Both verbs function figuratively as metaphors for deflowering a virgin, for Eve has been made to witness a kind of ravishing. She is then invited to take her turn: "happie Creature, fair Angelic *Eve*," croons the dream speaker, "Partake thou also; happie though thou art,/ Happier thou mayst be, worthier canst not be" (5.74–6). His words are all the more sinister in that we hear in them echoes of the opening scenes of *Macbeth*, when the doomed Duncan calls Macbeth "worthy" and the witches equivocate with Banquo (1.2.24): "Lesser than Macbeth, and greater./ Not so happy, yet much happier" (1.2.65–6).

Eve's unhappiness at having dreamed of disobedience is signaled in the "Tresses discompos'd, and glowing Cheek" (*Paradise Lost* 5.10) that Adam observes when he awakens her. (He has another occasion to observe her glowing cheek, after she has eaten the forbidden fruit [9.887].) Unlike the dream-speaker, who extols the shadowy beauty of the night, Adam awakens Eve to the joys of the day: "the morning shines, and the fresh field/ Calls us" (5.20–1), he whispers to her. Upon waking, Eve at once tells Adam of her dream, for in their unfallen state they keep nothing from each other. His first response is to assure her that her suffering is his: "The trouble of thy thoughts this night in sleep/ Affects me equally" (5.96–7). Neither Adam nor Eve understands why she has dreamed such a dream, although he ventures an explanation based on what he understands about the workings of "Fansie" (akin to fantasy or imagination) upon experience (5.102). It is not a particularly satisfying explanation, but it leads him to articulate a fundamental principle: "Evil into the mind of God or Man/ May come and go, so unapprov'd, and leave/ No spot or blame behind" (5.117–19), he states. That is, because Eve does not *endorse* the action depicted in the dream, a dream for which she is not responsible, she remains innocent. Remembering this principle might have helped Adam find a different response to Eve's fall in Book 9, although he remembers and repeats a version of his avowal that *her* suffering is *his* suffering. Upon hearing Eve's story of eating the fruit, he says: "mee with thee hath ruind, for with thee/ Certain my resolution is to Die" (9.906–7). But he says it to himself, not to Eve, and this failure to share his thoughts undermines his claim that they share everything. In their unfallen state in Book 4, however, "all was cleard" after Eve tells Adam her dream, and he comforts her (5.136). The narrator's words imply that the incident has left no spot or blame on their untroubled existence. But it *does* produce from Eve "a gentle tear [. . .] From either eye" (5.130–1), the first tears in paradise.

Separation

The fact that Eve is frightened rather than allured by the induced dream suggests that another function of the incident is to teach Satan that he needs to find a different temptation strategy, one that does not assume Eve to be vain about her beauty, that does not threaten her chastity or her faithfulness to her husband, and that allows her to convince *herself* to eat the fruit. Satan of course quickly devises such a plan. The argument that Adam and Eve have at the beginning of Book 9 sets up conditions under which his new plan can more easily succeed. Almost 200 lines of Book 9 are devoted to the argument, for which there is no basis in Genesis. Critical discussions of the argument tend to center on how to regard Eve's proposal, "Let us divide our labours" (9.214). The poem withholds her motivation for the suggestion, but scholars have generally attributed to her either a desire to assert her independence or a concern about how to garden more efficiently. Critical consensus ends there. Whether she has found the proper way to express her independence, and indeed whether she ought to be expressing independence in the first place, are questions that have provoked much critical debate. So, too, have questions about her attitude toward gardening: is she correct to claim that their "dayes work" is "brought to little" by their constant interruptions for conversation (9.224)? Has she properly understood the nature and purpose of their task in the garden? Has she overvalued efficiency and productivity? Critical debate about Adam's initial response to Eve's suggestion has been almost as extensive. Does he judiciously assess, or does he exaggerate, his (the husband's) need and ability to guard her (the wife)? It is the implication that she is less able than Adam to fend off an attack from the enemy that causes Eve to answer Adam "As one who loves, and some unkindness meets," a sign that the argument has entered the territory of hurt feelings (9.271). Adam reads the sign and acquiesces to her leaving (Bennett 1983: 400). Should he instead have *insisted* that she stay with him? He had, after all, just stated the principle that "The Wife, where danger or dishonour lurks,/ Safest and seemliest by her Husband staies,/ Who guards her, or with her the worst endures" (9.267–9). Yet Adam deeply values Eve's decisiveness, her confidence in her own judgment: "so absolute she seems/ And in her self compleat, so well to know/ Her own," as he puts it to Raphael (8.547–9). In her presence, he confesses, "All higher knowledge [. . .] falls/ Degraded, Wisdom in discourse with her/ Looses discount'nanc't, and like folly shewes" (8.551–3).

The tension between husband and wife in Book 9 has, in fact, been anticipated by tension between Adam and Raphael in Book 8. In response to Adam's impassioned acknowledgement of his love and respect for Eve, Raphael's brow contracts. He warns Adam against "attributing overmuch to things/ Less excellent" (8.565–6). *Things* is ambiguous and, quite possibly, offensive to Adam, for the archangel seems to have in mind not only Eve's "outside" (though "fair [. . .] And worthy"), but also that "absoluteness" that Adam admires in her (8.568). Raphael directs particular criticism toward Adam's delight in "the sense of touch whereby mankind/ Is propagated" (8.579–80). The terms in which Raphael speaks of Adam and Eve's lovemaking betrays a failure to understand the nature of human sexuality – perhaps not surprisingly, given the very different nature of angelic sexuality. In answer to Adam's question, Raphael admits: "Whatever pure thou in the body enjoy'st [. . .] we enjoy/ In eminence, and obstacle find none/ Of membrane, joynt, or limb, exclusive barrs" (8.622–5). Raphael, in effect, is calling human physicality an "obstacle." Adam knows that that "obstacle" is the source of paradisal bliss, a word with both physical and spiritual significance: "Milton understood the erotic importance of the barrier" (Kerrigan and Braden 1986: 43). Raphael does not understand. Nor does he understand the importance of lovemaking for the sustaining and renewing of a marital relationship over time. Angels, after all, "neither marry, nor are given in marriage," according to the Bible (Mark 12:25), and Milton nowhere argues that they are.

Let us return to the argument in Book 9. Although there is disagreement about the motivation for and wisdom of Adam's "Go" (9.372), critical opinion largely concedes that the argument between the first couple is, from beginning to end, fully understandable and indeed all too familiar to most readers. A categorical condemnation of either Adam or Eve would seem to be a condemnation of the condition that defines human communication: the necessity for interpretation, which inevitably entails the possibility of *mis*interpretation. In short, the style in which Milton represents the argument between Adam and Eve makes it seem "natural," as if it has been drawn from life (in a way that the grand oratorical flourishes of Satan, or the pure, severe pronouncements of God do not). That which is made to seem "natural" is also made to seem inevitable. As Joseph Addison observed in 1712, "It is such a Dispute as we may suppose might have happened in *Paradise*, had Man continued happy and innocent" (Shawcross 1970: 205). Its apparent inevitability leads us to conclude that if *this* argument had not aided Satan's plans, the next argument, or the one after that, *would* have. The main point about this argument, or any loving argument between husband and wife, is that it has two sides: *both* partners participate in it and *both* contribute to its outcome. The argument in Book 9 is part of a clear refusal in *Paradise Lost* to allow readers easily and complacently to blame Eve or Adam alone for the Fall, or to blame one "more" than the other.

The poem thus stands in opposition to a centuries-long misogynistic tradition that dissects Genesis 3 for evidence of Eve's culpability. Medieval and Renaissance biblical commentators, who agree that Adam's "fall is the more important to the human race" (Williams 1948: 123), nonetheless compete in listing the particular sins that Eve's fall comprises. The Protestant commentator David Paraeus (whose work Milton knew well) finds 17 such sins: "idleness, in not cultivating Paradise; curious presumption; lack of consideration for Adam and their descendants; doubt; infidelity; disdain of her station; pride; ambition; idolatry; inordinate appetite; depravity of the will; concupiscence of the eyes; incontinency of the hands; intemperance of the taste; contumacy; apostasy; detestable ingratitude" (Williams 1948: 121–2). Milton does not deny Eve's faults, but in *De Doctrina Christiana* he attributes to Eve alone (as opposed to both of them) only negligence "of her husband's welfare" (*CPW* 6.383). Milton gives full weight to the Bible's statement that Eve was deceived – and that Adam was not (1 Tim. 2:14).

Satan's temptation strategy, refined and honed after his first failure, appeals this time to Eve's intimate knowledge and love of the created world. The tempter appears not as an angelic being but as one of the creatures she cherishes; he speaks to her not (primarily) of her own surpassing beauty but of the virtues of a tree in her beloved garden. When she finally convinces herself to eat, she uses the pronoun "I" only once, for she is thinking not of her own advancement (that thought comes *after* she has fallen), but of how to improve "our" condition (9.745–79). Satan, in short, uses what is most admirable about Eve – her nurturing of community – against her. "Here grows the Cure of all, this Fruit Divine,/ Fair to the Eye, inviting to the Taste,/ Of vertue to make wise," she declares (9.776–8). She is wrong, of course, for the fruit possesses no special "vertue." But the narrator of *Paradise Lost* refrains from angry condemnation, only an implied pun betraying reproach: "So saying, her rash hand in evil hour/ Forth reaching to the Fruit, she pluck'd, she eat" (9.780–1).

Eve's words explicitly reiterate the biblical account at Genesis 3.6, which dignifies her action by providing reasons for it: "And when the woman saw that the tree *was* good for food, and that it *was* pleasant to the eyes, and a tree to be desired to make *one* wise, she took of the fruit thereof, and did eat, and gave also unto her husband with her; and he did eat." One might expect the Bible to endorse the ancient stereotype that represents women as irrational or childishly thoughtless. It is the biblical Adam, however, who is represented as eating the fruit without pausing for thought. Although horrified, Milton's Adam, too, knows instantly what he will do upon hearing Eve's story: "mee with thee hath ruind, for with thee/ Certain my resolution is to Die" (*Paradise Lost* 9.906–7). Adam has been praised for sacrificing all for love and condemned for weakly "Submitting to what seemd remediless" (9.919). He ought, some scholars have argued, to have asked God to divorce him from Eve: divorce would have "provided Adam with his remedy" (Burden 1967: 170). In this view, Adam's self-sacrifice springs at best from a misguided notion of heroism and at worst from a terror of loneliness. But if Adam has overvalued the bond of flesh in their marriage, he has not undervalued the bond of heart and soul. In Milton's arguments for divorce, it is only the absence of "heart and soul" that means a marriage should be dissolved. Eve is fallen, but Adam still loves her. The poem, finally, allows neither easy condemnation nor easy approval of Adam's resolution.

As both share the blame, both share the consequences. Having fallen, Adam and Eve are inflamed with "Carnal desire" for each other (9.1013); burning "in Lust," they take "thir fill of Love and Loves disport" (9.1015, 1042) (see Aers and Hodge 1979); and when their lust has run its course, they quarrel long and harshly. The sequence of events is significant: union undertaken only to solace the flesh dis-unifies the heart and soul. Milton names the engines of disunity: "Anger, Hate,/ Mistrust, Suspicion, Discord," with "sensual Appetite" claiming power over "sovran Reason" (9.1123–4, 1129–30). These "high Passions" have selfishness at their center and locate all faults and failings in the other (9.1123). The pun that the narrator had gently used of Eve at 9.780–1 is crudely wielded by Adam as the argument begins: "O *Eve*, in evil hour thou didst give eare/ To that false Worm" (9.1067–8). The pun amounts to his saying that evil has nothing to do with him; it belongs solely to Eve. She is just as determined to accuse him. He blames her for "wandring" (9.1146). She blames him for *allowing* her to wander, or rather for not being "firm and fixt" enough to *disallow* it (with perhaps an implied sexual insult) (9.1160). Mutual accusation is inherently unresolvable. Thus the end of Book 9 does not bring an end to Adam and Eve's "vain contest," and in Book 10, Adam indulges in a long, self-pitying, misogynistic soliloquy (9.1189, 10.720–844). Its length is significant. It forces readers to experience the tedious futility of a mind that refuses to admit its own culpability. When Eve approaches Adam, interrupting his diatribe, he responds curtly, viciously: "Out of my sight, thou Serpent" (10.867). It is undoubtedly the low point of their relationship. Yet it evokes from Eve *the* crucial action in bringing about reconciliation. She refuses to be "repulst" (10.910); she approaches Adam again and asks for his forgiveness. Their reconciliation can then begin. The fact that Milton represents Eve as taking the first step (literally and figuratively) toward reconciliation is another sign that *Paradise Lost* does not endorse the well-established literary and theological tradition of heaping opprobrium on her (see Gallagher 1990: 96–114).

Milton represents reconciliation as a process, one not accomplished without difficulty. When Eve asks forgiveness for her part in the Fall, she blames herself alone for what has happened: "me, sole cause to thee of all this woe," she says to Adam (10.935). Her offer of self-sacrifice – she plans to ask God "that all/ The sentence from thy head remov'd may light/ On me [...] Mee mee onely just object of his ire" – has been described as Christ-like (10.933–6). But by putting the offer in the context of her exaggerated self-blame, Milton allows us to see that Eve is again overestimating her importance. Only the Son can make an offer of self-sacrifice that has meaning for human destiny. Adam responds to Eve's words by acknowledging his own role in the Fall: her "frailtie and infirmer Sex" were "To me committed and by me expos'd," he states (10.956, 957). Milton's point is clear: when Adam and Eve accept individual responsibility for the Fall, they *share* responsibility for it, and they are reconciled. The sharing is essential. When Eve approaches Adam, she articulates the principle that she and he belong together. Indeed, her first words to him, "Forsake me not thus, *Adam*," are a plea not to let their marriage fail (10.914). The union of heart, soul, and body that Adam and Eve enjoyed so completely and so effortlessly before the Fall can be attained after the Fall only with patience and care, and then only imperfectly. But it *is* union. That they have understood how to make a marriage work in the fallen world is made clear when Adam says to Eve: "But rise, let us no more contend, nor blame/ Each other [...] but strive/ In offices of Love, how we may light'n/ Each others burden in our share of woe" (10.958–61). Neither Adam nor Eve knows what their "share of woe" will be, nor do they entirely understand as yet that woe will be mixed with happiness. But we may see their loving determination to lighten each other's burden as an adult articulation of what love may accomplish in a fallen world. That *Paradise Lost*

represents one version of a whole, complete, and perfect union between a man and a woman in no way diminishes its representation of a necessarily less than perfect union that never ceases to strive for wholeness and completeness.

It is the fundamental law of the poem's universe that "Heavn'ly love shall outdoo Hellish hate" (3.298). *Paradise Lost* is not a tragedy, nor does it record a tragedy, for evil cannot triumph against Milton's beneficent and omnipotent God. But for human beings, the post-lapsarian world is one in which good and evil are inextricably mixed: they "grow up together almost inseparably" (*CPW* 2.514). It is a condition of life as *we* know it, for after the Fall, Adam and Eve's experience begins to coincide with ours. The Son's judgment on Adam and Eve (based on Genesis 3.16–19) is thus not a punishment but a spelling out of what existence in a fallen world necessarily entails. "Children," says the Son to Eve, "thou shalt bring/ In sorrow forth, and to thy Husbands will/ Thine shall submit, hee over thee shall rule" (10.194–6). The Son's words simply articulate the realities of human life: child bearing and rearing *is* a prolonged and fraught process, and physical strength *is* often used to control those who are weaker. To Adam, the Son says that the ground, unbidden, will bring forth thorns and thistles: "In the sweat of thy Face shalt thou eat Bread,/ Till thou return unto the ground" (10.205–6). Most people must indeed work to feed themselves, and all of us will die. And yet there is good even in what, after paradise, looks like evil. Eve's bringing forth children (though in pain) and Adam's bringing forth crops to feed his family (though with sweat) mean that both are participants in the creative process that began when the Creator commanded the earth to "bring forth" (Gen. 1.11, 24) and his creatures to "Be fruitful, and multiply" (Gen. 1.28). Moreover, the fruitfulness that God commands and enables begins at once, as soon as Adam and Eve pray for forgiveness. At the end of Book 10, they return to the place of judgment, "and both confess'd/ Humbly thir faults, and pardon beg'd, with tears/ Watering the ground" (10.1100–2). This figurative planting yields what the Son calls the "first fruits on Earth," their repentant hearts (11.22). These "first fruits" in turn yield others – most immediately, Adam and Eve's renewed marital love. After the harsh name-calling that follows the Fall, Adam begins again to address Eve with titles of respect: "Haile to thee,/ *Eve* rightly call'd, Mother of all Mankind,/ Mother of all things living" (11.158–60). Eve, for her part, promises never again to wander: "let *us* forth," she says (emphasis added), "I never from thy side henceforth to stray"

(11.175–6). It is significant that Eve becomes pregnant only *after* they leave the garden of Eden, the surest sign that the physical, emotional, and spiritual fulfillment provided by a loving marriage in a fallen world is *also* a "Fruit / Of that Forbidden Tree" (1.1–2).

References and Further Reading

Aers, David and Hodge, Bob (1979). "'Rational burning': Milton on Sex and Marriage." *Milton Studies* 13: 3–33.

Bennett, Joan (1983). "'Go': Milton's Antinomianism and the Separation Scene in *Paradise Lost*, Book 9." *Publications of the Modern Language Association* 98: 388–404.

Burden, Dennis H. (1967). *The Logical Epic: A Study of the Argument of* Paradise Lost. London: Routledge and Kegan Paul.

Fowler, Alastair (ed.) (1998). *Paradise Lost*. By John Milton. 2nd edn. London: Longman.

Froula, Christine (1983). "When Eve Reads Milton: Undoing the Canonical Economy." *Critical Inquiry* 10: 321–47.

Gallagher, Philip J. (1990). *Milton, the Bible, and Misogyny*. Edited by Eugene R. Cunnar and Gail L. Mortimer. Columbia: University of Missouri Press.

Gilbert, Sandra K. (1978). "Patriarchal Poetry and Women Readers: Reflections on Milton's Bogey." *Publications of the Modern Language Association* 93: 368–82.

Haller, William (1946). "Hail Wedded Love." *English Literary History* 13: 79–97.

Hume, Patrick (1695). *Annotations on Milton's* Paradise Lost. London: Jacob Tonson.

Kerrigan, William, and Braden, Gordon (1986). "Milton's Coy Eve: *Paradise Lost* and Renaissance Love Poetry." *English Literary History* 53: 27–51.

McColley, Diane Kelsey (1983). *Milton's Eve*. Urbana: University of Illinois Press.

McColley, Diane Kelsey (1989). "Milton and the Sexes." In Dennis Danielson (ed.), *The Cambridge Companion to Milton* (pp. 147–66). Cambridge: Cambridge University Press.

Martin, Catherine Gimelli (ed.) (2004). *Milton and Gender*. Cambridge: Cambridge University Press.

Milton, John (1732). *Milton's Paradise Lost*. Edited by Richard Bentley. London.

Milton, John (1953–82). *Complete Prose Works of John Milton* [*CPW*]. Edited by Don M. Wolfe. 8 vols. New Haven and London: Yale University Press.

Milton, John (1998). *The Riverside Milton*. Edited by Roy Flannagan. Boston: Houghton Mifflin.

Patterson, Annabel (2001). "Milton, Marriage and Divorce." In Thomas N. Corns (ed.), *A Companion to Milton* (pp. 279–93). Oxford: Blackwell.

Karen L. Edwards

Shawcross, John T. (ed.) (1970). *Milton: The Critical Heritage*. London: Routledge and Kegan Paul.

Turner, James Grantham (1987). *One Flesh: Paradisal Marriage and Sexual Relations in the Age of Milton*. Oxford: Clarendon Press.

Walker, Julia M. (ed.) (1988). *Milton and the Idea of Woman*. Urbana: University of Illinois Press.

Webber, Joan Malory (1980). "The Politics of Poetry: Feminism and *Paradise Lost*." *Milton Studies* 14: 3–24.

Williams, Arnold (1948). *The Common Expositor: An Account of the Commentaries on Genesis 1527–1633*. Chapel Hill: University of North Carolina Press.

Chapter 10

The Ecology of *Paradise Lost*

Juliet Lucy Cummins

The tensions we see today between the forces of scientific and economic progress and those of ecological conservation have their origins in debates surrounding the emergence of modern science in the seventeenth century. As science became more utilitarian, and as natural philosophers increasingly tended to objectify nature, ecological voices of the time responded by asserting the continuity between human beings and the natural world and the need to respect and preserve it. Early modern debates about the proper relationship between human beings and the natural world were played out in a variety of cultural forms, including literary texts, the writings of natural philosophers, and tracts about practical topics such as gardening, farming, and forestry. Milton enters these debates in his vision of unfallen life in *Paradise Lost*, and in the poem's presentation of nature as animate and intimately connected with human identity. In keeping with Scripture, Milton portrays human beings as exercising dominion over other created things, as is fitting for the "Master work" of Creation, "the end/ Of all yet don" (*Paradise Lost* 7.505–6). Nevertheless, his unfallen Adam and Eve are remarkable in the extent to which they are integrated into their environment, and the animals, plants and other created things in Milton's paradise are unusual in their active demonstration of both individuality and inherent goodness.

Milton's epic challenges mechanistic and instrumental conceptions of the world which gained in popularity over the seventeenth century and which tended to support a construction of nature as a tool or commodity to be used for achieving the ends of "man." The man Voltaire dubbed the father of experimental philosophy, Francis Bacon, explores and develops such ideas in *New Atlantis* (1624), his utopian vision of scientific and social advancement. Bacon depicts a world in which the "various orchards and gardens" are not so much for "respect[ing] beauty" as for appreciating "variety of ground and soil" and conducting scientific practices, such as "all conclusions of grafting, and inoculating" and putting plants to "medicinal use." Similarly, the "beasts and birds" are used "not only for view or rareness, but likewise for dissections and trials, that thereby we may take light what may be wrought upon the body of man" (Bacon 1996: 482). While Bacon also wrote about nature in more sympathetic and complex ways at other times (see Mathews 1996: 406–25), the understanding of nature as a commodity provided by God for man's material advantage was to become very influential among natural philosophers in mid to late seventeenth-century England.

The ideology which Bacon represents in his fictional world was, however, strongly resisted in some quarters. The mid-century philosophy of vitalism or animist materialism, another form of seventeenth-century scientific thought, adopted the ancient view that all things – even things usually considered inanimate such as stones – were infused with "the power of reason and self-motion" (Rogers 1996: 1). As John Rogers explains it, "[e]nergy or spirit, no longer immaterial, is seen as immanent within bodily matter, and even nonorganic matter, at least for some vitalists, is thought to contain within it the agents of motion and change" (1996: 1–2). The idea that all things contain spirit and the capacity for motion tended to break down oppositions between human beings and the natural world. In doing so, it supported an empathetic attitude toward nature, and provided grounds for resisting its manipulation in the name of natural philosophy. This perspective was in sympathy with what would now be called ecological thought – with the idea that "all of the living organisms of the earth" are "an interacting whole," to use the language of the historian of ecology Donald Worster (1994: x). Although Worster claims that the modern history of ecology begins in the eighteenth century, the vitalist movement of the mid-seventeenth century, and the development of horticultural ideas by writers such as John Evelyn after the English Civil Wars, provides a strong tradition of ecological thinking at least half a century earlier.

Milton's Ecological Resistance to the New Science

Milton's representation of nature in *Paradise Lost* expresses resistance to the prevailing mechanistic and instrumental forms of natural philosophy, while still reflecting other forms of contemporary thinking about the natural world. The once orthodox scholarly position that Milton's scientific views were primarily based on classical and medieval sources has recently been subject to intense scrutiny, and a new consensus has emerged that Milton was conversant with contemporary scientific ideas, and that he explores such ideas in his poetry and prose. Catherine Gimelli Martin has demonstrated persuasively similarities between Milton's epistemology and that of Francis Bacon and some of the new scientists (2001a, 2001b), while Angelica Duran has contended that "Milton's mature poetry [. . .] seriously engages with the similarities of relational mathematics and human activity" (2003: 69). Karen Edwards's study of Milton's representations of nature shows that there are continuities between Milton's treatment of natural things and those of contemporary natural historians and experimental philosophers. She registers, for example, "the sense of astonishment and exhilaration" the well-known seventeenth-century scientist Robert Hooke expresses in his preface to *Micrographia* (1665) at being able to view miniscule creatures through the microscope (1999: 7), and compares this to the delight apparent in Milton's description of the Creation of plants and animals in *Paradise Lost*. She also finds "surprising confluences" between Milton's work and that of Robert Boyle and other experimentalists (1999: 47). While Milton and contemporary practitioners of the new science shared certain views and approaches to knowledge, it is important to acknowledge that Milton's poetry also resists some of the dominant scientific assumptions of his day. This is particularly apparent in Milton's vitalist depiction of nature in *Paradise Lost*, which implicitly critiques the objectification and exploitation of nature often connected with the new science.

The new science that emerged from humanist natural philosophy depended to a certain extent on the construction of a dichotomy between human beings and nature in order to justify human intervention into and manipulation of natural things. To take an extreme example, vivisection can be presented as a legitimate form of activity only if the animal is objectified and constructed as the other (not-human) in the interests of pursuing the exalted goal of furthering human knowledge. This is apparent in Robert Hooke's description of an experiment performed in 1664 on a live dog in which he "wholly opened the thorax, and cut of all the ribs, and opened the belly" in order to "make some enquiries into the nature of respiration" (Jardine 1999: 116). And yet such oppositions between humans and animals are inevitably unstable. As Erica Fudge argues, in early modern writings generally "the animal is represented as the antithesis of the human" but "the desire to make a clear separation between the species" is constantly undermined by the writing (2000: 4). Discourse about vivisection, for example, tends to deconstruct itself, since "[t]he absolute animality of the human body is revealed even as humanness is expressed" (2000: 92). Poetry is perhaps better suited than scientific discourse to recognizing such paradoxes and to exploring the complexities of human identity in relation to animals. Milton's epic participates in the cultural ambivalence about human beings' part in nature, constructing the human as at once separate from and part of the animal world.

In *Paradise Lost* created things in the unfallen world subsist along a dynamic continuum of being. Milton transforms the medieval chain of being, in which everything had its assigned and inviolable place, into an organic, material structure which allows creatures to grow toward God. In doing so, he rejects the new scientists' utilitarian conception of animals and plants, adapting to a contemporary form of the medieval sense of nature's vitality and the concept of a direct connection between all created things and the Creator. The archangel Raphael explains to Adam that all things participate in a cycle of being with God as their origin and ultimate destination: "O *Adam*, one Almightie is, from whom/ All things proceed, and up to him return,/ If not deprav'd from good, created all/ Such to perfection, one first matter all" (5.469–72). All things are made of the "first matter" which is an aspect of God, in accordance with the vitalist idea of the inseparability of spirit and matter. Raphael describes the continuum of being to Adam using the metaphor of a plant. According to Milton's "winged Hierarch" all created things are "in thir several active Sphears assignd/ Till body up to spirit work" (5.468, 477–8). This means that each thing is capable of evolving to a higher state of material and spiritual being, just as a plant moves from its denser lower regions to its more refined leaves and flowers:

> So from the root
> Springs lighter the green stalk, from thence the leaves

> More aerie, last the bright consummate floure
> Spirits odorous breathes: flours and thir fruit
> Mans nourishment, by gradual scale sublim'd
> To vital Spirits aspire, to animal,
> To intellectual, give both life and sense,
> Fansie and understanding, whence the Soule
> Reason receives, and reason is her being.
>
> (5.479–87)

In this metaphorical tree of life, human beings, while differing in some significant ways from plants, animals, and spirits, nevertheless share an identity and participate in an organic whole. Milton reinforces the identification of Adam and Eve with the natural world through the metaphors and similes which describe them: Adam is "earths hallowd mould,/ Of God inspired" (5.321–32) and the vulnerable yet sufficient unfallen Eve is the "fairest unsupported Flour" (9.432). Such poetic imagery undercuts empirical and mechanist constructions of nature, whereby the natural world consists of discrete, mechanically ordered things with no necessary relation to each other.

As can be seen in the image of the tree of life, Milton's vision of human beings' relationship to other created things focuses upon the divine goodness dispersed throughout nature rather than on the divinely granted human right to control other creatures. Human beings are at a refined level of the tree, their "intellectual" Spirits and capacity for "discursive" reason distinguishing them from the beasts (5.485, 488). However, they are also an integral part of the scale of being, and depend on the lower orders for both being and sustenance: "flours and thir fruit/ Mans nourishment" (5.482–3). Human beings differ from animals in that they mirror God's "Image, not imparted to the Brute" (8.441) and in that God gives them "Dominion" over "all other Creatures that possess/ Earth, Aire and Sea" (4.429–32). And yet the dominion Adam and Eve are given is more like a responsibility for other creatures than a form of mere control or authorized exploitation; as Diane Kelsey McColley argues, Milton represents "human dominion as beneficent care" (2001: 72; see also Theis 1996: 65–6 and Jordan 2001: 134). In the King James translation of the relevant passage in Genesis, God says: "let them have dominion over the fish of the sea, and over the fowl of the air, and over the cattle, and over all the earth, and over every creeping thing that creepeth upon the earth" (Gen. 1:26). The repeated use of the word "over" emphasizes the differences between the first human beings and the

animals, and the passage was often cited in justification of instrumental approaches to nature and experiments upon living things. In
Milton's vitalist poem, on the other hand, Adam and Eve are given
dominion over the "*other* Creatures" (emphasis added), subtly drawing
attention to their common origins and status as creatures.

Adam's report of his first conversation with his Creator recognizes
the delicate position of authority human beings hold within creation,
and the connections between the first human beings and the animals
of Eden. God replies to Adam's request for a companion with a re-
minder of the animals' human-like abilities: "know'st thou not/ Thir
language and thir wayes, they also know,/ And reason not contempt-
ibly" (8.372–4). The point of the conversation is to elicit from Adam
the idea that he wants fellowship "fit to participate/ All rational
delight, wherein the brute/ Cannot be human consort" (8.390–2), but
the attribution of both a form of language and reason to animals is
unorthodox and challenges the man/brute dichotomy. Eve reinforces
this understanding that animals are rational when she observes to
Satan, in his serpent disguise, that she is surprised to hear him talk,
but not surprised to hear him express "human sense" because she has
observed in animals' "looks/ Much reason, and in thir actions oft
appeers" (9.554, 558–9). This attributes to Eve an extraordinary sympathy with animals, and gives to animals a degree of dignity unparal-
leled in contemporary depictions. Significantly in a poem championing
human freedom, Milton's portrayal of the natural world as animate
implies that created things are all, to a lesser extent, free. Milton
associates reason with liberty (see, for example, 12.83–5), suggesting
that animals possessing reason must also possess a form of freedom
which is manifested in the poem in their capacity to evolve towards
God and in the spontaneous way in which created things praise the
Creator.

While Adam and Eve individually acknowledge animals' rational
capacity, and evince their respect for nature, the morning hymn they
compose together dramatically and powerfully demonstrates their
harmony and continuity with other natural things. The hymn in
Book 5 is a poetic adaptation of Psalms 19 and 148, the Canticle
"Benedicite, omnia opera," and the hymn "Somno refectis" (attributed to St Ambrose), but it transforms these sources by allowing
Adam and Eve to sing their praise of their Maker in unity with the
rest of Creation. The hymn is "pronounc't or sung" by Adam and Eve
"Unmeditated" (5.148–9), while other created things spontaneously
praise God in individual forms which harmonize with each other. The

hymn dramatically illustrates the idea that natural things are animate and self-willed, and that their unity resides in their relationship to God. With "prompt eloquence," Adam and Eve praise God's "glorious works" and observe how the rest of creation also praises him, even "thy lowest works" which "declar/ Thy goodness beyond thought and Power Divine" (5.149, 153, 158–9). Their description of the various created things which praise God is itself a form of tribute, and their response to their Creator is at one with that of all Creation: the "Sons of light,/ Angels" who rejoice "with songs/ And choral symphonies," the "Sun" or "Soule" of the world who "sound[s] his praise/ In thy eternal course," the "wandring Fires" or planets which "move/ In mystic Dance not without Song," the "Birds" whose voices "singing up to Heaven Gate ascend," "every Plant" which "in sign of Worship wave," and even the "Elements" whose "ceasless chang/ Varie[s] to the Maker still new praise" (5.160–98). Just as Milton's voice merges with those of the angels in Book 3 (see 412–15), so too here angels, human beings, animals, plants, and nonliving things are unified in their mutual relationship of thankfulness to God.

Vitalist images and ideas in *Paradise Lost* create an ecological perspective upon the world that places God at the center of earthly life. This is particularly apparent in Milton's depiction of the earth. As Richard J. DuRocher argues, Milton "adapts Stoic scientific and literary accounts of the Earth as a living organism" (1996: 94) in his poetry. The earth is an "all-bearing Mother," producing food for humans and angels, and it is an active participant in Creation, responding to God's call to produce "Soul living in her kind" accordingly: "The Earth obey'd, and straight/ Op'ning her fertile Womb teem'd at a Birth/ Innumerous living Creatures, perfet forms,/ Limb'd and full grown" (7.453–6). The creatures that emerge from the earth's womb are "living Soules," idiosyncratic and with their own distinct experiences, from the "Shoales/ Of Fish that with thir Finns and shining Scales/ Glide under the green Wave, in Sculles that oft/ Bank the mid Sea" to the "tawnie Lion, pawing to get free/ His hinder parts, then springs as broke from Bonds,/ And Rampant shakes his Brinded main" (7.388, 400–3, 464–6). Milton's detailed, animate account of Creation celebrates the earth's fertility, and glories in variety and individuality. Raphael describes the animals not merely in relationship to human beings but in possession of their own integrity and value. Such an account undermines contemporary scientific constructions of nature as predominantly instrumental and as operating mechanically. Carolyn Merchant argues that the development of modern science in

seventeenth-century England brought about a symbolical transformation of nature from a nurturing mother figure to a "female to be controlled and dissected through experiment" (1980: 189). While the
transformation was not as simple nor as absolute as Merchant claims
(see Soble 1998), the portrayal of the male natural philosopher acting
upon nature, conceived of as an inert female, did become common in
natural philosophical discourse. Milton's poetry insists instead on the
female earth's inherent spirituality and goodness (a stance that has
interestingly been associated with early modern women writers in
their resistance to "masculinist" science [Bowerbank 2004: 17–19]).

Milton's unorthodox portrayal of nature suggests that the world is
a rich reflection of divine glory. All created things are naturally good
because they all consist of the "first matter" that is an aspect of God,
and all are interdependent. In Milton's "theology of nature," the proper
relationship between creatures is one of mutual exchange based on
responsibility, nurture, obedience, and gratitude (Rudrum 2000: 39,
McColley 1999: 125). Thus, in the Garden, Adam and Eve look after
the natural world: Eve "tend[s] Plant, Herb and Flour" just as Satan
perceives the angels "watch and tend/ Thir earthly Charge" (9.206,
156–7). The human duty to look after the garden is expressed in
Genesis, where God put Adam "into the garden of Eden to dress it
and to keep it" (Gen. 2:15). However, as Anthony Low notes, Milton
is one of very few early modern writers to take this command seriously (1992: 67). Eve conceives of their role as one of gentle discipline as they "direct/ The clasping ivy where to climb" or "redress"
the growth of roses, while Adam talks of the "reform" of "yon flowery
arbours" (9.216–17, 219, 4.625–6). Nature seems to invite their participation: the "dropping gums [. . .]/ Ask riddance" just as the fruit
trees "needed hands to check/ Fruitless embraces" (4.630–2, 5.214–
15). The beasts also recognize human dominion, "more duteous at
[Eve's] call,/ Then at *Circean* call the Herd disguis'd," because Circean
enchantment is unnecessary to secure their natural obedience (9.521–
2). The responsiveness of created things to each other is characteristic
of the paradisal world in which human beings are fully integrated
with their surroundings.

Satanic Objectification of Nature

Milton's critique of the commodification and objectification of the
earth is evident in his attribution of such attitudes and practices to the

fallen angels. The poem opens with the depiction of the fallen angels in their new habitat of Hell, a grim perversion of the new world Adam and Eve will inhabit in Book 4. In Hell, Milton presents a Satanic version of the predominant seventeenth-century view of nature as an object or a resource ripe for exploitation. Led by Mammon, the fallen angels metaphorically rape the landscape of Hell, taking from the "womb" of a hill "metallic Ore" with which to build a "Fabrick huge" which becomes "*Pandæmonium*, the high Capital/ Of Satan and his Peers" (1.673, 710, 756–7). Milton's condemnation of mining forms part of a tradition stretching back to ancient times, but is also a response to the increase in mining and in writings defending mining in seventeenth-century England. According to Milton's monist theology, the disturbance of the hill's womb is a real violation of the sanctity of a (really) female body. Milton explicitly connects Mammon's activities with those of men who "by his suggestion taught,/ Ransack'd the Center, and with impious hands/ Rifl'd the bowels of thir mother Earth/ For Treasures better hid" (1.685–8), a grotesque vision we revisit in the incestuous vision of Sin and Death when Satan embarks on his journey to Earth. This exploitation corrupts the natural processes of generation that occur when the "fruitful" female Earth interacts with the "vigour" of the beams of the male Sun which would be "barren" and "unactive else" (8.94–7). The error of Mammon and his demonic and human followers lies in their conception of nature as purely instrumental, and their failure to recognize the value of "aught divine" (1.683). The contrast between the devils' conception of earth in terms of a resource (producing "metallic Ore" [1.673] and gold) and the narrative depiction of it as a gendered, generative body underscores their error. The reification of matter paradoxically leads them to destroy the material world, and to fail to recognize its inherent spirituality and creativity.

Milton's disapproving attitudes toward the exploitation of the earth's bounty are also evident in his depiction of the biblical Tubulcain (unnamed in the poem) "at the Forge/ Labouring" (11.564–5). Michael tells Adam that he "formd/ First his own Tooles; then, what might else be wrought/ Fusil or grav'n in mettle" (11.571–3). While Tubulcain is not a miner, the vision of him draining "liquid Ore [. . .] Into fit moulds" to make metal objects recalls the fallen angels extracting "massie Ore" from the ground of Hell and pouring it into "A various mould" (1.703, 706). The parallel emphasizes the resemblances between the damaged earth and the landscape of Hell, just as the "farr greater part" of humanity resembles the fallen angels in its common alienation from God (12.533). Implicit in these activities that violate the sanctity of Creation is a denial of creaturely gratitude toward the Creator. This becomes explicit when Michael describes the race of Cain (to which Tubulcain belongs) as "Inventers rare,/ Unmindful of thir Maker, though his Spirit/ Taught them, but they his gifts acknowledg'd none" (11.610–12). Tubulcain's failure to acknowledge the divine gifts which enable him to create sharply distinguishes him from the unfallen creatures who praise God spontaneously, and from the fallen but regenerate poet who acknowledges the illumination of the Spirit from the outset (1.17–26).

The violation of nature is at its most heinous when Satan uses the "materials dark and crude" underlying the surface of Heaven to create gunpowder (6.478). Satan perverts the natural processes of conception and birth, by taking these materials from "thir dark Nativitie" and placing them "pregnant with infernal flame" into phallic "Engins long and round" (6.482–4). The word "Nativitie" alludes to the alchemical idea that the influence of stellar bodies can generate minerals or metals in the earth, but the devils abort such natural gestation by penetrating heaven's surface and taking its "crude" materials before they have time to develop. Again, Milton connects the devils' activities with those of the fallen human race, as Raphael conjectures that "Like instrument" may be "devise[d]" by men (6.504–5). Like the race of Cain, Satan is an "inventer" who attributes his creative abilities to himself, without acknowledging his Maker (6.499). This error is at its most pointed when Satan tells Abdiel that he is "self-begot, self-rais'd," the logical extension of the kind of arrogant thinking Milton satirizes in his portrayal of mining and technological innovation (5.860). In response to Satan's "invention" the not-yet-fallen angels take "Th' originals of Nature in thir crude/ Conception" and "with suttle Art" construct "thir Engins and thir Balls/ Of missive ruin" (6.511–19). When the cannons are fired, Milton's imagery again suggests that Satan and his crew are committing a bodily assault on nature due to their inability to understand their own divinely ordained relationship to the environment: "From those deep-throated Engins belcht, whose roar/ Emboweld with outragious noise the Air,/ And all her entrails tore, disgorging foule/ Thir devilish glut" (6.586–9). The "embowelling" of the air and the tearing of "her entrails" again suggests the violation of a female body, but this time it is not a rape but rather a hideous mutilation.

Satan's antipathy to an ecological conception of his place in the world is symptomatic of a distinctly modern conception of selfhood.

170

Satan conceives himself in terms of alienation and abstraction from others and from his environment, a self-concept he expresses in his soliloquy in Book 4. As Matthew Jordan argues, soliloquy in *Paradise Lost* is "inseparable from a consciousness of self as an entity set over against an object confronted as alien and external" (2001: 122). Satan's soliloquy addresses the Sun "with no friendly voice," manifesting his general hostility to the universe around him (4.36). The division Satan constructs between self and environment is self-defeating, however, as he cannot escape the alienation which he has come to embody: "Me miserable! Which way shall I flie/ Infinite wrauth, and infinite despaire?/ Which way I flie is Hell; my self am Hell" (4.73–5). Satan's recognition that he has become the place of his exile ironically recalls his earlier claim that he is "[o]ne who brings/ A mind not to be chang'd by Place or Time./ The mind is its own place, and in it self/ Can make a Heav'n of Hell, a Hell of Heav'n" (1.252–5).

In his depiction of Satan, Milton dramatically illustrates the dangers of separating both mind from body and mind from place, a phenomenon exhibited most powerfully in Milton's own time by the development of the Cartesian theory of mind. In René Descartes's formulation, the very foundation of knowledge is the mind itself, conceived of as alienated both from the body and from the world. This gives rise to the logic of *cogito ergo sum*, "I think therefore I am." Milton attributes a similar kind of subjectivism to Satan in *Paradise Lost*. As Ken Hiltner points out in *Milton and Ecology*, Milton's portrayal of Satan "is a scorching indictment of subjectivism: far from the freedom the subjectivist Satan has imagined, [. . .] he is nonetheless constrained by the mind itself" (2003: 22). In the organic, animate universe of *Paradise Lost*, mind and matter are integrated and subjectivism is both a denial of reality and a form of arrogance. The drive to mastery inherent in Satan's desire to "make a Heav'n of Hell" depends upon his willful blindness to the nature of a universe in which Hell is the fallen angels' "fit habitation" and in which their "gross" bodies by sin "impaird" are no longer fit for heavenly soil (6.876, 661, 691). Most fundamentally, Satan's ambition to radically transform his environment denies his status as a creature, divinely begot, and the implications such status has for his interconnectedness with other created beings and things.

Satan introduces into human consciousness the idea of an opposition between the subject and the natural world when he enters the garden to tempt Eve, and so also establishes the potential for dominating nature. As Karen Edwards argues (see chapter 9 of this volume), Satan's temptation strategy appeals "to Eve's intimate knowledge and love of the created world," but Satan cleverly perverts that knowledge and turns her love of nature into idolatry. The temptation scene begins with Satan idolizing Eve, thereby detaching her from her part in nature conceived as an organic whole. His suggestion that she "shouldst be seen/ A Goddess among Gods, ador'd and serv'd/ By Angels numberless" begins this process (9.546–8). The word "serv'd" subtly hovers in meaning between the service Adam and Eve have known in Eden (the "voluntary service" God requires and is given because his creatures "freely love" [5.529, 539]) to something closer to Satan's "Servility" which contends with "freedom" (6.169). As Satan's temptation develops, his objectification of both Eve and the fruit becomes more powerful. Eve becomes "Empress of this fair World" and the fruit which originally is a sign, becomes instead an object of desire – "those fair Apples" – and finally an object of idolatry – "Sacred, Wise, and Wisdom-giving Plant" (9.568, 585, 679). Eve fatally accepts Satan's construction of the world when she makes the mistake of seeing nature as commodified and isolated from a greater system of meaning. She objectifies the fruit, addressing it as "Best of Fruits" and ultimately succumbs to her desire for what has become in her mind the "Fruit Divine" (9.745, 776). In her newly fallen state, echoing Satan, Eve addresses the tree directly: "O Sovran, virtuous, precious of all Trees/ In Paradise" (9.795–6). As Achsah Guibbory argues (see chapter 8 of this volume), this speech "is at once a soliloquy and an address to a tree" which dramatizes "Milton's view that idolatry is ultimately self-worship." Eve misconceives the tree's proper relationship to God at the same time that she misconceives her own, falsely attributing autonomy to herself and the tree in an imagined world in which the Creator is figuratively displaced.

Eve's Fall can also be understood in part as a rejection of her connectedness with the earth. Under Satan's influence, Eve starts to see both God and nature as alien and untrustworthy. God becomes "hee [. . .] who forbids [the fruit's] use," the punishment of death becomes uncertain, and the "Beasts" are conceived as rivals for whom the fruit may be "reserv'd" (9.750, 768). As Ken Hiltner argues, Eve attempts to transcend the natural world, apparently attracted by Satan's description of her as "Goddess humane" and the desire for abstract knowledge (9.732). Eve "forgets that she [. . .] is rooted in the Earth": she "seeks to pull herself free of Creation (to 'uproot' herself from The Garden) so as to gain a God's-eye view of Creation" (2003: 45–6). Later, Adam is also attracted by the promise of "attain[ing]/ Proportional ascent," which is of course what Raphael promised him, "If ye be found obedient" (9.935–6, 5.501). This is a reversal of the medieval Christian view that the Fall was caused by the first humans being too "earthy" by not being sufficiently removed from the demands of the body (Hiltner 2003: 47). While Milton portrays the Fall as involving Eve's subjection to her bodily desire for the fruit, and Adam's submission to his desire for Eve, he also suggests that the Fall occurs due to Adam's and Eve's pursuit of transcendence and denial of their embeddedness in the natural world.

Ecology in a Fallen World

Milton forcefully registers the ecological devastation caused by the Fall in the response of the animate earth. When Eve eats the forbidden fruit, the narrative voice remarks that, "Earth felt the Wound" (9.782). Similarly, after Adam eats the fruit, "Earth trembl'd from her entrails" (9.1000). The Earth's physical responsiveness to human sin has the consequence that the Fall "clearly includes ecological consequences. Milton's focus on the wounded Earth at the pivotal moment of the human drama shows how closely interconnected is the health of human and natural bodies" (DuRocher 1996: 115). This is evident in the changes wrought in the human body when God tells the Son that Adam and Eve will be expelled from Paradise by natural law: "Those pure immortal Elements that know/ No gross, no unharmoneous mixture foule,/ Eject him tainted now" (11.50–2). Sin changes the very bodies of Adam and Eve, making them incompatible with their "native soile," just as it taints the wider Earth that they will now inhabit (11.270). The Earth is affected "with cold and heat/ Scarce tolerable," the winds become blusterous, and "Beast now with Beast gan war, and Fowle with Fowle,/ And Fish with Fish" (10.653–4, 665, 710–11). Nature is no longer congenial and responsive to Adam and Eve, and this is a direct result of their sin, as the Son tells Adam: "Curs'd is the ground for thy sake, thou in sorrow/ Shalt eate thereof all the days of thy Life;/ Thorns also and Thistles it shall bring thee forth/ Unbid" (10.201–4). The environment, like the human condition, has been dramatically altered, and will remain so until the Second Coming when the Son will "raise/ From the conflagrant mass, purg'd and refin'd,/ New Heav'ns, new Earth" (12.547–9). Some of the images Michael presents to Adam illustrate the wholesale human destruction of the ecological balance which inhered in Paradise, particularly the battlefield "Where Cattle pastur'd late, now scatterd lies/

173

With Carcasses and Arms th'ensanguind Field/ Deserted" and the construction of the Tower of Babel from the "black bitminous gurge" or whirlpool boiling from underground (11.653–5, 12.41). In Milton's London of the 1660s, where, according to John Evelyn, "the weary *Traveller*, at many Miles distant, sooner smells, then sees the City to which he repairs," the gap between Paradise and the contemporary environment must have seemed great indeed (Evelyn 1661: 6, cited in Edwards 1999: 194).

Milton emphasizes this distance between Paradise and the fallen world in *Paradise Lost*, and makes readers acutely conscious of what has been forfeited, while at the same time constructing continuities between the present world and that of the idyllic past. Eve powerfully registers the loss of place when she responds to the news that she must leave Paradise with the lament, "O unexpected stroke, worse then of Death!/ Must I leave thee Paradise? Thus leave/ Thee native soile [. . .]?" (11.268–70). Although Eve later accepts her "banishment," the loss of place is real and significant, and her lament expresses the loss of humankind (12.619). The Paradise in which both spirit and body are in perfect harmony, both for human beings and in the world at large, is no longer attainable. Michael encourages Adam to seek instead the "paradise within," a shadow of the original state of purity in which "inner and outer exist in seamless union" (12.587; Sherry 2003: 81, 85), and a state of mind which is necessarily cognizant of the complexities and uncertainties of the fallen world.

Milton, nevertheless, does not set up an absolute dichotomy between unfallen and fallen life, but rather presents the latter as a tainted version of the former. As Karen Edwards warns, it "is easy to underestimate the degree of continuity between Adam and Eve's pre- and postlapsarian life. Everything changes at the Fall – but not completely, not beyond recognition" (1999: 199). After all, Milton's depiction of Creation and of Paradise is largely based on the creatures and plants in his own world. The "Shoales/ Of Fish" and "tawnie Lion" Raphael describes are part of the complex of creatures inhabiting the natural world in the seventeenth century, just as the paradisal trees are based on travellers' and botanists' accounts of trees growing in other countries around the globe (Edwards 1999: 154–65). The point of Milton's portrayal of a world that remains vital, animate, and creative is to rebut mechanist constructions of the Earth's functioning in the present, not to produce nostalgia for something which has been irrevocably altered.

The continuity between the unfallen and fallen worlds in *Paradise Lost* has ecological significance, because it implies humankind's ongoing responsibility for nature and the present value of created things. An important part of Michael's consolation of Adam and Eve is an assurance that the divine presence in the natural world continues after the Fall, not merely in human beings but also in animals and in the earth itself:

> His Omnipresence fills
> Land, Sea, and Aire, and every kinde that lives,
> Fomented by his virtual power and warmd:
> [. . . . .
> . . .] doubt not but in Vallie and in plaine
> God is as here, and will be found alike
> Present.
>
> (11.336–8, 349–51)

The earth is, as Michael advises, "no despicable gift," but rather an extraordinarily rich tapestry of created things that demonstrates and partly embodies God's glory, as it continues to produce "Varietie without end" (11.340, 7.542). Adam's fallen and reformed sense of the value of other fallen creatures and human responsibility for them is evident in his response to his vision of Noah's ark, when he tells Michael: "I revive/ At this last sight, assur'd that Man shall live/ With all the Creatures, and thir seed preserve" (11.871–3). Where Bacon sought in *The New Organon* to recover man's "dominion over creation" through the "arts and sciences" in an attempt to achieve "an improvement in man's estate" (Bacon 1863, Aphorism LII), Milton's focus is always on discovery of the moral and spiritual aspects of such dominion. In *Paradise Lost*, as in *Of Education*, Milton shows that "by orderly conning over the visible and inferior creature" it is possible to "arrive [. . .] cleerly to the knowledge of God and things invisible" and thus, at least partly, to "repair the ruins of our first parents by regaining to know God aright" (366–9). Thus, Milton approaches redemption through a sense of human beings' relatedness to Creation and the relatedness of Creation to God.

Raphael's advice to Adam to "be lowlie wise" (8.173) applies equally to the epic's readers, who are encouraged to appreciate, understand, and respond to the natural world as an ongoing gift of the divine spirit. The lessons Milton teaches are those of empathy and humility; these are lessons that destabilize the hierarchies upon which the exploitation of others – animals, plants, fellow human beings, and Earth – depend. The recognition of the integrity and otherness of the natural world, coupled with an acknowledgement of one's place in it, is what Milton's epic portrays as the proper (and natural) response to God's bounty. As Adam and Eve leave Paradise to choose "Thir place of rest, and Providence thir guide" (12.647), the promise of place still offers human beings, including the readers of Milton's seventeenth-century poem, the chance to reconnect with the earth and, through the Creation, with the Creator.

References

Bacon, Francis (1863). *The New Organon or True Directions Concerning the Inter- pretation of Nature* [1620]. Trans. James Spedding, Robert Leslie Ellis and Douglas Denon Heath. In vol. 8 of *The Works*. Boston: Taggard and Thompson. At www.constitution.org/bacon/nov_org.htm. Maintained by the Constitution Society.

Bacon, Francis (1996). *Francis Bacon: Selections*. Edited by Brian Vickers. Oxford: Oxford University Press.

Bowerbank, Sylvia (2004). *Speaking for Nature: Women and Ecologies of Early Modern England*. Baltimore: Johns Hopkins University Press.

Duran, Angelica (2003). "The Sexual Mathematics of *Paradise Lost*." *Milton Quarterly* 37: 55–76.

DuRocher, Richard J. (1996). "The Wounded Earth in *Paradise Lost*." *Studies in Philology* 93: 93–115.

Edwards, Karen (1999). *Milton and the Natural World: Science and Poetry in Paradise Lost*. Cambridge: Cambridge University Press.

Evelyn, John (1661). *Fumifugium, or The Inconveniencie of the Aer and Smoak of London Dissipated*. London.

Fudge, Erica (2000). *Perceiving Animals: Human and Beasts in Early Modern English Culture*. London: Macmillan.

Hiltner, Ken (2003). *Milton and Ecology*. Cambridge: Cambridge University Press.

Jardine, Lisa (1999). *Ingenious Pursuits: Building the Scientific Revolution*. London: Little Brown and Company.

Jordan, Matthew (2001). *Milton and Modernity: Politics, Masculinity and Paradise Lost*. Basingstoke and New York: Palgrave.

Low, Anthony (1992). "Agricultural Reform and the Love Poems of Thomas Carew; With an Instance from Lovelace." In Michael Leslie and Timothy Raylor (eds), *Culture and Cultivation in Early Modern England* (pp. 63–80). Leicester: Leicester University Press.

Martin, Catherine Gimelli (2001a). "The Sources of Milton's Sin Recon- sidered." *Milton Quarterly* 35: 3–8.

Martin, Catherine Gimelli (2001b). "'What if the Sun Be Centre to the World?': Milton's Epistemology, Cosmology, and Paradise of Fools Reconsidered." *Modern Philology* 99.2: 231–65.

Mathews, Nieves (1996). *Francis Bacon: The History of a Character Assassination.* New Haven: Yale University Press.

McColley, Diane Kelsey (1999). "Ecology and Empire." In Balachandra Rajan and Elizabeth Sauer (eds), *Milton and the Imperial Vision* (pp. 112–29). Pittsburgh: Duquesne University Press.

McColley, Diane Kelsey (2001). "Milton's Environmental Epic: Creature Kinship and the Language of *Paradise Lost.*" In Karla Armbruster and Kathleen R. Wallace (eds), *Beyond Nature Writing: Expanding the Boundaries of Ecocriticism* (pp. 57–73). Charlottesville: University Press of Virginia.

Merchant, Carolyn (1980). *The Death of Nature: Women, Ecology and the Scientific Revolution.* New York: HarperCollins; with new preface 1990.

Milton, John (1959). *Of Education.* Preface and notes by Donald C. Dorian. In vol. 2 of *Complete Prose Works of John Milton.* Edited by Don M. Wolfe. New Haven: Yale University Press.

Milton, John (1998). *The Riverside Milton.* Edited by Roy Flannagan. Boston: Houghton Mifflin.

Rogers, John (1996). *The Matter of Revolution: Science, Poetry, and Politics in the Age of Milton.* Ithaca: Cornell University Press.

Rudrum, Alan (2000). "For then the Earth shall be all Paradise: Milton, Vaughan and the Neo-Calvinists on the Ecology of the Hereafter." *Scintilla* 4: 39–52.

Sherry, Beverley (2003). "A 'paradise within' Can Never be 'happier farr': Reconsidering the Archangel Michael's Consolation in *Paradise Lost.*" *Milton Quarterly* 37: 77–91.

Soble, Alan (1998). "In Defense of Bacon." In Noretta Koertge (ed.), *A House Built on Sand: Exposing Postmodernist Myths about Science* (pp. 195–215). Oxford: Oxford University Press.

Theis, Jeffrey S. (1996). "The Environmental Ethics of *Paradise Lost*: Milton's Exegesis of Genesis I–III." *Milton Studies* 34: 61–81.

Worster, Donald (1994). *Nature's Economy: A History of Ecological Ideas.* 2nd edn. Cambridge: Cambridge University Press.

Chapter 11

The Messianic Vision of *Paradise Regained*

David Gay

A charming anecdote tells how *Paradise Regained* became a sequel *to Paradise Lost*. Thomas Ellwood visited Milton at Chalfont St Giles, where Milton lived during the London plague of 1666. Milton had asked Ellwood to read the manuscript of *Paradise Lost*:

> He asked me how I liked it, and what I thought of it; which I modestly, but freely told him, Thou hast said much here of *Paradise Lost*; but what hast thou to say of *Paradise found*? He made me no Answer, but sate some time in a Muse: then brake off that Discourse, and fell upon another subject.
>
> After the Sickeness was over, and the City well cleansed and become safely habitable again, he returned thither. And when afterwards I went to wait on him there [. . .] He shewed me his Second Poem, called *Paradise Regained*; and in a pleasant Tone said to me, This is owing to you: for you put it into my head, by the question you put to me at Chalfont; which before I had not thought of. (MacKellar 1975: 1–2)

We can only speculate on what Milton was thinking as he "sate some time in a Muse," but speculation can lead to some good questions. Ellwood may have believed that he motivated Milton to write a sequel; in fact, Milton had thought a great deal about paradise found long before this encounter. In the early 1640s, Milton included themes such as "Christ born," "Christ Crucifi'd," and "Christ risen" in his outlines for possible dramas. In particular, he thought that "Christus patiens," or Christ's sufferings in the Garden of Gethsemane, could "receav noble expressions" (*CPW* 8.559–60). He subsumed many of these ideas into *Paradise Lost*, where we find glimpses of a restored paradise: in the narrator's expectation of the Messiah in the opening lines of the poem, "till one greater Man/ Restore us, and regain the blissful Seat," or the Son's redemptive action, "in thee/ As from a second root shall be restor'd," or Eve's dream of the incarnation: "By mee the Promis'd Seed shall all restore" (1.4–5, 3.287–8, 12.623). Michael's promise to Adam of a "paradise within thee, happier far" also reveals a restored if metaphoric paradise (12.587).

Perhaps Milton wondered why the recovered paradise and the Son who is the agent of its recovery were not more impressive to Ellwood. John Shawcross suggests that Ellwood moved Milton "to make the Son's example more explicit than it was to the average reader of *Paradise Lost*" (1988: 13). Singing "Recover'd Paradise to all mankind" in a sequel would mean exploring the Son's example in a new way (*Paradise Regained* 1.2). In *Paradise Lost*, Raphael portrays the Son's triumph over Satan from the higher plane of eternity, and Michael shows Adam the Son's redemptive sacrifice in the distance of earthly history. In *Paradise Regained*, Milton portrays the Son's point of view more immediately by entering into his thoughts, memories, conflicts, and expectations. The character of the Son – called Jesus in his incarnate, human form – now shapes or "focalizes" readers' perceptions of the world.

By portraying Jesus' point of view, Milton constructs what I will call the "messianic vision" of *Paradise Regained*. "Messiah," a Hebrew word meaning "anointed one," places the Son at the center of Milton's theology and poetry. For readers, the Messiah is both the object and the source of vision. Presenting the Messiah as the object of vision – the hero we observe – Milton invites readers to witness actions that redefine heroism. Presenting the Messiah as the source of vision – the point of view through which we observe Satan's temptations – Milton involves his readers imaginatively in Jesus' encounter with the fallen world. Jesus' vision is both critical and redemptive, as it leads him to reject Satan's temptations. At the same time, Jesus formulates his messianic mission more positively beyond the moment of temptation toward a redemptive vision that articulates values of justice and liberty as alternatives to servitude and tyranny. Temptation brings the hero to a deeper understanding of what a Messiah is, how the Messiah should act in the world, and how the messianic vision can be accessible to others. Milton's messianic vision asks readers to witness Jesus' triumph over temptation, and to engage more actively in his critical and redemptive perceptions of the world.

Vision and Doctrine: The Gospel according to Milton

Ellwood was uniquely privileged to read Milton's manuscript. What would Milton assume about his contemporary readers? He would assume that the Bible shaped their thinking about nearly everything. It is certainly central to Milton's major poems. *Paradise Lost* expands upon the first three chapters of Genesis and concludes by surveying the entire Bible. *Samson Agonistes* is grounded in the "Old Testament." *Paradise Regained* focuses on the beginnings of the "New Testament," or that part of the Christian Bible called the Gospel. "Gospel" is a vital term throughout Milton's writings. In *The Reason of Church Government*, for example, he writes that God "ordain'd his Gospell to be the revelation of his power and wisdome in Christ Jesus" (*CPW* 1.750). He also calls it a "mighty weaknes" capable of overthrowing the "weak mightines of mans reasoning" (*CPW* 1.827). As Adam remarks to Michael in *Paradise Lost*, it is a power "Subverting worldly strong, and worldly wise" (12.568). Milton's Jesus embodies this subversive, paradoxical power.

Milton develops his concept of the Gospel through the vantage point he creates for his readers. Our vantage point starts like that of the angels in Heaven (Rushdy 1992: 126). God invites Gabriel – and us – to witness the contest:

> *Gabriel*, this day by proof thou shalt behold,
> Thou and all Angels conversant on Earth
> With man or men's affairs, how I begin
> To verify that solemn message late,
> On which I sent thee to the Virgin pure
> In *Galilee*, that she should bear a Son
> Great in Renown, and call'd the Son of God.
> (1.130–6)

Like the angels, we watch as Jesus vanquishes Satan. God's speech, however, ensures that the three temptations are not viewed as a simple spectacle. Instead, the temptations are the justification of God's prior word or "solemn message." This "day" is not ordinary time.

Indeed, *Paradise Regained* represents two days. It is, instead, a complex, prophetic time that relates past to present, Earth to Heaven, Jesus to God. In the same way, Jesus focalizes the temptations for readers in order to preserve these relationships. He does so by interpreting biblical texts that arise from his combat with Satan, and thereby involves us in active reading. What kind of reader is Milton's Jesus? Critical of received opinions, complacent reading, and exploitative politics, Jesus is Milton's paragon of critical reason in confrontation with the world.

Milton's messianic vision combines Jesus' rejection of temptation with the development of the "Gospel." New questions now arise. Why did Milton choose this episode in the life of Jesus? Why not write about the biblical moment more often associated with regaining and redemption, Christ's Passion and resurrection? The young Milton abandoned a poem entitled "The Passion," finding the subject *"to be above the years he had, when he wrote it."* Yet, his inclusion of the work in his *Poems* (1645) indicates that he considered this poem to be presentable and important, even in its unfinished form. Other early poems such as the ode "On the Morning of Christ's Nativity" and "Upon the Circumcision" link Christ's infancy proleptically to his Passion. In the ode, for example, the prediction of Christ's eventual atoning sacrifice interrupts the celestial music that celebrates his nativity:

> The Babe lies yet in smiling Infancy,
>> That on the bitter cross
>> Must redeem our loss;
> So both himself and us to glorify.
>
> (151–4)

Other features of the ode anticipate Milton's depiction of the earlier stages of Jesus' messianic mission in *Paradise Regained*. For example, the ode recreates the tradition that Christ's birth silenced the pagan oracles (Hughes 1957: 42). The ode also shows Christian vision superseding classical myths and fables in the routing of the pagan gods (173–228). Similarly, in *Paradise Regained*, Satan is the agent of false "oracles, portents and dreams" (1.396), while Jesus enters the world as God's "living Oracle," the source of "all truth requisite for men to know" (1.460, 464). In both the ode and *Paradise Regained*, the conflict between truth and falsehood prefigures Jesus' ultimate victory over Satan through his death and resurrection; even so, why did Milton not choose to write about the Passion as a mature poet?

The episode of the three temptations in the wilderness was not an alternative to the Passion for Milton. The episode is a positive choice. This episode allowed Milton to imagine the Gospel in its formative stages. The temptations also look to the future by marking Jesus' transition from private to public life. Satan invites Jesus to replicate mundane patterns of heroism, oppression, and imperialism. Rejecting these patterns, Jesus meditates "How to begin, how to accomplish best/ His end of being on Earth, and mission high" (2.113–14). "How to begin" becomes the center of interest for readers. As readers, we know that Jesus is the Messiah and will prevail, just as we know that Adam and Eve will fall in *Paradise Lost*. How Jesus will prevail, rather than whether he will prevail, holds our interest.

Satan and his followers wonder who Jesus is: "Who this is we must learn, for man he seems/ In all his lineaments, though in his face/ The glimpses of his Father's glory shine" (1.91–3). Even this speech does not question that Jesus is the Messiah. It really asks how humanity and divinity are linked in the person of Jesus. Certain features of Jesus' identity should interest us, therefore, because they reflect his relationship to God. These relationships are points of Christian "doctrine," or the conceptual teachings of the Christian church throughout its history.

"Christology" is that part of doctrine that ponders the relationship between the divine and the human in the person of Jesus Christ. The Latin treatise entitled *De Doctrina Christiana*, attributed to Milton, is heretical in its Christology (Lieb 2002). Dissenting from the orthodox doctrine of the Trinity, in which God consists of three coequal and coeternal persons – Father, Son, and Holy Spirit – the treatise argues that the Son is subordinate to the Father and begotten "within the bounds of time" (*CPW* 6.209). In his earlier "On the Morning of Christ's Nativity," Milton affirmed the "Trinal Unity" of the Christian deity (11). In this later treatise, the subordination of the Son is heretical: it goes against accepted Christian teaching. An orthodox or "right thinking" person would call this error rather than truth.

How does this information affect our experience of the poem? There are other heretical statements in the treatise, but searching *Paradise Regained* for such heresies will prove unrewarding. The poem stimulates us to think about Jesus' nature and example without imposing any heretical opinion on us. It is helpful to consider the doctrinal ideas expressed in Milton's prose in a broader context. The preface to *De Doctrina Christiana* offers us this context. It states that its opinions come from an honest search for truth through reading, and it urges us to make our own, informed choices as readers. (Interestingly, "heresy" comes from the Greek word for choice.) The treatise thus makes a political point about the freedom to read. The relation between a free society and the freedom to read is typical of Milton's political vision, as *Areopagitica* shows. This political vision offers us a context in which to view Milton's particular theological choices. Milton's heresies result from his careful reading. Similarly, *Paradise Regained* appeals to us as thoughtful readers and not as potential heretics. In fact, the poem portrays a conflict between two readers: Jesus resists temptation by interpreting the texts that Satan exploits. In constructing his messianic vision, Milton makes important claims about the politics of reading in general, and the politics of scriptural interpretation in particular.

A particular Christological concept shows how Milton uses doctrine to enhance his messianic vision. Jesus has a human nature, as Milton emphasizes in his rendition of the temptations. Scriptural texts support this emphasis. Philippians 2:7 states that Christ "made himself of no reputation, and took upon him the form of a servant, and was made in the likeness of men." The phrase "made himself of no reputation" in the King James Bible is a rendering of the Greek "emptied himself." That Jesus emptied himself of his divinity is an orthodox idea, that is, not heretical. This "emptying," or in Greek "kenosis," is a stage in the myth of incarnation (Lieb 1989: 38–52). "Myth" means that we are examining the Incarnation as a narrative structure (readers of literature should avoid the pejorative notion of "myth" as merely meaning something false or fabricated). The stages of this myth are pre-existence, as Christ exists before his earthly incarnation in Heaven; kenosis, as he sets aside eternal glory to take human form; and exaltation, in his resurrection and return to heavenly glory (Pelikan 1971: 256). As in the Son's narrative of his incarnation in *Paradise Lost* (3.238–40), this voluntary emptying relinquishes divine power so that Jesus can comprehend suffering in human form. Jesus vanquishes Satan "by wisdom" rather than by supernatural power, enhancing his exemplary heroism.

In his human nature, Jesus grows and matures in time. Hugh MacCallum observes that Jesus' early years combine "continuity and discovery" with a deepening "knowledge of himself and his office" (1988: 136; *Paradise Regained* 1.196–292). Matthew, Mark, and Luke, called the "synoptic" Gospels because they have many stories in common, emphasize a Jesus who grows and matures. Dayton Haskin suggests that Milton's Jesus "is the figure of the Synoptic tradition, who 'increased in wisdom and stature, and in favour with God and

David Gay

man'" (1994: 152–3). John, a Gospel different in style and content from the synoptics, does not depict Jesus' growth or early years. John, however, still influences *Paradise Regained* in its use of longer speeches, and in its emphasis on the image of light (Revard 1984). The synoptic Jesus who develops from childhood to the moment of temptation is important to the construction of the messianic vision in the poem. This is so because Scripture – the means of Jesus' growth into self-knowledge – provides a template of stories, teachings, and prophecies that shape Jesus' messianic identity.

That template is called "typology": reading the Bible, and getting more meaning out of it, by comparing and contrasting characters and events from different texts. Typological comparisons originate in the Hebrew Bible, called the "Old Testament" in the Christian Bible (Rosenberg 1984). Drawn subsequently into the "New Testament," with its Messiah who appears in the fullness of time, Christian typology treats figures and events in the Old Testament as "types" of Jesus. Milton calls these forerunners "shadowy types" in *Paradise Lost*, which recalls the idea of "foreshadowing" in many literary works. Old Testament types prefigure Christ, who is the ultimate "antitype" in the Christian frame of reference. In Romans 5:14, Paul tells us that Adam "prefigures" Christ who is "the second Adam." Hence, a premise of *Paradise Regained* is that Jesus, by overcoming temptation, succeeds where Adam failed. Typology tells us more about how people read the Bible in Milton's time, and about how Jesus interprets Scripture in *Paradise Regained*.

The typology of Adam and Jesus enhances *Paradise Regained* as a sequel to *Paradise Lost*. But Milton presents us with even more types of Jesus. Job, for example, is important to Milton's plan for the poem (Lewalski 1966). In his great sufferings, Job is a type of spiritual warrior who, like Jesus, undergoes a purposeful or "good" temptation that strengthens his faith and patience (*CPW* 8.338–9). Moses, Elijah, David, Joshua, and other Old Testament figures referred to in the poem also foreshadow the Messiah. Moses' 40-year journey in Exodus prefigures Jesus' 40-day sojourn in the wilderness. In a sermon on Christ's temptation, Bishop of Winchester, leading Anglican scholar, and translator of the King James Bible (1611) Lancelot Andrewes (1555–1626) shows that this kind of typological thinking was common: "Moses, when he entered into his calling at the receiving of the Law, fasted forty days (Deut. 9.9). So Elias, at the restoring of the same Law, did the like (1 Kings 19.8)" (Andrewes 1967: 491). Jesus recalls these figures in his rejection of the first temptation:

184

> In the Mount
> *Moses* was forty days, nor eat nor drank,
> And forty days *Eliah* without food
> Wander'd this barren waste; the same I now:
> Why dost thou then suggest to me distrust,
> Knowing who I am, as I know who thou art?
> (1.351–6)

Here, Jesus cites Deuteronomy 8:3. In fact, the core responses to all three temptations come from this fifth book of the Torah. Deuteronomy 6:13 is the core response to the second temptation, for example, and Deuteronomy 6:16 to the third. As Jesus identifies with Moses (the giver of the law) and Elijah (a prophet), we observe that typology pertains not only to characters but also to key parts of the biblical canon. Law and prophecy, in other words, are typological phases of biblical revelation. It is useful to view the Christian Bible as presenting seven such phases: creation, revolution, law, wisdom, prophecy, gospel, and apocalypse (Frye 1982: 105–38). The first five comprise the Old Testament. In *Paradise Regained*, the Gospel draws from these five prior phases. As Jesus explores the Scriptures, this typological sequence supports his messianic identity:

> straight I again revolv'd
> The Law and Prophets, searching what was writ
> Concerning the Messiah, to our Scribes
> Known partly, and soon found of whom they spake
> I am; this chiefly, that my way must lie
> Through many a hard assay even to the death,
> Ere I the promis'd Kingdom can attain,
> Or work Redemption for mankind, whose sins'
> Full weight must be transferr'd upon my head.
> (1.259–67)

Jesus focuses his vision, not simply on himself, but on the "promis'd Kingdom." A central theme in the Gospels, this "kingdom" redefines the relationship between the individual and society for Jesus and his followers. Satan's temptations ask Jesus to conform to an unjust society. Jesus refuses. He cannot, however, point to actual examples of a visionary kingdom in the way that Satan can point to Rome. Like the "paradise within" in *Paradise Lost*, the visionary kingdom speaks to the inward potential of readers, and begins with communities nurtured by dialogue, reading, and interpretation. One illustration of this community occurs when Mary and Joseph bring the infant Jesus to the Temple. "Just *Simeon* and Prophetic *Anna*" recognize him on the steps (1.255). The carefully selected adjectives "Just" and "Prophetic" bring together two of the phases of revelation Jesus explores: law and prophecy.

It would be easy to overlook minor characters like Simeon and Anna in a poem so dominated by Jesus and Satan, but these figures show the potential of Jesus' visionary kingdom. Mary is the most important minor character in the brief epic, and of course a major focus of Christian doctrine because she conceives the incarnate Christ in the full mystery of his being. In the opening lines of his earlier ode "On the Morning of Christ's Nativity," Milton reflects on Mary's doctrinal significance:

> This is the Month, and this the happy morn
> Wherein the Son of Heav'n's eternal King,
> Of wedded Maid, and Virgin Mother born,
> Our great redemption from above did bring.
> (1–4)

Virgin Maid and *wedded Mother* would fit our ordinary human experience; "wedded Maid" and "Virgin Mother," however, are both paradoxical statements, showing Milton's delight in the mystery of Christ's conception. Balancing this opening, Milton closes the ode with a charming Nativity scene:

> But see! The Virgin blest,
> Hath laid her Babe to rest.
>   Time is our tedious Song should here have ending;
> Heav'n's youngest-teemed Star
> Hath fixed her polisht Car,
>   Her sleeping Lord with Handmaid Lamp attending:
> And all about the Courtly Stable,
> Bright-harness'd Angels sit in order serviceable
> (237–44)

Milton evokes these Nativity scenes in *Paradise Regained*, but differently. Here, it is less the paradox of doctrine and more the irony of suffering that informs the character of Mary:

> In such a season born when scarce a Shed
> Could be obtain'd to shelter him or me

186

> From the bleak air; a Stable was our warmth,
> A Manger his.
>
> (2.72–5)

The Mary of *Paradise Regained* is the introspective figure of Luke 2:19: "Mary kept all these things, and pondered them in her heart." She is a mother who contemplates the pattern and meaning of her son's life from the time of his birth to the time of his family's flight into Egypt to escape a "Murd'rous King" (2.66–104) to the time of his baptism and temptation. Traditionally called the "second Eve," she is Milton's model of a thoughtful reader as she patiently synthesizes her son's sayings: "But I to wait with patience am inur'd;/ My heart hath been a storehouse long of things/ And sayings laid up, portending strange events" (2.102–4). Dayton Haskin remarks that Mary's heart is like a "commonplace book," or "storehouse" of sayings one might write down to remember (1994: 136–7). Mary's experience as a reader is indeed profound. *De Doctrina Christiana* defines the inward possession of Scripture as the ideal result of reading:

> We have, particularly under the gospel, a double scripture. There is the external scripture of the written word and the internal scripture of the Holy Spirit which he, according to God's promise, has engraved upon the hearts of believers, and which is certainly not to be neglected. (*CPW* 6.587)

The inner scripture, typified by Mary, becomes the basis of Jesus' vision of the "promis'd kingdom." It is therefore important to Milton's politics as well as his poetics. To explore this point, we can turn to Satan and his three temptations.

Vision and Confrontation: The Three Temptations

Matthew and Luke present the three temptations in different orders. Matthew's order is the temptation to turn stones into bread, the temptation of Jesus to cast himself down from the pinnacle of the temple, and the temptation to rule the kingdoms of the world. Luke reverses Matthew's sequence of the last two, placing the world second and the temple third. As the first canonical Gospel, Matthew took precedence in tradition (Pope 1962: 54). Matthew's version was, and still is, the Gospel reading for the first Sunday in Lent (the 40-day period leading to Easter) in the *Book of Common Prayer*, the official guide to worship of the Church of England (Church of England 1559). Illustrating this precedence, Lancelot Andrewes used Matthew for his sermons on the three temptations. Why, then, did Milton prefer Luke? Luke has interesting artistic possibilities. Luke's sequence makes for a spectacular climax at the pinnacle of the temple. Luke's second temptation may have been just as interesting artistically to Milton. If the third temptation provides a great climax, the second allows for a prolonged critical analysis of the fallen world. An extensive critique of the present world is well suited to Milton's artistic and political temperament.

Each temptation subsumes traditional ideas about the biblical event and emphasizes a specific sin; and each rejection establishes a specific component or "office" of the Messiah's role. These three sins and three offices comprise a "triple equation" that offers a way of comparing Adam's fall to Jesus' triumph: "the three sins which Christ refused to commit were, in essence, the same three which had caused Adam's fall: gluttony, vain glory, and avarice" (Pope 1962: 51–2). Shawcross argues that Jesus' refusals inculcate specific virtues that counter these vices: temperance in relationship with the self; prudence in relationship with community; fortitude in relationship with God (1988: 51). This symmetry between Jesus and Adam is once again typological.

Tradition can be flexible. While earlier biblical commentators associated the first temptation with gluttony, later commentators argued that Jesus' hunger in the desert is quite real. Adam and Eve are forbidden a specific fruit amidst the bounty of the Garden of Eden, but no law forbids Jesus from satisfying his natural hunger from his self-imposed fast, as Milton emphasizes in *Paradise Regained*:

> But now I feel I hunger, which declares
> Nature hath need of what she asks; yet God
> Can satisfy that need some other way,
> Though hunger still remain: so it remain
> Without this body's wasting, I content me,
> And from the sting of Famine fear no harm,
> Nor mind it, fed with better thoughts that feed
> Mee hung'ring more to do my Father's will.
>   (2.252–9)

The leading Protestant reformer of the sixteenth century, Jean Calvin, saw the first temptation as an invitation to distrust God (Pope 1962:

57). Calvin's influence shows up in Andrewes' opinion: "There is small likelihood that one should sin in gluttony, by eating bread only," he argues, and the "temptation therefore is to distrust" (Andrewes 1967: 497).

Milton's Satan tempts Jesus to distrust Scripture as well as God by placing objective, material displays of power above spiritual teaching. When Satan asks him to turn stones into bread, however, Jesus remains grounded in Scripture: "Think'st thou such force in Bread? is it not written/ (For I discern thee other then thou seem'st)/ Man lives not by Bread only, but each Word/ Proceeding from the mouth of God" (1.347–50). Here, Jesus defines his first office: prophet, or vehicle of God's word.

The second temptation is to avarice through the acquisition of power (Shawcross 1988: 51). In refusing the kingdoms of the world, Jesus understands his second office: King in relation to the promised kingdom. Satan offers global power in three spheres: military, imperial, and intellectual. Religion is a common element in these spheres, as Satan invites Jesus to make religion a motive for domination instead of redemption. How does Jesus understand the relationship between politics and religion in the second temptation?

To answer this question, we need to know more about the relationship between religion and politics in Milton's time. Here we encounter a "rich religious and socio-political matrix" in which "politics and religion were closely connected" (chapter 1 of this volume; Loewenstein 2001: 243). Milton lived in a deeply biblical culture. Historian Christopher Hill remarks that the "Bible was central to the whole of the life of the society" (1993: 4). The Bible shaped political and religious arguments. In the 1640s, Milton challenged the traditional organization of the church, argued for divorce, and championed the freedom of the press, all from his sense that the Gospel promotes liberty. Freedom of religion was an issue for the many radical religious "sects" at this time. The Quakers (and Thomas Ellwood was a Quaker) tried to work out the principles of the Gospel for their communities. At times, however, these "nonconformists" suffered persecution, exile, and imprisonment for their beliefs and practices. John Bunyan was a Baptist preacher who wrote much of the *Pilgrim's Progress* in jail where he was placed for refusing to give up his ministry. Religion permeated society in Milton's time, but the separation of church and state was an emerging principle that Milton endorsed. Addressing religious toleration in his *A Treatise of Civil Power* (1659), Milton argued that "it is not lawful for any power on earth to compel in matters of religion" (Milton 1957: 839). His Jesus illustrates an individual resisting coercive power.

In the political sphere, the Restoration of monarchy in 1660 frustrated Milton's hopes for republican government. Despite this frustration, he continued to invest his idea of liberty in the Gospel. *The Readie and Easie Way to Establish a Free Commonwealth*, written at great risk to oppose the return of monarchy, makes a "precept of Christ" into a political point: "Ye know that the princes of the Gentiles exercise dominion over them, and they that are great exercise authority upon them. But it shall not be so among you: but whosoever will be great among you, let him be your minister" (Matt. 20:25–6). This precept reinforces the Gospel paradox: serving God is empowering; weakness can be a form of strength. *Paradise Regained* expresses the paradox of "mighty weakness": "His weakness shall o'ercome Satanic strength" (1.160). Yet, as David Loewenstein points out, Milton did not sympathize with extreme groups such as the Fifth Monarchists, who hoped to bring in the reign of Christ by the "violent remodelling of society" (2001: 256). Jesus dismisses real violence, yet proclaims his "promis'd kingdom" through a kind of spiritual violence:

> Know therefore when my season comes to sit
> On *David's* Throne, it shall be like a tree
> Spreading and overshadowing all the Earth,
> Or as a stone that shall to pieces dash
> All Monarchies besides throughout the world,
> And of my Kingdom there shall be no end:
> Means there shall be to this, but what the means,
> Is not for thee to know, nor me to tell.
>
> (4.146–53)

While expressing this metaphoric violence, Jesus remains guarded in Satan's presence about the "means" he will use. Is this "means" the Gospel itself? Is it a foreshadowing of his death and resurrection? Jesus' circumspection exercises readers who, unlike Satan, are not excluded from the visionary kingdom.

The relationship of actual violence to spiritual violence is one of parody. Parody is an important aspect of the second temptation. Jesus must reject each component of the temptation, whether war, empire, or intellect. He can also identify in each component certain semblance or demonic parody of a feature of the kingdom that can be redeemed. Thus, in dismissing war and conquest, depicted in the Parthian Empire poised to the east of Jerusalem, Jesus calls militarism an "argument of human weakness, not strength." He rejects military force, but is involved in a spiritual combat with Satan. Like violence, militarism is a parody of spiritual warfare. True spiritual warfare, in contrast, characterizes the Gospel as a subversive, paradoxical power, and therefore advances the "promis'd kingdom."

Rome presents a demonic parody of government envisioned in the "promis'd kingdom." Satan presents "great and glorious *Rome*, Queen of the Earth" as the center of the world, including Milton's own "*British* West" (*Paradise Regained* 4.45, 77). Satan's Rome is a lavish architectural display designed for spectacles of power. Its "Statues and Trophies, and Arcs" might remind Milton's contemporaries of the displays of restored monarchical power (4.37). The coronation parade of Charles II moved through arches and by statues that flattered the restored regime (Knoppers 1994: 96–122). Some supporters of monarchy even promoted a kind of messianic fervor in Charles's return to power, since at his return Charles was 30, the age traditionally ascribed to Jesus when he began his public mission. Yet Charles's court soon became notorious, as Milton warned it would in *The Readie and Easie Way*, for indulgence and luxury. Jesus dwells for 20 lines on a similar decadence in Rome (*Paradise Regained* 4.125–41). After surveying Rome's excess, he asks, "What wise and valiant man would seek to free/ These thus degenerate, by themselves enslav'd,/ Or could of inward slaves make outward free?" (4.143–5).

In its decadent phase, Rome declines from virtue (frugality and temperance) to vice (lust and ambition). Satan seeks to assimilate Jesus into this pattern. Jesus is unmoved by the spectacle, however, noting that the "wise and valiant man" finds no counterpart for his virtue in existing states and empires. Abandoning the spectacle of history, Satan latches on to the word "wise" to tempt the intellectual side of Jesus' character. He now offers Jesus a kingdom of the mind. He turns to Athens because of Jesus' apparent addiction to "contemplation and profound dispute" (4.213). He also sees that Jesus' intellect is iconoclastic, or hostile to images and ideas that reinforce earthly power. Finding this intellect threatening, Satan tries to sequester Jesus in an academic paradise. The episode evokes Eden as a quiet, pastoral retreat. Athens, the tranquil "Olive Grove of *Academe*," is a parody of paradise (4.244). Was the mature Milton thinking of his youthful days at Cambridge or his private studies at Horton? Satan offers education as an escape. For Milton, education must lead to engagement with the world (see chapter 4 of this volume).

The second temptation also invites Jesus to imagine how his gospel might spread throughout the world. Christianity has traversed the globe over time, often justifying conquerors and colonizers as well as pilgrims and exiles. Columbus wondered if Eden might be found in the fertile estuaries of the Americas. Embracing the wilderness, English Puritans later settled in New England seeking religious liberty and community (Keeble 2002). Missionaries, whether Catholic or Quaker, traveled the world to proclaim their understanding of the Gospel.

The Athenian temptation thus evokes an influential moment in the spread of Christianity. The Acts of the Apostles record Paul's missionary journeys through the ancient Mediterranean world. Dayton Haskin compares Jesus' rejection of learning to Paul's speech to the Athenians in Acts 17:16–32. Speaking at the Areopagus (the ancient site of oratory from which Milton took the title of his *Areopagitica*), Paul proclaims the Gospel in opposition to the Greco-Roman gods. In Colossians 2:8, Paul separates Scripture and philosophy: "Beware lest any man spoil you through philosophy and vain deceit, after the tradition of men, after the rudiments of the world, and not after Christ." Writing against heresy in the late 2nd century, Tertullian, one of the Latin "fathers" of the Christian Church, attacked "human wisdom which pretends to know the truth, whilst it only corrupts it, and is itself divided into its own manifold heresies, by the variety of its mutually repugnant sects. What indeed has Athens to do with Jerusalem? What concord is there between the Academy and the Church?" (1884: 9). Tertullian's is perhaps the most strident response to the question of "Athens and Jerusalem" in early Christianity.

Milton was a very scholarly poet. He owed much to classical literature and philosophy in the development of his poetic vocation and political principles. For this reason, Jesus' seemingly harsh rejection of Athens has troubled readers. How could Milton, of all people, reject the riches of learning? We need to see this rejection in the context of this temptation. Satan offers classical wisdom as a substitute for the Gospel and its teachings. Substitution, if accepted, means that the Gospel would never appear at all. Jesus would interpret Euripides and Aeschylus instead of Moses and Elijah. Satan offers these tragedians as "teachers best/ Of moral prudence, with delight receiv'd/ In brief sententious precepts, while they treat/ Of fate, and chance, and change in human life" (4.262–5). These themes recall the pastimes of Hell in *Paradise Lost* (2.557–69). For Jesus, however, fate is really Satan's misreading of providence: "Alas! what can they teach, and not mislead;/ Ignorant of themselves, of God much more,/ And how the world began, and how man fell/ Degraded by himself, on grace depending?" (*Paradise Regained* 4.308–11). How "the world began, and how man fell" locate the Messiah in the design of time. Jesus refuses to withdraw from history.

Jesus also uses this temptation to formulate more of his future ministry. He defines wisdom not as a cultural trophy but as the inner possession of the faithful: "he who receives/ Light from above, from the fountain of light,/ No other doctrine needs, though granted true" (4.288–90). Here we can see the appeal of this episode to Milton's radical contemporaries. The Quakers, for example, found God's presence in "inward illumination," and considered the Holy Scriptures as a "declaration of the fountain, and not the fountain itself" (Bettenson 1967: 253). Bunyan, though wary of Quaker claims to an inner light, still found that the Spirit illuminates scripture. Milton shows support for persecuted religious groups in affirming the "Light from above" (Loewenstein 2001: 266–76; Knott 1980: 128). At the same time, light is an expansive, archetypal symbol. In John's Gospel, Jesus is the "light of the world" (8:12; 9:5). Light cannot be confined to any one doctrine or group. With his penchant for parody, Satan seeks to replace the light of grace that guided the authors of Scripture with "Nature's light," the light that guided the pagan philosophers (4.227). Jesus does not reject nature's light, but he does subordinate it to the "divinely taught" prophets (4.357). Satan, as usual, seeks to substitute philosophy for Scripture; Jesus, in contrast, seeks the right relationship between them.

The third temptation is an act of violence. Satan carries Jesus to the pinnacle of the temple in Jerusalem and tempts him to cast himself down. The temptation here is to pride or "vainglory" in a manifestation of Jesus' status as the Son of God. In resisting this temptation, Jesus adds the third component of his messianic identity by confirming his role as priest. Hebrews 4:15–16 emphasizes Jesus' human nature in relation to his priesthood: "For we have not an high priest which cannot be touched with the feeling of our infirmities; but was in all points tempted like as we are, yet without sin. Let us therefore come boldly unto the throne of grace, that we may obtain mercy, and find grace to help in time of need." Tempted to usurp God's place, Jesus instead clarifies his role as mediator between humanity and divinity.

Jesus' final rejection of Satan is concise: "Also it is written,/ Tempt not the Lord thy God; he said, and stood" (4.560–1). The core precept is simply "Tempt not the Lord thy God." Milton, however, presents the precept as a sequence of three actions: writing; saying; standing. The sequence illustrates the myth of incarnation: Jesus, the word made flesh, embodies past writing in the present moment. The climax presents not just the objective image of Jesus' triumph over Satan but also a set of relationships connecting the past to the present, and readers to both God and sacred writing through the pronoun "thy." This is the complex, prophetic moment of God's earlier prediction (1.130–6).

The totality of these relationships creates a visionary moment that we could call apocalyptic. "Apocalypse" is the final typological phase of revelation beyond the Gospel. When Jesus stands, Satan falls, "smitten with amazement" (4.562). This moment foreshadows the ultimate defeat of Satan in Revelation at the end of the Bible. The apocalypse, often assumed to predict the world's end, must here be conceived internally (Frye 1982: 135–8). Like the vision Michael gives to Adam at the end of *Paradise Lost*, the climax of *Paradise Regained* presents a mature idea of the apocalypse. Revelation is not a sudden end of the world. It is a vision that guides readers through fallen history. As *Paradise Lost* ends with the reunion of Adam and Eve, and with the world, not dissolved, but "all before them," so *Paradise Regained* ends with the second Adam reuniting with the second Eve, as Jesus "Home to his Mother's house private return'd." As in *Paradise Lost*, the ending of *Paradise Regained* has a way of returning us to the world we have to live in.

Vision and Criticism: Reading Milton Now

In 1804, the painter and poet William Blake was working on a poem called *Milton* (one of Blake's illustrations for that poem is the cover illustration of this volume). In *Milton*, Blake uses the theme of temptation he found in his reading of *Paradise Regained*. The poem *Milton* relates Blake's struggle to resist the pressures of fashion and marketability in order to follow his own artistic vision. This was more than a personal temptation for Blake. His genius was to discern, out of the circumstances that produced his temptation, a range of forces affecting the whole of England in his time. Inspired by Milton's depiction of the kingdoms of the world in *Paradise Regained*, Blake perceived these forces in prolonged war, in growing imperialism, in economic oppression, in social injustice, and in intellectual error. Resisting these forces required vision. For Blake, vision meant that the imagination has both a critical and a creative role to play in the world. Blake

194

aligned his unique vision with the biblical prophetic tradition emphasized by Milton. This alignment did not, however, lead Blake merely to revere Milton as a cultural icon. To the contrary, it led him to struggle deeply with Milton by criticizing his ideas. Blake's critique of Milton raises issues of gender, patriarchy, politics, and religion, areas where Blake found Milton the cultural icon and Milton the political radical to be at odds.

A similar activity energizes critical work on Milton and literature today. Milton justly belongs in the canon of major Western authors, yet recent scholarship has also sought to regain the radical Milton by setting him more among his contemporaries. While acknowledging that important work, this essay has primarily reclaimed "vision" as a critical term. Is it a useful term? What implications might it hold for us in our ongoing work? Writing within a tradition of radical Christianity, with a special emphasis on biblical prophecy, Blake defined vision in terms of his, and Milton's, artistic identification with the iconoclastic, revolutionary, imaginative figure of Jesus. Both poets sought to recover this figure, through imaginative work, from its exploitation by mundane powers and interests. In undertaking this work, both Blake and Milton discovered an important synergy between their creative and critical faculties. Milton is a formidable poet, and Milton's Jesus is a formidable critic. In our unique historical moments and different cultural contexts, we can consider how Milton's critical vision links his poetic and polemical roles. *Paradise Regained* affirms that criticism impelled by the imagination's encounter with past, present, and future worlds is a vital enterprise.

References

Andrewes, Lancelot (1967). *Seven Sermons upon the Temptation of Christ in the Wilderness. The Works of Lancelot Andrewes*, vol. 5. New York: AMS Press.

Bettenson, Henry (ed.) (1967). *Documents of the Christian Church*. Oxford: Oxford University Press.

Church of England (1559). *Booke of Common Praier, and Administration of the Sacramentes, and other Rites and Ceremonies in the Churche of Englande*.

Frye, Northrop (1982). *The Great Code: The Bible and Literature*. Toronto: Academic Press.

Haskin, Dayton (1994). *Milton's Burden of Interpretation*. Philadelphia: University of Pennsylvania Press.

Hill, Christopher (1993). *The English Bible and the Seventeenth-Century Revolution*. London: Penguin.

Hughes, Merritt Y. (1957). "Preface to 'On the Morning of Christ's Nativity.' " In *John Milton, Complete Poems and Major Prose*. Edited by Merritt Y. Hughes. New York: Odyssey Press.

Keeble, N. H. (2002). "Wilderness Exercises: Adversity, Temptation, and Trial in *Paradise Regained.*" *Milton Studies* 42: 86–105.

Knoppers, Laura Lunger (1994). *Historicizing Milton: Spectacle, Power and Poetry in Restoration England.* Athens: University of Georgia Press, 1994.

Knott, John (1980). *The Sword of the Spirit: Puritan Responses to the Bible.* Chicago: University of Chicago Press.

Lewalski, Barbara (1966). *Milton's Brief Epic: The Genre, Meaning, and Art of* Paradise Regained. Providence: Brown University Press.

Lieb, Michael (1989). *The Sinews of Ulysses: Form and Convention in Milton's Works.* Pittsburgh: Duquesne University Press.

Lieb, Michael (2002). "*De Doctrina Christiana* and the Question of Authorship." *Milton Studies* 41: 172–230.

Loewenstein, David (2001). *Representing Revolution in Milton and his Contemporaries.* Cambridge: Cambridge University Press.

MacCallum, Hugh (1988). "Jesus as Teacher in *Paradise Regained.*" *English Studies in Canada* 14.2: 135–51.

MacKellar, Walter (ed.) (1975). *A Variorum Commentary on the Poems of John Milton. Vol. 4: Paradise Regained.* London: Routledge and Kegan Paul.

Milton, John (1953–82). *Complete Prose Works of John Milton* [*CPW*]. Edited by Don M. Wolfe. 8 vols. New Haven and London: Yale University Press.

Milton, John (1957). *John Milton, Complete Poems and Major Prose.* Edited by Merritt Y. Hughes. New York: Odyssey Press.

Pelikan, Jaroslav (1971). *The Christian Tradition: A History of the Development of Doctrine. Vol. 1: The Emergence of the Catholic Tradition (100–600).* Chicago: University of Chicago Press.

Pope, Elizabeth (1962). Paradise Regained: *The Tradition and the Poem.* New York: Russell and Russell.

Revard, Stella (1984). "The Gospel of John and *Paradise Regained*: Jesus as 'True Light.' " In James H. Sims and Leland Ryken (eds), *Milton and Scriptural Tradition: The Bible into Poetry* (pp. 142–59). Columbia: University of Missouri Press.

Rosenberg, Joel (1984). "Biblical Narrative." In Barry W. Holz (ed.), *Back to the Sources: Reading the Classic Jewish Texts* (pp. 31–8). New York: Summit.

Rushdy, Ashraf H. A. (1992). *The Empty Garden: The Subject of Late Milton.* Pittsburgh: University of Pittsburgh Press.

Shawcross, John (1988). Paradise Regain'd: *Worthy T'Have Not Remain'd So Long Unsung.* Pittsburgh: Duquesne University Press.

Tertullian (1884). *On Prescription against Heretics.* In vol. 2 of *The Writings of Quintus Sept. Flor. Tertullianus.* Edited by John Kay et al., trans. Peter Holmes. 3 vols. Edinburgh: T. T. Clark.

Chapter 12

The Nightmare of History: *Samson Agonistes*

Louis Schwartz

Of History, Providence, and the Sound of Falling Temples

I first confronted *Samson Agonistes* at about the time I also first discovered modern literature and philosophy, and ever since that time I have associated three passages with one another. They have haunted me for years in both the classroom and the library, as I have tried to make sense of the very strong and disquieting responses I have had to Milton's poem as both a teacher and a scholar. In the first passage, from Joyce's *Ulysses*, Stephen Daedalus expresses a distinctly modern terror at the probable meaninglessness of human history, a desire to wake up from the nightmare of seeing history in a particular way:

> – History, Stephen said, is a nightmare from which I am trying to awake.
>   From the playfield the boys raised a shout. A whirring whistle: goal. What if that nightmare gave you a back kick?
> – The ways of the Creator are not our ways, Mr Deasy said. All human history moves towards one great goal, the manifestation of God.
>   Stephen jerked his thumb towards the window, saying:
> – That is God.
>   Hooray! Ay! Whrrwhee!
> – What? Mr Deasy asked.
> – A shout in the street, Stephen answered, shrugging his shoulders.
>   (Joyce 1986: 28)

Stephen is wearily skeptical about both the old, no longer quite so comforting platitudes expressed by Mr Deasy and the likelihood of ever finding something equally comforting to replace them. In the second passage, from *Samson Agonistes* itself, Samson's father and the chorus of Danites confront a historical event whose nightmarish terror is evident, but whose meaning is not yet clear:

> *Manoa.* I know your friendly mind and – O what noise!
> Mercy of Heav'n! what hideous noise was that?
> Horribly loud, unlike the former shout.
>   *Chorus.* Noise you call it or universal groan
> As if the whole inhabitation perish'd?
> Blood, death, and deathful deeds are in that noise,
> Ruin, destruction at the utmost point.
>   (*Samson Agonistes* 1508–14)

As we will see later, their shock at the noise of blood, death, and ruin sets them struggling on a path toward a conclusion very like Mr Deasy's. The context makes it hard to take their version as merely a platitude – these are, after all, people in the midst of bloody conflict – but that does not, as we will also see, make it any easier for a reader to simply accept.

In the third passage, from the second essay of *On the Genealogy of Morals*, Friedrich Nietzsche suggests a cold hard fact about all historical conflict and change:

> I end with three question marks; that seems plain. "What are you really doing, erecting an ideal or knocking one down?" [. . .] But have you ever asked yourselves sufficiently how much the erection of *every* ideal on earth has cost? How much reality has to be misunderstood and slandered, how many lies have had to be sanctified, how many consciences disturbed, how much "God" sacrificed every time? If a temple is to be erected *a temple must be destroyed:* that is the law – let anyone who can show me a case in which it is not fulfilled! (Nietzsche 1967: 95)

Like Nietzsche's essay, Milton's poem asks difficult questions: Can God's voice be heard in "Blood, death, and dreadful deeds [. . .] Ruin and destruction?" Can ideals be erected or affirmed on earth at all, given that doing so always entails not just the destruction of other ideals, but the destruction of the human beings and communities that stand for them? How do we know when our ideals are worth the destruction that will inevitably attend their assertion? Can we be awakened to action in history and know that what we are moved to do is right?

That the poem asks, but never clearly or simply answers, such questions is only one reason it has always been Milton's most controversial work. *Samson Agonistes* is, in a word, troubling. It not only represents the world of cultural and religious conflict in a way that renders that world more uncertain than it might have seemed to us before (especially if we were apt to see it the way Mr Deasy does), it also presents more interpretive dilemmas than any of Milton's other major works. In this essay, I would like to suggest that there is a close relationship between the interpretive ambiguities of the poem and its ultimate purpose in casting a cold eye on the terrible human problem of how terrible violence can be wielded in good cause. In the end, I think that Milton does come to some conclusions about the problem. They are not, however, comforting ones. They are, instead, designed to awaken us to the nature of our most basic commitments, and they offer a scouring calculus concerning what these might cost as they impel us to action.

Uncertainties

The uncertainties of the poem, its "uncertain world," as John Shawcross has termed it, are considerable (Shawcross 2001). We do not know exactly when it was written, why it was published in the same volume as *Paradise Regained*, whether we are to take it as independent from that work, a companion to it, or as an afterthought. Some have thought it a relatively early work, perhaps even unfinished. Others have treated it as the culminating masterpiece of Milton's long career. As a Christian work that uses a Greek generic form to tell an ancient Hebraic story, it has presented scholars and critics with a host of theological and theoretical questions: How are we to understand tragedy in a Christian context? How are we to understand the historical and/or typological relationship between the Hebrew story and the Christian one that it precedes and perhaps prefigures? How are the conventions of classical tragedy affected by the sacred material, and vice versa? Some have wondered to what extent we should consider performance conventions in reading and interpreting the text. Even if we decide, as Milton himself suggests in his introductory note, to treat it as a poem to be read rather than as a script to be performed, we still have to deal with the fact that as a drama it presents the actions, reactions, and perspectives of a set of characters without telling us which ones (if any) express the truth as the author would like us to see it. There is no narrator to tell us what to think about what the characters say and do, no one to tell us what they are thinking; even the Chorus seems to lack any reliable authority.

Because the text itself does not provide clear answers to the many questions it raises, readers have often looked, instead, to the various traditions and contexts on which it draws. There are, however, several such contexts to choose from, and each suggests its own possible meanings and presents its own problems. Of primary interest, of course, have been the Judaic and Christian interpretive traditions that have surrounded Milton's biblical source (Judges 13–16). These traditions have seemed to some to be more or less univocal, presenting Samson as flawed, but heroic, a hero of Israelite nationalism, a zealous iconoclast. In Hebrews 11, Paul presents him as a "Hero of Faith," a vindicator of God who wrought miracles on behalf of Israel, helping to pave the way in history for the final fulfillment of the covenant in Christ. To other scholars, however, the traditions have seemed more vexed and varied. These scholars have tended to concentrate on Samson's considerable human flaws and on the inconclusiveness of his mission to free Israel from Philistian bondage.

The political resonance of the Samson figure for any number of sides in the complicated debates and conflicts of Milton's own era have also been examined in minute detail, as has its applicability to a number of theological problems central to the Reformation. Such examinations have led many critics to conclude that Milton meant the poem to comment on the religious turmoil of his age. The fact, furthermore, that its story so clearly suggests certain perennial Miltonic obsessions has led many critics to see the poem as a major or even final statement on matters like temptation, fall, and redemption; on Milton's anxieties about his parallel careers as poet, polemicist, and political appointee; and on the larger, related question of how believers can know that they are executing God's will in the course of their lives. Others have seen in the poem a debate between Milton's humanism and the more radical aspects of his Protestantism, a debate over when believers have to leave human reason behind and open themselves to divine impulses or commands that may be irrational or suprarational.

The fact that aspects of the narrative obviously but inconsistently parallel aspects of Milton's life has led to a wide variety of biographical readings. Uncertainties about the date of composition (suggestions have ranged from the early 1640s to the years just prior to its publication in 1671) have made it difficult to establish the poem's proper local context, but this has certainly not stopped anyone from speculating. Scholars and critics have argued over the years that we should see the tragedy in terms of everything from Milton's disquiet about his blindness to the problems he encountered early in his first marriage, from his debate in print with Salmasius over the execution of Charles I to his despair over the ultimate failure of the revolution that brought about that execution. Some have suggested that the tragedy is a call to arms, others a defeated man's revenge fantasy, still others an older and wiser warrior's exhausted rejection of political action and political violence.

Some critics in recent years have worried in both scholarly journals and the popular press about how we should see the poem in light of twenty-first century world politics. Is Samson "a suicide bomber?" (see especially Carey 2002). Is Milton advocating Samson's action, suggesting a justification for it? How free are we to apply that justification, if it is there? How can we best understand Milton's approach to the political violence of his own age so that we can gauge the significance of his poem for ours? Contemplation of these issues has led many readers to extreme statements of either censure or apology.

Looking over all of this lively and at times heated debate, some critics have concluded that the poem is hopelessly ambiguous, expressive of Milton's unresolved ambivalence, perhaps an artistic failure. Some have thought, on the other hand, that the poem is purposely designed to introduce problems that Milton had decided were, in fact, unsolvable, or that it is designed to make us confront the indeterminate nature of our condition itself. Milton, of course, believed that the outcome of events in the created universe was ultimately determined by God's will, but he was also keenly aware of how difficult it sometimes could be to perceive that will amid the host of uncertain signs that often confronts us. God's face, as the poem's final chorus notes, is often hidden. Some critics – Stanley Fish most prominently – have, therefore, suggested that the poem is designed to dramatize precisely such moments of tense epistemological uncertainty – moments when we know there is a right choice, but we feel impulses in more than one direction and do not know which ones to credit. Samson is alone with his inner impulses; he acts on faith that these are from God, but there is no way for either him or us to know for sure. His final choice may or may not be right, and Milton is as much in the dark about it as we are. Others critics have suggested that Milton withholds an explicit or unalloyed statement of the truth from us in order to force us to come to our own conclusions. In some readings, we are asked to do this by exercising reason, in others by opening ourselves to contemplation of those disquietingly nonrational impulses of divine will I mentioned earlier.

The tragedy, in any case, certainly dramatizes one man's coming to a conclusion about divine will, by reason or by faith, and then acting on his conclusion, and it is the nature of that conclusion and act, much more so than the ambiguities that surround them, that has given interpretation of the poem so much moral, political, and theological urgency. This is because, whatever its author may have intended it to mean in the context of his own life and times – some possibilities are more plausible than others, but there are certainly more than one – the poem's violent setting gives it a wide applicability to a kind of event that is tragically common in human history. The ancient tribal and religious warfare that gave birth to the Samson narrative in the first place, the religious and political conflicts of the seventeenth century that Milton witnessed and in which he participated, and whatever atrocities or triumphs are reported in tomorrow's paper, along with a host of other, similarly bloody historical events and episodes, all have a way of collapsing into one another like the pillars of Dagon's Temple whenever we try and come to terms with the way Milton thought to represent Israelite and Philistine in conflict.

I would like to suggest that Milton meant this to happen. After all, he chose to tell an ancient story that he thought of as historical, and that he knew could and probably would be taken in a number of ways given contemporary circumstances. In the process, he referred to a set of theological, political, and philosophical frameworks (some of which, but not all of which, were native to the story's original context) in such a way as to inspire more questions than he managed to answer. Furthermore, despite what the famous last lines of the poem suggest, the few answers he did provide do not, I believe, leave our minds calm and our passions spent – even if we accept the story's conclusion as just. Instead, I would like to suggest that even the most believing readers, with the most traditional approach to Samson's heroism and regeneration, are invited to tremble in the face of what the Chorus calls a gift, the "new acquist/ Of true experience" (1755–6). Milton's poem offers a strikingly open-eyed vision of what can, and even what must, happen when human and divine wills collide and collude on the stage of human history.

Hard Questions

While the gift of new experience that the poem offers us is indeed a mixed blessing, given as it is by a catastrophic and morally disquieting event, it is presented as a gift nonetheless (one that, after all, was first given, as far as Milton was concerned, in the Scripture). This, however, only makes it all the more disquieting. Milton's presentation of the concluding episode, in fact, gives almost free rein to both the comforting and the disquieting. The way Milton announces the horrible climax, for example, and then represents a sequence of responses to it is typically mixed and complex. Even those who stand to benefit from the destruction (Manoa, the Chorus of Danites, the Hebrew Messenger who tells the tale) are all at first deeply unnerved by what has happened, and not just because they have lost their son, champion, and/or compatriot. Milton registers a powerful initial distress in the first speech of the Messenger who describes for us the destruction of the temple and the death of Samson: "O whither shall I run, or which way fly/ The sight of this so horrid spectacle/ Which erst my eyes beheld and yet behold?/ For dire imagination still pursues me" (1541–4). The Messenger's words echo Satan's in Book 4 of *Paradise Lost*: "which way shall I fly/ Infinite wrath, and infinite despair?" (73–4). He is caught between a vision of infinite wrath and a possible response of infinite despair. The infinite – God's will – has crashed into the finite – human will in opposition to God's – and destroyed it. Even the faith of a believer (one who does God's will, or at least tries) can be, these lines suggest, shaken by the sight of such a collision, its sheer cost in human terms. The Messenger, however, does not fall into despair, but gradually, instead, makes his peace with the wrathful, destroying will of the God the Chorus later describes as "our living Dread" (1673). He remains uncertain for a while, but does finally manage, along with Manoa and the Chorus, to work his way through to an acceptance, even a celebration, of what has happened. It is, indeed, with a considerable amplification of this final celebration that Milton chooses to end the play.

The horror remains, however, some of it in the language of the final celebration itself, some of it simply hovering in our sense that the way through to certain comforts depends on where we, finally, place our loyalties. That Milton fully expects us to side with the Israelites might seem a given, but that does not mean that the poem somehow keeps us from imagining how things looked from the perspective of the Philistines. The poem is designed to allow us such an imagining, maybe even to require it of us, even if in the end we admit that Milton does want us to think like an Israelite (then as a Christian who has inherited the grounds of his or her own faith from the Israelites). The language of the consolation itself is uneasily balanced between a rational, Boethian sense of the final goodness and justice of providence (that all is best "found in the close") and a rather frank bloody-mindedness modeled on the kind of rhetoric, both zealous and vengeful, to be found in many places in the Hebrew Scriptures (for example, in the last verses of the Song of Deborah, Judges 5:28–31). The Chorus is delighted, for example, to imagine that the Philistines were killed while drunken at their idolatrous feast, just when they thought they were celebrating their own victory (*Samson Agonistes* 1669–86). Both the Chorus and Manoa take time to imagine, again with relish, the "years of mourning,/ And lamentation" that their enemies will face (1712–14, 1752–4). That such heated emotion, turned first to a kind of cold-bloodedness, is carried over into the stately and ostensibly comforting final choral speech of the poem is striking.

The tragedy catches us, I believe, between two rather forceful and seemingly opposed propositions: what has happened is unacceptably horrible, and what has happened was willed by God. Strictly speaking, this is impossible. If it was willed by God, it has to be acceptable. One way out of this problem is to simply decide that one or the other proposition is simply wrong. I do not think, however, that Milton is asking us to choose *between* the two propositions, as though the horror of the first should lead to the rejection of the second, or the truth of the second erase the horror of the first. Many readers have felt that Milton could not have meant us to see the end of the play as acceptable at all. See, for example, the different ways critics like John Carey, Irene Samuel, and Joseph Wittreich have argued for the undermining power of the darker implications I describe above, going so far as to suggest we reject Samson and his actions. On the other hand, critics like Mary Ann Radzinowicz and Anthony Low have argued convincingly that, even if the choral perspective is to some extent partial or incomplete, Milton's portrayal of Samson is, as a whole, in line with the traditional heroic view of his story, with Milton adding his own particular intellectual and theological emphases. The choice between these two perspectives is, I think, however, a false one.

I would like to suggest, instead, that *Samson Agonistes* challenges us to hold in our imaginations both a truth *and* its unacceptable manifestation. We are asked somehow to maintain our horror even as we are asked to commend the horrible action. Our situation is like that of the "warfaring Christian" in Milton's *Areopagitica*, who is asked to "apprehend and consider vice" fully before rejecting it and learning to prefer virtue. There is one crucial difference, however: while we are asked in *Samson Agonistes* "to apprehend and consider" participation in a terrible act, we are not then asked to reject it. Our willingness, instead, to consider the possibility that we might actually have to do something like it, that we must prefer doing so to any alternatives that might be available, is crucial to the poem's terrible power.

The question the play asks, therefore, is not "did God really command the wholesale slaughter of the Philistines in the temple of Dagon?" Milton's answer to that question is, I think, "yes." The real question the play asks, instead, is "how are we to feel and behave in the face of that 'yes'?" This question forces us to a consideration of what scholars of Milton's theology call his "antinomianism." "Antinomianism" is the strain in Christian thought, particularly strong in Reformation theology, that holds that Christians are freed by faith in Christ's sacrifice not only from the ritual laws of the Old Testament, but perhaps its moral laws as well, perhaps even from all manner of civil and natural law, what Samson refers to in his debate with Dalila over the politics of their marriage as "the law of nature, law of nations" (890). A true Christian, according to the logic of antinomianism, seeks and gets guidance directly from the Holy Spirit, wholly as a result of his or her faith in Christ's saving grace, and need not heed any earthly authority, or any outmoded religious strictures, unless prompted to do so by that grace.

Scholars have detected a distinctive antinomianism in Milton's thought, especially as it pertains to the right of a people to depose a tyrant, which, of course, not only entails law-breaking and the instigation of civil strife, but also collective and/or individual acts of violence. The right to take up arms against a tyrant also, perforce, licenses acts of deception, theft, even perhaps revenge. These actions, which Milton indirectly advocated in the cause of liberating English Christians from civil coercion, not only violated English law as it stood at the time, but also might be seen as violating several basic moral principles grounded both in natural reason and biblical revelation (see Bennett 1998 and 1989; Burns 1996; Worden 1995). Samson is himself "guilty," of course, of all of these things and more. He also, as many have noted, violates at least one specific commandment in the course of the drama – the commandment against participation in idolatrous rites – and perhaps several others in the course of his life (commandments concerning exogamy, theft, and sexual indiscretion) (Burns 1996; Shoulson 2001: 240–61). As a hero of faith, Samson, in other words – though not a Christian – is a model for a certain mode of Christian antinomianism, along with Abraham, David, and others listed in Hebrews 11.

The arguments of these critics suggest that we ask the question I have already raised in a slightly different way. What does it mean, we should ask, that in doing God's will in history it seems at times acceptable, or even necessary, to abrogate all that is acceptable not only to human reason, law, and custom, but even to God's will as manifest in his own commandments? I think that Milton prompts us to this question because he suspected that there was, in fact, no way to promote God's will *in certain historical circumstances* without committing an atrocity of one kind or another. And this leads to another question: what do we do with our human moral responsiveness when we feel called to commit such an act in God's behalf? How do we gird ourselves for the task, and how can we live with ourselves afterwards? It is in the face of this question, as Bennett's searching arguments in particular make clear, that the distinctively Miltonic, Christian nature of the poem's approach to tragedy is manifested. There is no other way, the poem suggests, for God's will to get done in history, and yet his will must be done.

"O change beyond report, thought, or belief!"

That following God's will should entail perpetrating Samson's kind of violence and that such violence should be necessary to ensuring for believers a free religious life are, to say the least, very uncomfortable ideas for twenty-first century readers to entertain, and for many readers the answers Milton suggests in the poem have seemed to run counter to the Milton that emerges from his other major works. This feeling of discontinuity has led some critics to argue with tremendous moral and scholarly energy that this is not what he meant at all. How could he have when Samson so strikingly contrasts with the less ambiguous (in some cases compellingly *un*ambiguous) images of Christian heroism that Milton offers us elsewhere: the temperance of the Lady in *A Mask*, the "better fortitude/ Of Patience and Heroic Martyrdom" and the power of "things deem'd weak" to subvert the "worldly strong" sung of in *Paradise Lost* (*PL* 9.31–2, 12.567–8), and above all the Son of *Paradise Regained*, whose story of resistance to temptation –

including the temptation to violence – was published in the same volume as Samson's and offers an immediate and striking interpretive foil?

The power this play has had to shatter the image of Milton that many readers develop from careful reading of the other major and minor works often comes, in fact, as an unpleasant shock. I know that it was for me the first time I read it as an undergraduate, and I have seen that experience repeated every time I have taught the play since then. *Samson Agonistes* inevitably occupies the terminal spot of my Milton syllabus, which is structured chronologically, and many students over the years have found it very difficult to reconcile what they read there with the image of Milton that tends to emerge from the earlier reading I have assigned them. This is, in part, because my teaching tends to emphasize texts like *Areopagitica* and *Paradise Lost*, which despite some alienating moments feel like harbingers of the modern modes of humanism, both secular and religious, that most of my students espouse. It is also because I teach in the United States, and the violent argument of the antimonarchical tracts seems so reasonable and historically inevitable to most students in the US. The violent conflict between King and Parliament seems like an early version of the US's own myth of national origin. The English Civil War also seems from a safe historical distance to have been a matter, mostly, of state-controlled violence (in a conflict over who would control the state). However barbarous they might actually have been, the actions of monarch and legislators, their armies, judicial courts, and executioners seem to many students to have been quite civilized in comparison with Samson's. My students find that they do not want to make the analogy between Milton's and Samson's political causes, even after I show them passages like those quoted in the work of critics like David Lowenstein, passages that show how common it was for Milton and other writers in the seventeenth century to do just that.

Students sometimes find the rejection of classical learning in *Paradise Regained* a little off-putting, but despite such moments, and despite the overall iciness they sometimes feel coming off of that text, they never seem to have much trouble seeing the Son as a culminating example of the ideals of temperance and faith that Milton had been celebrating since the 1630s. They can draw a line, in other words, between the Lady of *A Mask* rising from her chair and the Jesus of the brief epic balanced on the pinnacle of the temple, both upheld by grace and justified by trial. But the line between the Lady and Samson is more difficult to draw. Many of them also tend to distrust the idea that because the Samson story is a biblical story they are simply supposed to side with whomever the Good Book says are the "good guys," no matter how problematic their behavior might seem. It may be a mistaken overreading of what Milton means, but they take his criticisms of "custom" in *Areopagitica* and *The Tenure of Kings and Magistrates* very much to heart and apply them, naturally, exactly that far. In today's political climate, moreover, for many Christians, even for some Jews, let alone the few Muslim students I have taught over the years – certainly for the secular internationalists in any given class – just who the "good guys" really are is hardly clear anymore anyway.

As Alan Rudrum has observed in a recent essay defending those readings that insist on Samson's heroic stature, it has always been hard to teach this poem against the backdrop of whatever world-historical events are going on at any given time. He warns us about conflating our own moral and political responses with Milton's intentions, and he calls for readings that scrupulously attend to the poem's original historical context. The poem plainly, however, wants to be applied beyond its immediate historical contexts – both ancient and early modern – and as long as we do attend carefully to the textual details and the contextual materials, and as long as we are prepared for the difficult work of confronting both historical differences *and* historical similarities, we can and should do so.

It has been particularly difficult, as many have attested, to confront the poem in US classrooms – and perhaps any classroom where the text is taught – since September 11, 2001. Recently, for example, when I began discussing *Samson Agonistes* in class, my brightest student indignantly slammed her copy of Carey's *Complete Shorter Poems* on her desk as prelude to telling me that she simply did not believe that Milton could have written the poem. She said bluntly that the only justifications she could find in the work for the slaughter of the Philistines were identical in her mind to the justifications offered by Al Qaeda for attacking New York and Washington. She did not see that Milton had given her sufficient grounds for finding the Philistines collectively guilty, nor could she see that Samson, despite his self-characterization, was any better than Dalila in using their marriage for political ends. She was only slightly mollified when I told her that on both counts she was not alone in feeling this way, and that many prominent Miltonists had made similar arguments in print. This did not help enough, however, because she saw – I think quite clearly – that either I, her professor, was going to have to resolve all dispute by revealing the one thing she had missed, the one thing that would restore the passionate and generous but also rational poet she had come to love over the course of the semester, or she was going to have to break off her romance with him.

The class laughed when we put it in those terms, but there was a very serious feeling at the heart of my student's conclusion. The play seemed to present an aspect of Milton's personality and belief system that she could not embrace. She could no longer feel an easy intimacy with Milton's works, could not feel like they were a source of possible wisdom – something she *had* felt before, despite certain ideas that she also felt were to some extent anachronistic. She could not feel, for example, as she did about some of the rhetoric about gender in *Paradise Lost*, that the poem was rescued for her precisely by her sense of historical distance. She felt that Milton was, as we often say, "remarkably searching, even progressive, *for a man of his day*" when it came to women – even if he sometimes fell back on patriarchal rhetoric, and even if he did not go as far as she might have liked. She could perform a similarly apologetic exercise when it came to the backpedaling toward the end of *Areopagitica*, where modern readers are inevitably reminded of how the free exchange of ideas in the commonwealth means the free exchange of *Christian* ideas, and not even all of those. After all, the argument goes, we cannot expect a fully secular humanism from Milton and he, in any case, speaks in that same paragraph about tolerance and the "compassionat means" to be used "to win and regain the weak and the misled" (*CPW* 2.565).

The problem she was facing was especially acute because, for various reasons, I did fail to resolve the dispute to her satisfaction. And I regularly fail students when it comes to *Samson Agonistes*. I had been able all semester to explain these sorts of things, show the reasonable side of them, even more, show how Milton's reason itself often implied things beyond its own religious and cultural frameworks, things that we flatter ourselves with all the time (a free press, gender equality, etc.), ideas that emerged in embryo in the seventeenth century and that we can imagine ourselves as having brought to maturity or fulfilled by a kind of secular historical typology. Milton is our prophet, I implied over and again without ever actually saying it. But with Samson I could not do this. I had no framework for making acceptable sense out of what she had read. The striking historical *applicability* of the analogy with modern religious terrorism is, in fact, what made recourse to anachronism useless, and I could produce no fully convincing account of the Philistines' perfidy that seemed equal to the punishment meted out to them. I had to admit that the best arguments for the problem with the Philistines did not seem fully adequate to the atrocity. The best ones, I think, are those offered by Bennett in her discussions of marriage and tyranny (1989: 141–50; 1998), but as several critics have noted, it is striking that Milton seems to have had little interest in indicating in the tragedy itself any of the tyrannical or genuinely debauched behavior of which we might *imagine* the Philistines guilty. He even has Manoa tell us about his meeting with a number of "generous [. . .] and civil" leaders just before the temple comes crashing down on top of them (and with them his own hopes of ransoming his son) (*Samson Agonistes* 1457–71).

From my students' perspective, the Philistines held one truth and lived in accordance with it, and so did the Israelites. If the Philistines were wrong, why not show more clearly how, and why not use those more "compassionat means" mentioned in *Areopagitica* "to win and regain the weak and the misled"? Why not, even better, just live and let live? Unfortunately for the reasonable, modern Milton, his answers to these and other similar questions involve recognizing that at certain extremes, two perspectives do not mean two truths, and that the Philistines, even if they may be said to have been misled in their religious life, were certainly not weak in their political life. They were perfectly happy lording it over the Israelites who were being kept from freely living under the direct authority of God, not just their God, but Milton's – some Israelites were even tempted to worship Dagon themselves. Even if we agree with those critics who think Milton rejected Samson's particular reaction to such circumstances, this sort of foreign rule and the temptations it created were clearly, from his perspective, bad things, and there is nothing to suggest even in the most generous moments of Milton's portrayal of Philistian characters that they were amenable to either rational or compassionate persuasion (Bennett 1989). As Harold Skulsky puts it, and as my own earlier remarks suggest, "[t]he play generously makes room for evidence against its own conclusion – but that's not the same thing as not really coming to it" (1996: 101).

It is at this point in classroom discussion that I usually introduce a troubling thought. Maybe we simply have to give up our easy intimacy with Milton when we read this last published poetic work. His assumptions are not our assumptions, and by reading this text we can get a handle on those we have rejected. On the other hand, and even more troubling, what if we really do not have as much freedom to reject such assumptions as we think? After all, even if we argue God out of the picture, we might still find ourselves having to take up arms in defense of our own conceptions of liberty, our own values, however they are conceived. Maybe this poem is, deliberately or not, Milton's final warning to the future's tendency not simply to misread but to belittle the past freely. This warning is, I think, couched in his own fierce refusal to belittle the "pastness" of the period of the Judges. Milton makes a stark claim for *its* applicability to his own historical situation, despite certain differences, and it is by virtue of that move that it becomes prophetic also of ours (and in a way different from the sort of secular "prophesy" I spoke about before). I remind my students of the painful switching back and forth that Milton did in that troubling paragraph from *Areopagitica*. In that passage, Milton does back away from some of the more radical implications of his argument, but he enforces some other implications that are just as, though differently, radical. It is true that he says, "it is not possible for man to sever the wheat from the tares, the good fish from the other frie," and that "that must be the Angels Ministery at the end of mortall things" (*CPW* 2.564–5). This passage, like the allegory of the Lord's Temple, to which he refers in the sentence just before the one I quote, points in the direction of a tolerance that is rooted in a profound spiritual humility, a refusal to believe or claim that any mere mortal human has privileged access to the whole truth and can therefore say right off what can and cannot go into the building. The statement edges close to some forms of modern pragmatism or relativism (stopping short of claiming there *is* no truth at all). But in the rest of the paragraph, despite the suggestions about "compassionat means," Milton also makes it clear that he is willing to "extirpat" those who, in the end, refuse to give up their "Popery, and open superstition, which as it extirpates all religions and civill supremacies, so itself should be extirpat" (2.565). The root of the word "extirpate" comes from the Latin for clearing the ground of unwanted plants by uprooting them. By the late sixteenth century it was commonly used, however, in the stronger sense of "exterminate, or totally destroy (a class, sect, or nation); to kill off, and render extinct" (*Oxford English Dictionary* 3); and we all know the common modern words for that.

In bringing this up it is not my intention to make Milton into an advocate for genocide or ideological purging; but I do think that we should face the fact that he did believe there were circumstances in which an extirpation of some kind was the only proper course. The passage in *Areopagitica* presents, however, the *reasonable* version of this. You can feel his swerving away from persons to their ideas, his generous hope that the mistaken can be enlightened, his attempt to exclude only the very worst from the bright circle of "brotherly dis-similitude"; but you can also see the dark reality that haunts the edges of his vision. To recall the passage from Nietzsche I quoted at the beginning of this essay, if a temple is to be built, then one must also be destroyed. *Samson Agonistes* is Milton's attempt to stare steadily at the implications of that dark principle.

The great difficulty, of course, is that Milton is inviting us to stare as well, and if we do so, any smugness we might feel about our greater civility – or even worse, about the power of civility itself in the face of whatever *we* deem to be evil – falls away as quickly as any temple wall. What, after all, is even the modern pragmatist or relativist to do when someone wants to take away his or her freedom to be a mod-ern pragmatist or relativist? The equation of Milton and his Samson with twenty-first century religious terrorism, as it turns out, is only one possible turn of the figure. The battle of the liberal West against, say, Al Qaeda or some similarly hostile entity involves the attempt to extirpate what, from the liberal perspective, amounts to the modern equivalent of "tolerated Popery, and open superstition," modes of thinking that if they were allowed to govern civil life would them-selves extirpate civil life as the West knows and values it. Such extir-pation is, however, hardly the sort of action that liberalism itself values. The position of the violent defenders of modern civil life is, or should be, therefore, just as morally disquieting for generous and open-minded secularists as the analogous position is for Christian antinomians (or, for that matter, for their Jewish or Islamic counter-parts). All have to compromise values of compassion and tolerance in the act of defending those very values. The only comfort anyone has in such circumstances is a belief in the truth of the values themselves and the cold necessity that, ironically or tragically, requires they be defended by intolerant means. Milton is insisting, I believe, in the truth of his own values and principles, and in the process he forces us to recognize that even if we claim that we hold no truth at all, we may very well find ourselves having to defend even that position as true. I might be moved – and I should admit that I am moved – to take my pen and put "scare quotes" around that last word, but what really scares me is the possibility that I might be more fundamentally moved by circumstance to pick up a gun rather than a pen (or, as Milton found himself doing, a pen in justification of someone else's raised gun). As the passages I quoted at the start of this essay suggest, given the sort of back-kicks it has a tendency to deliver, for a character like Stephen Daedalus, a thinker like Friedrich Nietzsche, and for us no matter what our particular persuasions, there may be no awakening from the nightmare of history.

References and Further Reading

Bennett, Joan S. (1989). *Reviving Liberty: Radical Christian Humanism in Milton's Great Poems.* Cambridge: Harvard University Press.

Bennett, Joan S. (1998). "Asserting Eternal Providence: John Milton through the Window of Liberation Theology." In Stephen B. Dobranski and John P. Rumrich (eds), *Milton and Heresy* (pp. 219–43). Cambridge: Cambridge University Press.

Burns, Norman T. (1996). "'Then stood up Phinehas': Milton's Antinomianism, and Samson's." *Milton Studies* 33: 27–46.

Carey, John (1969). *Milton.* London: Evans Brothers.

Carey, John (2002). "A Work in Praise of Terrorism? September 11 and *Samson Agonistes. Times Literary Supplement,* Sept. 6, 15–16.

Fish, Stanley (2001). *How Milton Works.* Cambridge: Belknap Press of Harvard University Press.

Joyce, James (1986). *Ulysses.* New York: Vintage.

Kerrigan, William W. (1987). "The Irrational Coherence of *Samson Agonistes.*" *Milton Studies* 22: 217–32.

Krouse, Michael F. (1949). *Milton's Samson and the Christian Tradition.* Princeton: Princeton University Press.

Lieb, Michael (1994). *Milton and the Culture of Violence.* Ithaca: Cornell University Press.

Lieb, Michael (1996). "'Our living dred': The God of *Samson Agonistes.*" *Milton Studies* 33: 3–25.

Low, Anthony (1974). *The Blaze of Noon*: A Reading of Samson Agonistes. New York: Columbia University Press.

Lowenstein, David (1996). "The revenge of the saint: Radical religion and politics in *Samson Agonistes.*" *Milton Studies* 33: 159–80.

Milton, John (1953–82). *Complete Prose Works of John Milton [CPW].* Edited by Don M. Wolfe. 8 vols. New Haven and London: Yale University Press.

Milton, John (1957). *John Milton, Complete Poems and Major Prose.* Edited by Merritt Y. Hughes. New York: Odyssey Press.

Nietzsche, Friedrich (1967). *On the Genealogy of Morals.* Trans. and edited by Walter Kauffman. New York: Random House.

Radzinowicz, Mary Ann (1978). *Toward* Samson Agonistes: *The Growth of Milton's Mind.* Princeton: Princeton University Press.

Rudrum, Alan (2004). "Milton Scholarship and the *Agon* over *Samson Agonistes.*" *Literature Compass* 1: 1–24.

Samuel, Irene (1971). "*Samson Agonistes* as Tragedy." In Joseph A. Wittreich (ed.), *Calm of Mind: Tercentenary Essays on* Paradise Regained *and* Samson Agonistes (pp. 235–57). Cleveland: Case Western Reserve University Press.

Shawcross, John (2001). *The Uncertain World of* Samson Agonistes. Cambridge: D. S. Brewer.

Shoulson, Jeffrey S. (2001). *Milton and the Rabbis: Hebraism, Hellenism, and Christianity*. New York: Columbia University Press.

Skulsky, Harold (1996). *Justice in the Dock: Milton's Experimental Tragedy*. Newark: University of Delaware Press.

Wittreich, Joseph A. (1986). *Interpreting* Samson Agonistes. Princeton: Princeton University Press.

Wittreich, Joseph A. (2002). *Shifting Contexts: Reinterpreting* Samson Agonistes. Pittsburgh: Duquesne University Press.

Worden, Blair (1995). "Milton, *Samson Agonistes*, and the Restoration." In Gerald MacLean (ed.), *Culture and Society in the Stuart Restoration: Literature, Drama, History* (pp. 111–36). Cambridge: Cambridge University Press.

Part III

Reference Points

Select Chronology

"Speak of things at hand/ Useful"

Compiled by Edward Jones

Editor's note: This section takes its subtitle from a moment in *Paradise Lost* that is humorous and authentic for many instructors. After the archangel Raphael's account of the distant and awe-inspiring War in Heaven and his attempts to show the "relevance" of the rebel angels' disobedience to human obedience in Books 5 and 6, Adam begins Book 7 seeking to shift the discussion to the human world, "things at hand/ Useful." The humor lies in the disparity between student-Adam's practical-mindedness and teacher-Raphael's equally important attention to intense abstractions. Both are important. Similarly, this section attempts to ground the complex interpretations of parts I and II by providing biographical and historical context to contemporary readers.

The following chronology provides specific dates whenever possible to establish Milton's whereabouts, the occurrences of births, marriages, and deaths within his extended family, document numbers for identification purposes and composition and publishing dates of his writing. The last of these, especially regarding composition, should be deemed approximations at best. The second column, which lists events in the larger context of Milton's time, affords the opportunity to gauge the extent to which national and international events may have found their way into his private and public life. No overt links are made; however, implicit possibilities are registered through the selections chosen for inclusion.

For the readers' convenience, all dates are New Style, that is, using the Gregorian Calendar, which begins the new year on January 1st, opposed to the Julian Calendar in use in England until 1752, which starts the new year on March 25th.

Edward Jones

Events in John Milton's life		Events in Milton's time
JM is born in Bread Street (Dec 9) and baptized in the church of All Hallows, London (Dec 20).	**1608**	Shakespeare's *Pericles* debuts to great acclaim.
		Champlain founds a colony at Quebec.
	1609	Shakespeare's *Cymbeline* is performed late in the year or in the first months of 1610, most likely indoors at the Blackfriars Theatre.
		The British establish a colony in Bermuda.
		Moriscos (Christianized Muslims) are expelled from Spain.
		Galileo constructs his first telescope.
		The Dutch East India Company ships the first tea to Europe.
A tax assessment (E179/146/470) confirms the Miltons residing in the parish of All Hallows, London	**1610**	Galileo discovers the four largest moons of Jupiter (Jan 7).
Ellen Jeffrey, JM's maternal grandmother, is buried in All Hallows, London (Feb 26).	**1611**	Shakespeare's *The Winter's Tale* is performed at the Globe Theatre (May).
		The Authorized Version (King James Bible) is published.
		Shakespeare's *The Tempest* is performed at court (Nov 1).
		The Dutch begin trading with Japan.
		The First Presbyterian Congregation is established at Jamestown.
JM's sister Sara is baptized (Jul 15) and buried in All Hallows, London (Aug 6).	**1612**	Henry, Prince of Wales, dies.
		Charles I becomes heir to the throne.
	1613	A fire breaks out during a performance of Shakespeare's *Henry VIII* and destroys the Globe Theatre (Jun 29).

218

Events in John Milton's life		Events in Milton's time
JM's sister Tabitha is baptized in All Hallows, London (Jan 30).	**1614**	Shakespeare's *Two Noble Kinsmen* opens at the rebuilt Globe Theatre.
		Napier publishes tables of logarithms.
		The Dutch establish New Amsterdam in the area of present day New York City.
		Fire destroys parts of Stratford-upon-Avon.
		The first saltworks near Jamestown produce saltpeter, an important ingredient in gunpowder.
Tabitha Milton is buried in All Hallows, London (Aug 3).	**1615**	Part 2 of Cervantes's *Don Quixote* is published.
JM's brother Christopher is born (Nov 24 or Dec 1?) and baptized in All Hallows, London (Dec 3).		Lord and Lady Somerset are convicted of murdering Sir Thomas Overbury.
Between 1615 and 1621, JM begins his formal education at St Paul's.		George Villiers, the future Duke of Buckingham, becomes the new favorite of King James I.
Between 1615 and 1624, JM possibly writes "Philosophus ad Regem," "Apologus De Rustico et Hero," "Carminia Elegiaca," "Ignavus Satrapam Dedecet," and a prose theme on early rising.		
Eton College surveys the Milton Bread Street home (Oct 16).	**1617**	Henry Briggs publishes the first table of logarithms to base 10.
Between 1617 and 1619, Thomas Young tutors JM.		Widespread flooding in the Catalonian region of Spain kills 35,000 inhabitants.
An unknown artist, traditionally reported to be Cornelius Janssen, paints JM's portrait.	**1618**	The Bohemian Phase of the Thirty Years' War (through 1620) begins.
Thomasine Webber, the future sister-in-law of JM, is baptized in the church of St Clement Danes, Westminster (Oct 18).		The Synod of Dort convenes in the Netherlands.
		Sir Walter Ralegh is executed.

Events in John Milton's life		Events in Milton's time
Thomas Young serves as the chaplain to the English Merchant Adventurers in Hamburg (Apr).	**1620**	Bacon's *Novum Organum* is published.
JM's father is appointed a trustee of the Blackfriars Playhouse in London (Jul 4).		A Separatist congregation of pilgrims establishes a colony in Plymouth, Massachusetts.
		Cornelius van Druffell submerges a 270 foot long leather-covered vessel powered by 12 oarsmen 15 feet below the surface of the Thames.
JM's father publishes six musical settings in Thomas Ravenscroft's *The Whole Book of Psalms*.	**1621**	The Palatine Phase of the Thirty Years' War (through 1623) begins.
Richard Powell, JM's future father-in-law, acquires Forest Hill (Oct 2).		Oughtred constructs the first slide rule.
A tax assessment (E 179/289/31) verifies Richard Powell residing at Forest Hill (Jan).	**1622**	The Congregation for the Propagation of the Faith is established as a Catholic missionary organization.
Rate books for the parish of St Martin-in-the-Fields, Westminster, establish Edward Phillips, JM's future brother-in-law, as a resident (Apr 7).	**1623**	Bernini completes his *David*.
Edward Phillips marries JM's sister Anne in the parish church of St Stephen, Walbrook, London (Nov 22).		Prince Charles and Buckingham are unable to negotiate the Prince's marriage to the Spanish Infanta.
JM and his mother, Sara, sign Anne Milton's marriage settlement (Nov 27).		
Sometime during this year JM paraphrases Psalms 114 and 136.	**1624**	The Danish Phase of the Thirty Years' War (through 1629) begins.
		England declares war on Spain
JM's nephew John Phillips is baptized in St Martin-in-the-Fields, Westminster (Jan 16).	**1625**	James I dies (Mar 27) and is buried in Westminster Abbey (May 7).

Events in John Milton's life		Events in Milton's time

Events in John Milton's life

Mary Powell, JM's future wife, is baptized in the parish church of St Nicholas, Forest Hill (Jan 24).

JM is admitted to Christ's College, Cambridge (Feb 12) and matriculates at the University (Apr 9).

JM's niece Anne Phillips is baptized in St Martin-in-the-Fields, Westminster (Jan 12).

JM composes "Elegia I" (Apr?), "Elegia II" and "Elegia III" (Sep/Oct?), "In Obitum Praesulis Eliensis" (Oct?), "In Obitum Procancellarii Medici" (Oct–Nov?), "In Proditionem Bombardicam" (four epigrams on the Gunpowder plot [Nov?]), "In Inventorem Bombardae" (Nov?), and "In Quintum Novembris" (Nov).

JM writes Thomas Young in Hamburg and encloses "Elegia IV" (Mar 26).

JM signs an indenture in London for property in St Martin-in-the-Fields, Westminster (May 25).

JM signs a loan in London from his father to Richard Powell for 300 pounds (Jun 11). Powell will pay JM interest twice a year on this loan until he defaults on June 12, 1644.

JM's niece Anne Phillips is buried in St Martin-in-the-Fields, Westminster (Jan 22).

JM composes "On the Death of a Fair Infant" (Jan 23–Mar?).

Thomas Young accepts the living at Stowmarket in Suffolk and returns to England (Mar 27).

Events in Milton's time

Charles I ascends the throne (Mar 30) and marries the Catholic Henrietta Maria of France by proxy (May 1).

An outbreak of the plague kills thousands in London (Jul 8).

1626 Charles I is coronated at Westminster Abbey (Feb 2) and dissolves Parliament (Jun 15).

England engages in war with France (through 1629).

1627 Buckingham fails to liberate besieged Huguenots near La Rochelle.

1628 William Harvey publishes *De Motu Cordis* describing the first accurate account of the human circulatory system.

Czech educator John Comenius publishes *Didactica Magna*, which advocates teaching in the vernacular and universal education for men and women.

221

Events in John Milton's life		**Events in Milton's time**
JM's niece Elizabeth Phillips is baptized in St Martin-in-the-Fields, Westminster (Apr 9).		Buckingham is assassinated. William Laud becomes Bishop of London (Jul 4).
JM composes *At a Vacation Exercise, An Oration*, and *Prolusion 6* (all in July).		
JM's nephew John Phillips is buried in St Martin-in-the-Fields, Westminster (Mar 15).	**1629**	Parliament passes resolutions against religious innovations and taxes.
JM writes "Elegia Quinta" (Mar/Apr?), completes B.A. (July), and composes *Prolusion 2* (Oct) and "On the Morning of Christ's Nativity" and "Elegia Sexta" (both in Dec).		Charles I dissolves Parliament and begins the "Personal Rule" (Mar 2). The British establish a colony in the Bahamas. The Treaty of Susa concludes England's war with France.
During this year, JM composes *On Shakespeare*, probably Sonnets 1–6, Canzone, and "The Passion" (Mar), "Elegia Septima" (May), "Lines appended to Elegia Septima" and "Song: On May Morning" (both in May?).	**1630**	Van Dyck completes his *Samson and Delilah*. The Swedish phase of the Thirty Years' War (through 1635) begins. A remedy for malaria is introduced into Europe.
JM's nephew Edward Phillips is born most likely in August in the parish of St Paul's, Hammersmith, but neither the month nor the place has been definitively settled.		An outbreak of the plague devastates Venice and surrounding parts of Italy killing 500,000. The Treaty of Madrid concludes England's war with Spain.
JM writes "On the University Carrier" (two poems) and "Hobson's Epitaph" (Jan–Mar).	**1631**	The symbol for multiplication ("×") is introduced. John Donne dies.
JM's brother Christopher is admitted to Christ's College, Cambridge (Feb 15).		Vesuvius erupts and kills 3,000 (Dec 13).
JM's niece Elizabeth Phillips is buried in St Martin-in-the-Fields, Westminster (Feb 19).		A drought across much of Asia causes widespread famine.
A parish rate book (PAF/1/212) establishes JM's father as a resident of St Paul's, Hammersmith (Apr 30).		

Events in John Milton's life		**Events in Milton's time**

JM composes "An Epitaph on the Marchioness of Winchester" (Apr), *Naturam non pati senium* (Jun?), *De Idea Platonica quemadmodum* (Jun?), "L'Allegro" (?), "Il Penseroso" (?).

JM's brother-in-law Edward Phillips is buried in St Martin-in-the-Fields, Westminster (Aug 25).

JM's nephew John Phillips is born most likely in October in Hammersmith, but neither the month nor the place has been definitively settled.

Anne Milton Phillips marries Thomas Agar in the parish of St Dunstan in the East, London (Jan 5).

JM completes M.A. (Jul 3) and subsequently returns to his parents' home in Hammersmith.

JM's niece, Mary Agar, is baptized in the parish church of Kensington (Oct 10).

JM composes "Sonnet 7" and "Letter to a Friend" (Dec).

1632 Galileo publishes his *Dialogue Concerning the Two Chief World Systems.*

Rembrandt completes *The Anatomy Lesson of Dr Nicholas Tulp.*

A plague outbreak in France kills 80,000.

The first coffee shop in London opens for business.

Van Dyck becomes the Court painter.

Between 1633 and 1637, JM composes *Arcades*, "On Time," "Upon the Circumcision," and *A Mask*.

1633 Herbert's *The Temple* and Donne's *Poems* are published.

William Laud becomes Archbishop of Canterbury (Aug 6).

The first publication on first aid appears.

The Inquisitional Courts force Galileo to recant his belief in the Copernican system expressed in the 1632 *Dialogue*.

JM's *A Mask* is performed at Ludlow Castle (Sep 29).

1634 William Prynne loses his ears for publishing *Histrio-mastix* which criticizes Henrietta Maria (May 7).

Charles I issues the first requests for ship money (Oct 20).

Edward Jones

Events in John Milton's life		Events in Milton's time
Chancery record C24/600/37 confirms the Miltons residing in Hammersmith (Jan 8). They relocate to the village of Horton sometime between Jan 9, 1635 and May 12, 1636.	**1635**	The Franco-Habsburg Phase of the Thirty Years' War (through 1648) begins. The Dutch continue to trade at Nagaski, the only overseas contact with Japan's imperial government.
JM purchases Chrysostom's *Orationes LXXX*.	**1636**	Rembrandt completes *The Blinding of Samson*. Harvard College is founded.
JM's brother Christopher informs the court in Westminster that his father, now living in Horton, is too infirm to appear (Apr 1). JM's mother Sara dies (Apr 3) and is buried inside the Horton parish church of St Michael (Apr 6). A diocesan church inspection of St Michael's cites JM's father for an improper church seat (Aug 8). JM composes *Lycidas* (Nov). JM's brother Christopher takes up residence in the Inner Temple, London (Nov 26). JM's *A Masque Presented at Ludlow Castle, 1634*, dated 1637, is most likely published at the beginning of 1638.	**1637**	The first public opera house San Cassiano opens. Prynne, Bastwick, and Burton are mutilated (Jun 30). The introduction of the Laudian prayer book in Edinburgh occasions a riot (Jul 23). Descartes publishes his *Discourse on Method* in Venice.
JM's father lowers his church seat as recommended by the diocesan report (Feb 21). Christopher and Thomasine Webber Milton reside with JM's father in Horton. JM composes "Ad Patrem" (Mar?) and meets and corresponds with Sir Henry Wotton at Eton College (Apr 1–13).	**1638**	The first printing press in the American colonies is set up in Cambridge, Massachusetts. Henry Jacobs establishes the Particular Baptist movement outside London.

224

Events in John Milton's life	Events in Milton's time
JM sells land in St Martin-in-the-Fields, Westminster to Sir Matthew Lyster (May 15).	
JM begins a tour of the Continent (May) which includes visits to Florence (Jun through Sep), Rome (Oct and Nov), and Naples (Dec). During this time he composes *Ad Salsillum* (Nov?) and *Mansus* (Dec).	
JM's *Lycidas* appears in *Justa Edouardo King Naufrago*.	
Christopher Milton marries Thomasine Webber in the parish church of St Andrew Holborn, London (Sept 10). Subsequently they reside with JM's father in Horton.	

Events in John Milton's life		Events in Milton's time
JM travels back to Rome (Jan and Feb) and Florence (Mar).	**1639**	Rubens finishes his *Judgment of Paris*.
JM attends the debut of the first complete comic opera *Chi soffre, speri* by Mazzocchi and Marazzuoli, with the libretto by Rospigliosi, the future Pope Clement IX, in Rome (Feb).		Monteverdi composes *Vespers*. Roger Williams establishes a Baptist church in Providence, Rhode Island but eventually he abandons it.
JM visits Venice (Apr), Verona and Milan (May), and Geneva (May and Jun). He returns to England via France in July and during the remainder of the year possibly resides in Horton and St Brides, London.		Episcopacy is abolished in Scotland (Aug), and the Scottish Parliament is dissolved (Oct 31).
JM composes three *Ad Leonoram* poems (Feb?) and *Epitaphium Damonis* (Sep–Nov?).		
Sometime during this year, JM moves to St Bride's Churchyard, London and begins instructing his nephews Edward and John Phillips.	**1640**	*The Whole Book of Psalms*, arguably the first book published in Colonial America, appears.
JM takes land in Wheatley owned by Richard Powell (Jun 30?).		Joseph Hall publishes *Episcopacy by Divine Right* (Feb/Mar) which will be answered by JM's *Of Preletical Episcopacy*.

Edward Jones

Events in John Milton's life		Events in Milton's time
JM's niece, Sarah Milton, is baptized in St Michael's, Horton (Aug 11).		Portugal regains independence from Spain.
		Fermat develops modern number theory.
		The Scottish army invades England setting off the Second Bishops' War (Aug 20).
		Archbishop Laud is impeached (Dec 18).
A tax record (Guildhall MS 1503) confirms JM living in the parish of St Botolph, London on Aldersgate Street (Apr 29).	**1641**	Descartes publishes *Meditations*.
		The Grand Remonstrance identifies royal mismanagement as well as parliamentary solutions and future objectives.
A subsidy return (E 179/75/355) and churchwarden account identify Christopher Milton and his father as members of the parish of St Laurence, Reading (Apr).		
JM publishes *Of Reformation* (May 12–31), *Of Prelatical Episcopacy* (Jun/Jul?), and *Animadversions* (Jul?).		
JM's niece Anne Milton is baptized in St Laurence, Reading (Aug 27).		
JM publishes *The Reason of Church-Government* (Jan) and *An Apology* (Apr).	**1642**	Parliament closes the theaters.
		Flooding in China kills 300,000.
Christopher Milton takes the Protestation Oath in Reading (Feb–Mar).		Beriberi is clinically discovered.
		Galileo dies.
JM marries Mary Powell of Forest Hill (Jul?) who returns to her family a month after moving to London (Aug).		Pascal invents the adding machine and contributes to the development of differential calculus.
JM composes "Sonnet 8" (Nov?) and begins drafting *Paradise Lost*, the majority of which will be composed from 1656 to 1665?		Parliament issues the Nineteen Propositions limiting Charles I's power, but the King resists and the English Civil War begins.
		The first major battle of the English Civil War takes place at Edgehill (Oct 23).

226

Events in John Milton's life		Events in Milton's time

After the fall of Reading to Parliamentary forces (Apr.), JM's father relocates to his elder son's residence in London. While Christopher moves his family to the home of his mother-in-law Isabel Webber in the parish of St Clement Danes, Westminster.

JM's nephew, John Milton, is baptized in St Clement Danes, Westminster (Jun 29).

JM composes "Sonnet 9" and "Sonnet 10" between 1643 and 1645 and publishes *The Doctrine and Discipline of Divorce* (Aug 1).

1643 Parliament enacts laws of censorship.

The mercury barometer is invented.

Louis XIV ascends the French throne.

The Westminster Assembly is established and adopts Presbyterianism on the basis of the Solemn League and Covenant. It subsequently writes *The Directory for the Worship of God* (1645), *The Westminster Confession* (1646), and *The Longer and Shorter Catechisms* (1647).

JM publishes a revised edition of the *Doctrine and Discipline of Divorce* (Feb 2), *Of Education* (Jun 5), *The Judgement of Martin Bucer* (Aug 6), and *Areopagitica* (Nov 23).

Thomas Young, now a member of the Westminster Assembly, delivers *Hope's Encouragement*, a sermon to Parliament, which draws upon JM's *Doctrine and Discipline of Divorce* (Feb 28).

The Westminster Assembly summons JM to answer charges of unlicensed and unregistered printing (Dec 28).

1644 The Globe Theatre is torn down.

Descartes publishes his *Principles of Philosophy*.

The largest battle of the Civil War takes place at Marston Moor and is won by Parliamentary forces and the Scots.

JM publishes *Tetrachordon* and *Colasterion* (Mar 4).

JM's niece Sarah Milton is buried in St Clement Danes, Westminster (May 26).

Some time during this year JM composes *In Effigei Eius Sculptorem*.

JM reconciles with Mary Powell Milton and subsequently moves to a new home in the Barbican (Aug/Sep).

JM writes "Sonnet 11" (Sep–Nov?).

1645 William Laud is executed (Jan).

The first text discussing crop rotation is published in England.

The New Model Army is established and wins victory at the Battle of Naseby.

The English Prayer Book is abolished.

Events in John Milton's life		Events in Milton's time
JM's *Poems* is published (Jan 2).	**1646**	Massive flooding in Holland results in the death of 110,000.
JM writes the first draft of "Sonnet 13" (Feb 9).		Episcopacy is abolished.
Richard and Anne Powell and at least five of their children move into JM's Barbican home (after Jun 27).		The Long Parliament establishes Presbyterianism as the official national religion during the Civil War and Interregnum.
JM's daughter Anne is born (Jul 29), but no record of her baptism or place of birth have been found.		The Scots capture Charles I at Newark and the first Civil War ends (Jun).
JM writes "Sonnet 14" (after Dec 16).		
Between 1646 and 1648, JM composes the *Fifth Ode of Horace, Book 1* and possibly begins *Paradise Regained* (most of which will be written after 1665).		
JM may begin composing *Samson Agonistes*, but it is mostly likely revised in 1653 and after.		
JM's father-in-law Richard Powell dies in the Barbican residence (Jan 1).	**1647**	George Fox establishes the Society of Friends.
JM writes *Ad Jonnem Rousiam* (Jan 23), "Sonnet 12" (Jan?) and "On New Forcers of Conscience" (Jan/Feb?).		The Army Grandees and the Levellers debate constitutional reform in a series of meetings now known as the Putney Debates.
JM's nephew Thomas Milton is baptized in St Clement Danes, Westminster (Feb 2).		A cavalry force led by Cornet Joyce abducts Charles I from Holmby House and brings him to Newmarket as a prisoner of the New Model Army (Jun).
JM's father is buried inside the parish church of St Giles Cripplegate, London (Mar 15).		
JM moves his family to High Holborn (Sep/Oct?).		
JM translates Psalms 80–88 (Apr), begins drafting the *History of Britain*, and composes "Sonnet 15" (Aug).	**1648**	The Treaty of Westphalia concludes the Thirty Years' War.
		The second Civil War begins.

Events in John Milton's life		Events in Milton's time

JM's second daughter Mary is baptized in the parish church of St Giles-in-the-Fields, London (Nov 7).

JM writes *The Tenure of Kings and Magistrates* (Jan 15–29) which is published shortly thereafter (Feb 13).

JM is appointed Secretary for Foreign Tongues by the Council of State (Mar 15), a post he will hold for 11 years. He will draft, translate, and prepare letters of state first for the Council and later for the Secretary of State during the Protectorate.

JM moves his family from High Holborn to Charing Cross (Mar) and publishes *Eikonoklastes* (Oct/Nov?).

1649

The expelling of 140 MPs from the House of Commons, commonly referred to as Pride's Purge, takes place.

Charles I is tried (Jan 19–29) and executed (Jan 30).

Salmasius's *Defensio* appears in England (May) and an English translation of *Eikon Basilike* is published (Jul).

Monarchy and the House of Lords are abolished.

The Rump of the Long Parliament rules England until 1653.

Oliver Cromwell embarks on a military campaign against Irish Confederates.

JM composes the verse which appears in *Defensio Pro Populo Anglicani.*

JM successfully negotiates with the Goldsmiths' Company to receive a 7% rebate on his lease of the Red Rose property on Bread Street (Mar 12).

1650

Cromwell defeats the Irish and subsequently invades Scotland. As the Lord General of the New Model Army, he is victorious at the Battle of Dunbar.

The French infantry develop the bayonet.

The air pump is invented.

The Dutch create a world empire.

Rickets is clinically described.

JM's *Defensio Pro Populo Anglicano,* which reports its author to be in poor health, is published (Feb 24).

JM's son John is born in Scotland Yard (Mar 16).

On Aug 30 JM is reportedly living outside London. His whereabouts remain unknown until Oct 15 when he returns to Westminster and conducts negotiations with Herman Mylius.

1651

Hobbes's *Leviathan* is published.

The English Navigation Ordinances are passed to hamper Dutch trade.

Events in John Milton's life		Events in Milton's time
JM moves his family to a home in Petty France, Westminster (Dec 17).		
JM becomes completely blind (Mar).	**1652**	War between England and the United Provinces (Netherlands) begins and continues through 1654.
JM's third daughter Deborah is born (May 2).		
JM's wife Mary Powell Milton dies (May 5?).		
JM composes "Sonnet 16" (May).		
JM's son John dies (Jun 16?).		
JM composes "Sonnet 17" (Jul 3) and sends it to Sir Henry Vane.		
JM translates Psalms 1–8 into English over the course of six days (Aug 7–14).	**1653**	The Taj Mahal is completed at Agra, India.
		Cromwell dissolves the Rump Parliament (Apr 20).
		A Constituent Assembly installs Cromwell as Lord Protector under *The Instrument of Government* (Dec).
JM publishes *Defensio Secunda* (May 30) and sends three copies to Andrew Marvell at Eton.	**1654**	Pascal and Fermat publish their theory of probability.
		The First Protectorate Parliament convenes (through 1655).
JM writes "Sonnet 18" (May?) and "Sonnet 19" (Jul–Oct?).	**1655**	The British establish a colony at Jamaica.
JM's *Defensio Pro Se* is published (Aug 8).		Cromwell appoints Major Generals.
In the later part of the year, JM writes "Sonnet 20" (Nov?), and Sonnets 21 and 22 (Nov–Dec?).		
Thomas Young dies in Stowmarket (Nov 28).		
JM's niece Mary Milton is baptized in St Nicholas, Ipswich (Mar 29).	**1656**	An outbreak of the plague spreads from Sardinia to Naples resulting in the death of 400,000.

Events in John Milton's life		Events in Milton's time
JM marries Katherine Woodcock in a civil ceremony (Nov 12), but banns for the marriage were published on Oct 22, Oct 27, and Nov 3 in the bride's parish of St Mary the Virgin, Aldermanbury, London as well as in the parish of the groom, St Margaret's, Westminster.		Christiaan Hugyens, a Dutch mathematician and physicist, builds the first accurate pendulum clock based on Galileo's theory.
		Cataracts are found to be caused by the clouding of the eye's lens.
JM writes "Sonnet 23" sometime during the three year period of 1656 through 1658.		The Second Protectorate Parliament convenes.
JM's daughter Katherine is born in Petty France, Westminster (Oct 19).	**1657**	Parliament offers the title of King to Cromwell (Mar 31).
		Hot chocolate is introduced into England.
JM's wife Katherine Woodcock dies (Feb 3) and is buried in the parish church of St Margaret's, Westminster (Feb 10).	**1658**	Oliver Cromwell dies (Sep 3).
		Richard Cromwell is named Lord Protector.
JM's daughter Katherine dies (Mar 17) and is buried in St Margaret's, Westminster (Mar 20).		Red corpuscles are discovered.
JM publishes an edition of *The Cabinet Council* (May/Jun?).		
JM's revised edition of *Defensio Pro Populo Anglicano* is published (Oct).		
JM publishes *A Treatise of Civil Power* (Feb), *Considerations Touching the Likeliest Means* (Aug), "Letter to a Friend" (Oct), and *Proposals of Certain Expedients* (Oct–Dec).	**1659**	The Protectorate is abolished and the Rump Parliament is restored.
		The modern division sign is introduced.
JM publishes *The Readie and Easie Way* 1st edition (Feb) and 2nd edition (Apr), *The Present Means* (Mar), and *Brief Notes Upon a Late Sermon* (Mar/Apr).	**1660**	The first regularly published newspapers appear in England.
JM leaves Petty France and hides in Bartholomew Close (Apr).		Marcello Malpigni observes through a microscope the capillary network connecting veins and arteries.

Edward Jones

Events in John Milton's life		Events in Milton's time
Charles II returns to England (May 25).		Boyle proves experimentally that air is necessary for life.
JM is arrested, briefly imprisoned, and released (Dec).		Episcopacy is restored as the Stuart dynasty reascends the English throne with Charles II.
Upon his release from prison, JM resides in Jewin Street, London until Feb 24, 1663.	**1661**	Huygens develops a manometer for measuring the elasticity of gases.
		A modernized version of the *Book of Common Prayer* is adopted.
		The enactment of the Clarendon Codes (through 1665) aims to promote a presbyterian unity of worship.
Isaac Pennington introduces Thomas Ellwood to JM. Shortly thereafter Ellwood takes lodgings in Jewin Street and except for the "first-days of the week [. . .] went every day in the afternoon" and "read to him."	**1662**	The Act of Uniformity decrees the *Book of Common Prayer* the only legal form of worship.
		The Royal Society is established by a Royal charter.
A license is issued to JM's niece Ann Agar and David Moore to marry at either St Sepulchre's, London or St Gregory's, London (Dec 29).		Sir Henry Vane is executed.
JM marries Elizabeth Minshull (Feb 24) and moves to a home in Artillery Walk, Bunhill Fields, London.	**1663**	Roger L'Estrange labels JM's *Tenure* treasonous in *Considerations and Proposals.*
JM's nephew Edward Phillips is employed as a preceptor for John Evelyn's son (Oct 24).		
JM's *On Shakespeare* appears in the Third Folio.	**1664**	The Great Plague kills 100,000 in London.
The almanac *Poor Robin* ridicules JM as "blind Milton" (Nov).		The British capture New Amsterdam from the Dutch and rename it New York.
		The Second War with the Dutch begins (through 1667).

232

Events in John Milton's life		Events in Milton's time
		The First Conventicle Act penalizes those attending illegal Protestant services.
To escape the plague, JM relocates to Chalfont St Giles in Buckinghamshire with the help of Thomas Ellwood (Jul).	**1665**	Robert Hooke publishes the first diagnosis of cells and cell walls. Newton works on calculus.
JM returns to London (Feb). The Great Fire of London destroys JM's house in Bread Street (Sep 2).	**1666**	The Great Fire of London burns 80% of the City. The first cheddar cheese is produced in the English village of Cheddar.
JM signs a contract to publish *Paradise Lost* (Apr 27). *Paradise Lost* in ten books is published (Oct).	**1667**	Hooke invents the anemometer. Artificial respiration is successfully performed on an animal.
Two more issues of *Paradise Lost* are published. JM's nephew John Milton is admitted to Pembroke College, Cambridge (Jan 29). JM's nephew Christopher Milton is called to the bar (9 Feb); he is buried (Mar 12) in St Nicholas, Ipswich.	**1668**	Newton invents the reflecting telescope. John Dryden becomes Poet Laureate.
Two more issues of *Paradise Lost* are published. Christopher Milton becomes a justice of the peace in Ipswich (Jan 9). JM's *Accedence Commenc't Grammar* is published (Jun/Jul?). JM's nephew John Milton is buried in St Nicholas, Ipswich (Dec 29).	**1669**	The Italian city of Catanoia is destroyed by lava flow from the eruption of Mt Etna (Mar 11–Jul 15), resulting in the death of 20,000. Henry Brand discovers phosphorus.
JM's *History of Britain* is published (Nov).	**1670**	William Clement discovers the minute hand for clocks.

Events in John Milton's life		Events in Milton's time
JM's *Paradise Regained* and *Samson Agonistes* are published (May).	**1671**	Welsh Henry Morgan captures Panama for Great Britain.
An advertisement in the *Term Catalogue* for JM's *Artis Logicae* suggests that it has been published by May 13.	**1672**	The bubonic plague devastates Naples resulting in the death of 400,000.
JM's *Of True Religion* is published (Apr/May).	**1673**	The Test Act is passed effectively excluding Catholics from public office.
JM's brother-in-law Thomas Agar dies (Nov 1) and is buried (Nov 4).		
JM's *Poems*, 2nd edition is published (Nov 24).		
JM publishes *Epistolarum Familiarium* (May), *A Declaration of Letters Patent* (Jul), and *Paradise Lost* in 12 books (Jul 6).	**1674**	The Treaty of Westminster concludes the third Anglo-Dutch war.
JM's daughter Deborah marries Abraham Clarke in St Peter and St Kevin, Dublin (Jun 1).		
JM prepares oral will (Jul 20?).		
JM dies (Nov 9 or 10) and is buried inside the church of St Giles Cripplegate, London (Nov 12).		

Select Bibliography

"Much arguing, much writing, many opinions"

Compiled by J. Martin Evans

Editor's note: Electronic search engines have provided scholars with access to an enormous number of materials on any given subject, the likes of which Milton may not have been able to imagine when he penned *Areopagitica*, from which this select bibliography takes its secondary title. Given the limitations of time and human energy, the problem of course lies in how to select what to read, what Milton called (employing his characteristically digestive metaphors when talking of knowledge) "Wholesome meats" in contrast to the "Bad meats" that do find their way into print. This select bibliography strives to introduce readers to a strictly wholesome diet . . . and a spare one. Acknowledging again the fast pace of school terms and the desire to return to reading primary Miltonic texts rather than secondary Milton criticism, many of the entries are book chapters and journal articles rather than books.

This section attends to important topics and texts not covered in this volume for the sake of brevity, as well as complements the References and Further Reading sections at the end of each chapter. For the maximum benefit, the entries should be thought of as parts of conversations. Sometimes the conversations are expressed in the use of the same term in a title, as in the use of "bogey" in the articles about Adam and Eve in *Paradise Lost*. At other times, they are implied in titles that use "yet once more," echoing Milton's inscription of *Lycidas* into the pastoral tradition. Old and new criticism is included to help readers enter into and contribute to the conversation with a

strong sense of what has been said before. The organization of materials is itself a guide to how the best scholars have thought about
Milton's works.

For the reader's convenience, sections marked with an asterisk are
organized chronologically rather than alphabetically. Also, in order to
avoid unnecessary duplication, items that appear in the References
and Further Reading at the end of individual chapters have been
omitted here, with few exceptions.

MAJOR EDITIONS

Poems published in Milton's lifetime*

Anon. (1637). *A Maske Presented at Ludlow Castle, 1634*. London: Humphrey
Robinson.
J. M. (1638). *Justa Edouardo King Naufrago*. Cambridge: Thomas Buck and
Roger Daniel.
Milton, John (1645). *Poems of Mr. John Milton, Both English and Latin*. London:
Humphrey Moseley.
Milton, John (1667). *Paradise Lost. A Poem Written in Ten Books*. London: Samuel
Simmons.
Milton, John (1671). *Paradise Regained. A Poem. In IV Books. To Which is Added
Samson Agonistes*. London: John Starkey.
Milton, John (1673). *Poems, &c. upon Several Occasions*. London: Thomas Dring.
Milton, John (1674). *Paradise Lost. A Poem in Twelve Books*. London: Samuel
Simmons.

Poems published after Milton's death*

Milton, John (1688*). Paradise Lost* [. . .] *The Fourth Edition, Adorn'd with
Sculptures*. London: Jacob Tonson.
Milton, John (1695). *The Poetical Works of Mr. John Milton*. London: Jacob
Tonson.
Bentley, Richard (ed.) (1732). *Milton's Paradise Lost, A New Edition*. London:
Jacob Tonson.
Newton, Thomas (ed.) (1749–52). *Paradise Lost* [. . .] *A New Edition, with Notes
of Various Authors*, 3 vols. London: J. and R. Tonson and S. Draper.
Wharton, Thomas (ed.) (1785). *Poems Upon Several Occasions, English, Italian,
and Latin, with Translations, by John Milton*. London: J. Dodsley.
Todd, Henry J. (ed.) (1801). *The Poetical Works of John Milton, with the Principal
Notes of Various Commentators*. London: J. Johnson.

Fletcher, Harris F. (ed.) (1943–8). *John Milton's Complete Poetical Works Reproduced in Photographic Facsimile*. 4 vols. Urbana: University of Illinois Press.

Brooks, Cleanth and Hardy, John E. (eds) (1951). *Poems of Mr. John Milton: The 1645 Edition, with Essays in Analysis*. New York: Harcourt Brace.

Prose

Please note that Milton's numerous prose works were published during his lifetime. They are all collected in the following:

Milton, John (1953–82). *Complete Prose Works of John Milton* [*CPW*]. 8 vols. Edited by Don M. Wolfe. New Haven and London: Yale University Press.

Textual and bibliographical studies – general

Adams, Robert Martin (1955). "Empson and Bentley: Scherzo." In Robert Martin Adams (ed.), *Ikon* (pp. 112–27). Ithaca: Cornell University Press.

Adams, Robert Martin (1955). "The Text of *Paradise Lost*." In Robert Martin Adams (ed.), *Ikon* (pp. 60–111). Ithaca: Cornell University Press.

Bennett, Stuart (1988). "Jacob Tonson, an Early Editor of *Paradise Lost*?" *The Library* 10.3: 247–52.

Empson, William (1966). "Milton and Bentley: The Pastoral of the Innocence of Man and Nature." In *Some Versions of Pastoral* (pp. 123–55). London: Chatto and Windus/Penguin.

Lindenbaum, Peter (1991). "John Milton and the Republican Mode of Literary Production." *Yearbook of English Studies* 21: 121–36.

Lindenbaum, Peter (1995). "The Poet in the Marketplace: Milton and Samuel Simmons." In P. G. Stanwood (ed.), *Of Poetry and Politics* (pp. 249–62). Binghamton, NY: Medieval and Renaissance Texts and Studies.

McKenzie, Donald F. (1980). "Milton's Printers: Matthew, Mary and Samuel Simmons." *Milton Quarterly* 14: 87–91.

Moyles, R. G. (1985). *The Text of Paradise Lost*. Toronto: University of Toronto Press.

Oras, Ants (1931). *Milton's Editors and Commentators from Patrick Hume to Henry John Todd, 1695–1801*. London: H. Milford, Oxford University Press.

Textual and bibliographical studies – 1645 *Poems*

Carrithers, Gale H., Jr. (1981). "Poems (1645): On Growing Up." *Milton Studies* 15: 161–79.

Corns, Thomas (1982). "Milton's Quest for Respectability." *Modern Language Review* 77.4: 769–79.

Corns, Thomas (1984). "Ideology in the Poemata (1645)." *Milton Studies* 19: 195–203.

Evans, J. Martin (2000). "The Birth of the Poet: Milton's Poetic Self-Construction." *Milton Studies* 38: 47–65.

Hale, John K. (1991). "Milton's Self-Presentation of Poems [. . .] 1645." *Milton Quarterly* 25.2: 37–48.

Ingram, Randall (1996). "The Writing Poet: The Descent from Song in *The Poems of Mr. John Milton, Both English and Latin* (1645)." *Milton Studies* 34: 179–97.

Marcus, Leah S. (1991). "Milton as Historical Subject." *Milton Quarterly* 25.3: 120–7.

Moseley, Charles W. R. D. (1991). *The Poetic Birth: Milton's Poems of 1645*. Aldershot: Scolar Press.

Revard, Stella P. (1997). *Milton and the Tangles of Neaera's Hair: The Making of the 1645 Poems*. Columbia: University of Missouri Press.

Ricks, Christopher (1987). "Milton, I: Poems 1645." In Christopher Ricks (ed.), *New History of Literature, II*. New York: Bedrick.

MAJOR WORKS OF REFERENCE

Journals

Flannagan, Roy C. (1967–). *Milton Quarterly*, formerly Milton Newsletter. Athens: University of Ohio Press.

Labriola, Albert C. (1969–). *Milton Studies*. Pittsburgh: University of Pittsburgh Press.

Bibliographies*

Stevens, David Harrison (1930). *A Reference Guide to Milton from 1800 to the Present Day*. Chicago: University of Chicago Press.

Fletcher, Harris F. (1931). *Contributions to a Milton Bibliography 1800–1930*. Urbana: University of Illinois Press.

Huckabay, Calvin (1960). *John Milton: A Bibliographical Supplement 1929–1957*. Pittsburgh: Duquesne University Press.

Huckabay, Calvin (1970). *John Milton: An Annotated Bibliography, 1929–1968*. Pittsburgh: Duquesne University Press.

Shawcross, John T. (1984). *Milton: A Bibliography for the Years 1624–1700*. Binghamton, NY: Medieval and Renaissance Texts and Studies.

Klemp, Paul J. (1989). *The Essential Milton: An Annotated Bibliography of Major Modern Studies*. Boston: G. K. Hall.

Huckabay, Calvin (1996). *John Milton: An Annotated Bibliography, 1968–1988*. Edited by Paul J. Klemp. Pittsburgh: Duquesne University Press.

Indexes and concordances

Ingram, William and Swaim, Kathleen M. (eds) (1972). *A Concordance to Milton's English Poetry*. Oxford: Clarendon Press.

Le Comte, Edward (1961). *A Milton Dictionary*. New York: Philosophical Library.

Le Comte, Edward (1981). *A Dictionary of Puns in Milton's English Poetry*. New York: Columbia University Press.

Patterson, Frank A. (1940). *An Index to the Columbia Edition of The Works of John Milton*. 2 vols. New York: Columbia University Press.

Biographical studies (See also chapter 3)

Arthos, John (1972). *Milton and the Italian Cities*. London: Bowes and Bowes.

Barolini, Helen (1975). "Milton in Rome." *South Atlantic Quarterly* 74: 118–28.

Brown, Cedric (1995). *John Milton: A Literary Life*. Basingstoke: Macmillan.

Campbell, Gordon (1997). *A Milton Chronology*. Basingstoke: Macmillan.

Clark, Donald L. (1948). *John Milton at St Paul's School*. New York: Columbia University Press.

Di Cesare, Mario A. (ed.) (1991). *Milton in Italy: Contexts, Images, Contradictions*. Binghamton, NY: Medieval and Renaissance Texts and Studies.

French, J. Milton (1949–58). *The Life Records of John Milton*. 5 vols. New Brunswick: Rutgers University Press.

Hanford, James Holly (1925). "The Youth of Milton, an Interpretation of his Early Development." In *Studies in Shakespeare, Milton and Donne*. New York: Macmillan.

Hanford, James Holly (1964). "Milton in Italy." *Annuale Mediaevale* 5: 49–63.

Parker, William R. (1996). *Milton: A Biography*. 2nd edn., rev. Gordon Campbell. 2 vols. Oxford: Clarendon Press.

Wilson, A. N. (1983). *The Life of John Milton*. Oxford: Oxford University Press.

Commentaries* (See also chapter 3)

Hume, Patrick (1695). "Annotations on Milton's *Paradise Lost*." In *The Poetical Works of Mr. John Milton*. London: Jacob Tonson.

Addison, Joseph (1719). *Notes upon the Twelve Books of Paradise Lost*. London: Jacob Tonson.

Richardson, J. et al. (1734). *Explanatory Notes and Remarks on Milton's Paradise Lost. With the Life of the Author and a Discourse on the Poem*. London: J., J. and P. Knapton.

Hughes, Merritt Y. et al. (1970–5). *A Variorum Commentary on the Poems of John Milton*. 6 vols. New York: Columbia University Press.

Miner, Earl, Moeck, William and Jablonski, Steven (2004). *Paradise Lost, 1668–1968: Three Centuries of Commentary*. Lewisberg: Bucknell University Press.

Critical collections

Danielson, Dennis (ed.) (1999). *The Cambridge Companion to Milton*. 2nd edn. Cambridge: Cambridge University Press.
Evans, J. Martin (2003). *John Milton: Twentieth Century Perspectives*. 5 vols. New York: Routledge.
Hunter, William B., Jr et al. (1978–83). *A Milton Encyclopedia*. 9 vols. London: Associated University Presses.
Thorpe, James (ed.) (1950). *Milton Criticism: Selections from Four Centuries*. New York: Macmillan.

MILTON'S ILLUSTRATORS

Critical discussions

Allentuck, Marcia (1962). "Fuseli as Illustrator of Milton." *Studies in English Literature* 2: 151–3.
Baker, C. H. Collins (1948). "Some Illustrators of Milton's *Paradise Lost*, 1688–1850." *The Library* 3.1: 1–21; 3.2: 101–19.
Balston, Thomas (1949). "Some Illustrators of Milton's *Paradise Lost*". *The Library* 4.2, 146–7.
Behrendt, Stephen (1983). *The Moment of Explosion: Blake and the Illustration of Milton*. Lincoln: University of Nebraska Press.
Boorsch, Suzanne (1972). "The 1688 *Paradise Lost* and Dr. Aldrich." *Metropolitan Museum Journal* 6: 133–50.
Dunbar, Pamela (1980). *William Blake's Illustrations to the Poetry of Milton*. Oxford: Clarendon Press.
Gardner, Helen (1956). "Milton's First Illustrator." *Essays and Studies of the English Association* (n.s.) 9: 27–38.
Hughes, Merritt Y. (1961). "Some Illustrators of Milton: The Expulsion from Paradise." *Journal of English and Germanic Philology* 60.4: 670–9.
Labriola, Albert and Sichi, Edward (eds) (1988). *Milton's Legacy in the Arts*. University Park: Pennsylvania State University Press. Especially Estella Schoenberg, "Picturing Satan for the 1688 *Paradise Lost*" (pp. 1–20).
Ravenhall, Mary D. (1982). "Francis Atterbury and the First Illustrated Edition of *Paradise Lost*." *Milton Quarterly* 16.2: 29–36.
Ravenhall, Mary D. (1982). "Sources and Meaning in Dr. Aldrich's 1688 Illustrations of *Paradise Lost*." *English Language Notes* 19.3: 208–18.
Shawcross, John T. (1975). "The First Illustrations for *Paradise Lost*." *Milton Quarterly* 9: 43–6.

Svendsen, Kester (1961). "John Martin and the Expulsion Scene of *Paradise Lost.*" *Studies in English Literature* 1.1: 63–73.

Tufte, Virginia (1987). "Protection and Peril: Bernard Lens' View of Milton's Eden." *Milton Quarterly* 21.3: 90–6.

Tufte, Virginia (1988). "Evil as Parody in the Paradise that Was Lost: Three Illustrators Interpret Book IV." *Mosaic* 21.2: 37–58.

Waddington, Raymond B. (1985). "Louis Cheron's Illustration of Milton's Sin." *Milton Quarterly* 19.3: 78–80.

Welsh, Dennis M. (1985). "Blake's Critique of Election: Milton and the *Comus* Illustrations." *Philological Quarterly* 64.4: 492–531.

Wittreich, Joseph A., Jr (1974). "Milton's 'First' Illustrator." *Seventeenth-Century News* 32: 70–1.

MILTON'S INFLUENCE (See also chapter 2)

Anozie, Sunday O. (1987). "Soyinka and the Jihad of the Pen, or Style as Intertextuality." *Matatu: Journal for African Culture and Society* 1: 73–83.

Bostich, June (1973). "Miltonic Influence in *The Rape of the Lock.*" *Enlightenment Essays* 4: 65–72.

Brisman, Leslie (1973). *Milton's Poetry of Choice and its Romantic Heirs.* Ithaca: Cornell University Press.

Dahiyat, Eid A. (1986). "Milton and Franklin." *Early American Literature* 21.1: 44–8.

Foerster, Donald M. (1956). "Homer, Milton, and the American Revolt against Epic Poetry: 1812–60." *Studies in Philology* 53.1: 75–100.

Frank, Marcia (1993). "Staging Criticism, Staging Milton: John Dryden's *The State of Innocence.*" *Eighteenth Century* 34.1: 45–64.

Gordon, R. K. (1947). "Keats and Milton." *Modern Language Review* 42.4: 434–6.

Grierson, Herbert J. C. (1937). *Milton and Wordsworth, Poets and Prophets.* New York: Macmillan.

Griffin, Dustin (1982). "Milton and the Decline of Epic in the Eighteenth Century." *New Literary History* 14.1: 143–54.

Griffin, Dustin (1989). "Milton's Literary Influence." In Dennis Danielson (ed.), *The Cambridge Companion to Milton* (pp. 243–61). Cambridge: Cambridge University Press.

Grundy, Joan (1985). "Hardy and Milton." *Thomas Hardy Annual* 3: 3–14.

Hale, John K. (1984). "The Significance of the Early Translations of *Paradise Lost.*" *Philological Quarterly* 63.1: 31–53.

Herron, Carolivia (1987). "Milton and Afro-American Literature." In Mary Nyquist and Margaret W. Ferguson (eds), *Re-membering Milton: Essays on the Texts and Traditions* (pp. 278–300). New York: Methuen.

241

J. *Martin Evans*

Hogan, Patrick C. (1990). "Joyce's Miltonic Pamtomomiom and the Paradox Lust of *Finnegans Wake.*" *James Joyce Quarterly* 27.4: 815–33.

Howard, Leon (1935). "Early American Copies of Milton." *Huntington Library Bulletin* 7: 169–79.

Jarvis, Robin (1991). *Wordsworth, Milton, and the Theory of Poetic Relations.* Basingstoke: Macmillan.

Jenkins, Hugh (1998). "Jefferson (Re)reading Milton." *Milton Quarterly* 32.1: 32–8.

Jones, Frederick L. (1952). "Shelley and Milton." *Studies in Philology* 49.3: 488–519.

McArthur, Murray (1988). *Stolen Writings: Blake's Milton, Joyce's Ulysses and the Nature of Influence.* Ann Arbor: UMI Research Press.

McGann, Jerome J. (1974). "Milton and Byron." *Keats-Shelley Memorial Bulletin* 25: 9–25.

Moore, Leslie E. (1990). *Beautiful Sublime: The Making of Paradise Lost 1701–1734.* Stanford: Stanford University Press.

Pommer, Henry F. (1950). *Milton and Melville.* Pittsburgh: University of Pittsburgh Press.

Schulman, Lydia D. (1992). *Paradise Lost and the Rise of the American Republic.* Boston: Northeastern University Press.

Simmonds, James D. and Rajan, Balachandra (eds) (1978). "The Presence of Milton." *Milton Studies* 11 (special issue).

Wittreich, Joseph A., Jr. (1990). "The Illustrious Dead: Milton's Legacy and Romantic Prophecy." *Milton and the Romantics* 4: 17–32.

MILTON AND ART (See also chapter 2)

Daniells, Roy (1963). *Milton, Mannerism and Baroque.* Toronto: University of Toronto Press.

Frye, Roland Mushat (1978). *Milton's Imagery and the Visual Arts: Iconographic Tradition in the Epic Poems.* Princeton: Princeton University Press.

Roston, Murray (1980). *Milton and the Baroque.* London: Macmillan.

Trapp, J. B. (1968). "The Iconography of the Fall of Man." In C. A. Patrides (ed.), *Approaches to Paradise Lost* (pp. 223–65). Toronto: University of Toronto Press.

Tuve, Rosemond (1961). "Baroque and Mannerist Milton?" *Journal of English and Germanic Philology* 60.4: 817–33.

MILTON AND MUSIC (See also chapter 2)

Brennecke, Ernest (1938). *John Milton the Elder and his Music.* New York: Columbia University Press.

Davidson, Audrey (1968). "Milton on the Music of Henry Lawes." *Milton Newsletter* 2: 19–23.

Frank, Mortimer H. (1979). "Milton's Knowledge of Music: Some Speculations." In J. Max Patrick and Roger H. Sundell (eds), *Milton and the Art of Sacred Song* (pp. 83–98). Madison: University of Wisconsin Press.

Hadow, William Henry (1909). "Milton's Knowledge of Music." In Percy W. Ames (ed.), *Milton Memorial Lectures, 1908* (pp. 11–22). London: H. Frowde.

Hollander, John (1961). *The Untuning of the Sky: Ideas of Music in English Poetry, 1500–1700.* Princeton: Princeton University Press.

Hunter, William B., Jr. (1979). "Music of the Spheres; Milton and Music." In William B. Hunter Jr (ed.), *A Milton Encyclopedia* (vol. 5, pp. 165–74). 9 vols. London: Associated University Presses.

Mander, M. N. K. (1990). "Milton and the Music of the Spheres." *Milton Quarterly* 24.2: 63–71.

Maynard, Winifred (1973). "Milton and Music." In J. B. Broadbent (ed.), *John Milton: Introductions* (pp. 226–52). Cambridge: Cambridge University Press.

Morris, Brian (1968). "'Not without song': Milton and the Composers." In C. A. Patrides (ed.), *Approaches to Paradise Lost* (pp. 137–161). Toronto: University of Toronto Press.

Patrick, J. Max, and Roger H. Sundell (eds) (1979). *Milton and the Art of Sacred Song.* Madison: University of Wisconsin Press.

Spaeth, Sigmund (1963). *Milton's Knowledge of Music.* Ann Arbor: University of Michigan Press.

MILTON AND SCIENCE (See also chapter 10)

Curry, Walter C. (1957). *Milton's Ontology, Cosmogony and Physics.* Lexington: University of Kentucky Press.

Duran, Angelica. "The Sexual Mathematics of *Paradise Lost.*" *Milton Quarterly* 38.2: 55–76.

Friedman, Donald (1991). "Galileo and the Art of Seeing." In Mario A. Di Cesare (ed.), *Milton in Italy: Contexts, Images, Contradictions* (pp. 159–74). Binghamton, NY: Medieval and Renaissance Texts and Studies.

Gilbert, Allan H. (1922). "Milton and Galileo." *Studies in Philology* 19.2: 152–85.

Herz, Judith Scherer (1991). "'For whom this glorious sight?': Dante, Milton, and the Galileo Question." In Mario A. Di Cesare (ed.), *Milton in Italy: Contexts, Images, Contradictions* (pp. 147–57). Binghamton, NY: Medieval and Renaissance Texts and Studies.

Marjara, Harinder S. (1992). *Contemplation of Created Things: Science in Paradise Lost.* Toronto: University of Toronto Press.

J. Martin Evans

McColley, Grant (1937). "Milton's Dialogue on Astronomy." *Publications of the Modern Language Association* 52.3: 728–62.
McColley, Grant (1937). "The Astronomy of *Paradise Lost.*" *Studies in Philology* 34.2: 209–47.
Nicolson, Marjorie H. (1935). "Milton and the Telescope." *English Literary History* 2.1: 1–32.
Nicolson, Marjorie H. (1956). *Science and Imagination.* Ithaca: Great Seal Books.
Nicolson, Marjorie H. (1960). *The Breaking of the Circle: Studies in the Effect of the "New Science" upon Seventeenth-Century Poetry.* New York: Columbia University Press.
Svendsen, Kester (1956). *Milton and Science.* Cambridge, MA: Harvard University Press.
Walker, Julia (1989). "Milton and Galileo: The Art of Intellectual Canonization." *Milton Studies* 25: 109–23.
Webster, Charles (1975). *The Great Instauration: Science, Medicine and Reform, 1626–1660.* London: Duckworth.

"ON THE MORNING OF CHRIST'S NATIVITY"
(See also chapter 11)

Tradition

Allen, Don Cameron (1954). "The Higher Compromise." In Don Cameron Allen (ed.), *The Harmonious Vision: Studies in Milton's Poetry* (pp. 24–40). 2nd edn. Baltimore and London: Johns Hopkins University Press.
Broadbent, J. B. (1960). "The Nativity Ode." In Frank Kermode (ed.), *The Living Milton* (pp. 12–31). London: Routledge and Kegan Paul.
Cook, Albert S. (1909). "Notes on Milton's 'Ode on the Morning of Christ's Nativity.'" *Transactions of the Connecticut Academy of Arts and Sciences* 15: 307–68.
Cullen, Patrick (1969). "Imitation and Metamorphosis: The Golden-Age Eclogue in Spenser, Milton, and Marvell." *Publications of the Modern Language Association* 84: 1,559–70.
Erlich, Victor (1975). "Milton's Early Poetry: Its Christian Humanism." *American Imago* 32: 77–112.
Evans, J. Martin (1993). "A Poem of Absences." *Milton Quarterly* 27: 31–5.
Hyman, Lawrence W. (1970). "Christ's Nativity and the Pagan Deities." *Milton Studies* 2: 103–12.
Kingsley, Lawrence W. (1972). "Mythic Dialectic in the Nativity Ode." *Milton Studies* 4: 163–76.
Patrides, C. A. (1965). "The Cessation of the Oracles: The History of a Legend." *Modern Language Review* 60: 500–7.
Quint, David (1999). "Expectation and Prematurity in Milton's Nativity Ode." *Modern Philology* 97.2: 195–219.

Swaim, Kathleen M. (1971). " 'Mighty Pan': Tradition and an Image in Milton's Nativity Hymn." *Studies in Philology* 68: 484–95.

Swanson, Donald (1989). "Milton's 'On the Morning of Christ's Nativity': The Virgilian and Biblical Matrices." *Milton Quarterly* 23.2: 59–66.

Tuve, Rosemond (1957). "The Hymn 'On the Morning of Christ's Nativity.' " In *Images and Themes in Five Poems by Milton* (pp. 37–72). Cambridge, MA: Harvard University Press.

Genre

Dobin, Howard (1983). "Milton's Nativity Ode: 'O What a Mask Was There.' " *Milton Quarterly* 17.3: 71–80.

Fry, Paul H. (1980). *The Poet's Calling in the English Ode*. New Haven: Yale University Press.

Jacobs, Laurence H. (1974). " 'Unexpressive Notes': The Decorum of Milton's Nativity Ode." *Essays in Literature* 1: 166–77.

Nelson, Lowry, Jr. (1961). *Baroque Lyric Poetry*. New Haven: Yale University Press.

Rollinson, Philip B. (1975). "Milton's Nativity Poem and the Decorum of Genre." *Milton Studies* 7: 165–88.

Shafer, Robert (1918). *The English Ode to 1660*. Princeton: Princeton University Press.

Shuster, George N. (1940). *The English Ode from Milton to Keats*. New York: Columbia University Press.

Narrator

Friedman, Donald M. (1969). "Harmony and the Poet's Voice in Some of Milton's Early Poems." *Modern Language Quarterly* 30: 523–34.

Halpern, Richard (1987). "The Great Instauration: Imaginary Narratives in Milton's 'Nativity Ode.' " In Mary Nyquist and Margaret W. Ferguson (eds), *Re-membering Milton* (pp. 3–24). New York: Methuen.

Kastor, Frank S. (1968). "Miltonic Narration: 'Christ's Nativity.' " *Anglia* 86: 339–52.

MacCallum, Hugh (1978). "The Narrator of Milton's 'On the Morning of Christ's Nativity.' " In Patricia Bruckmann and Jane Couchman (eds), *Familiar Colloquy* (pp. 179–95). Ottawa: Oberon Press.

General

Barker, Arthur E. (1941). *The Pattern of Milton's Nativity Ode*. University of Toronto Quarterly 10.2: 167–81.

Behrendt, Stephen (1976). "Blake's Illustrations to Milton's Nativity Ode." *Philological Quarterly* 55: 65–95.

Doherty, M. J. (1989). "Salvation History, Poetic Form and the Logic of Time in Milton's Nativity Ode." *Milton Studies* 25: 21–42.

Entzminger, Robert L. (1981). "The Epiphanies in Milton's Nativity Ode." *Renaissance Papers* 25: 21–31.

Goekjian, Gregory F. (1985). "Deference and Silence: Milton's Nativity Ode." *Milton Studies* 21: 119–35.

MacLaren, I. S. (1981). "Milton's Nativity Ode: The Function of Poetry and Structures of Response in 1629." *Milton Studies* 15: 181–200.

Meier, T. K. (1970). "Milton's Nativity Ode: Sectarian Discord." *Modern Language Review* 65: 7–10.

Morris, David B. (1971). "Drama and Stasis in Milton's 'Ode on the Morning of Christ's Nativity.'" *Studies in Philology* 68: 207–22.

Rajan, Balachandra (1968). "'In order serviceable.'" *Modern Language Review* 63: 13–22.

Romano, J. R. (1981). "'Heaven's youngest teemed star.'" *Milton Quarterly* 15.3: 80–8.

Sherry, Beverley (1983). "Milton's 'mystic nativity.'" *Milton Quarterly* 17.4: 108–21.

Smith, George W., Jr (1978). "Milton's Method of Mistakes in the Nativity Ode." *Studies in English Literature* 18.1: 107–23.

Stapleton, Laurence (1953–4). "Milton and the New Music." *University of Toronto Quarterly* 23: 217–26; repr. in Arthur E. Barker (ed.), *Milton: Modern Essays in Criticism* (pp. 31–42). New York: Oxford University Press, 1965.

SONNETS (See also chapter 5)

Editions

Honigmann, E. A. J. (1966). *Milton's Sonnets*. London: Macmillan.

General

Finley, John H., Jr (1937). "Milton and Horace: A Study of Milton's Sonnets." *Harvard Studies in Classical Philology* 48: 29–73.

Hanford, James Holly (1921). "The Arrangement and Dates of Milton's Sonnets." *Modern Philology* 18.9: 475–83.

Harrington, David V. (1966). "Feeling and Form in Milton's Sonnets." *Western Humanities Review* 20: 317–28.

Jones, Edward (1994). *Milton's Sonnets: An Annotated Bibliography, 1900–1992*. Binghamton, NY: Medieval and Renaissance Texts and Studies.

Mazzaro, Jerome (1988). "Gaining Authority: John Milton at Sonnets." *Essays in Literature* 15.1: 3–12.

McCarthy, William (1977). "The Continuity of Milton's Sonnets." *Publications of the Modern Language Association* 92.1: 96–109.

Mengert, James G. (1981). "The Resistance of Milton's Sonnets". *English Literary Renaissance* 11.1: 81–95.

Mueller, Janel (1987). "The Mastery of Decorum: Politics as Poetry in Milton's Sonnets." *Critical Inquiry* 13.3: 475–508.

Schlueter, Kurt (1995). "Milton's Heroical Sonnets." *Studies in English Literature* 35.1: 123–36.

Stoehr, Taylor (1964). "Syntax and Poetic Form in Milton's Sonnets." *English Studies* 45: 289–301.

LYCIDAS (See also chapter 6)

Anthologies

Harrison, Thomas P., Jr (ed.) (1939). *The Pastoral Elegy: An Anthology*. Austin: University of Texas.

Kirkconnell, Watson (1973). *Awake the Courteous Echo: The Themes and Prosody of Comus, Lycidas and Paradise Regained*. Toronto: University of Toronto Press.

The tradition

Alpers, Paul (1972). "The Eclogue Tradition and the Nature of Pastoral." *College English* 34: 352–71.

Evans, J. Martin (1983). *The Road from Horton: Looking Backwards in "Lycidas."* Victoria, Canada: University of Victoria Press.

Hanford, James Holly (1910). "The Pastoral Elegy and Milton's *Lycidas*." *Publications of the Modern Language Association* 25.3: 403–47.

Hunt, Clay (1979). *"Lycidas" and the Italian Critics*. New Haven: Yale University Press.

Kay, Dennis (1990). *Melodious Tears: The English Funeral Elegy from Spenser to Milton*. Oxford: Clarendon Press.

Lambert, Ellen Z. (1976). *Placing Sorrow: A Study of the Pastoral Elegy Convention from Theocritus to Milton*. Chapel Hill: University of North Carolina Press.

Martz, Louis L. (1972). "Who is Lycidas?" *Yale French Studies* 47: 170–88.

Mayerson, Caroline W. (1949). "The Orpheus Image in 'Lycidas.'" *Publications of the Modern Language Association* 64.2: 189–207.

Pigman, George W. III (1985). *Grief and English Renaissance Elegy*. Cambridge: Cambridge University Press.

Prince, F. T. (1954). *The Italian Element in Milton's Verse*. Oxford: Clarendon Press.

Riley, Joanne M. (1977). "Milton's *Lycidas*: New Light on the Title." *Notes and Queries* (n.s.) 24: 545.

Sacks, Peter M. (1985). *The English Elegy: Studies in the Genre from Spenser to Yeats*. Baltimore: Johns Hopkins Press.

Smith, Eric (1977). *By Mourning Tongues: Studies in English Elegy*. Ipswich: Boydell Press.

Wittreich, Joseph A., Jr (1979). *Visionary Poetics: Milton's Tradition and his Legacy*. San Marino, CA: Huntington Library.

Speaker

Baker, Stewart A. (1971). "Milton's Uncouth Swain." *Milton Studies* 3: 35–53.

Berkeley, David Shelley (1974). *Inwrought with Figures Dim: A Reading of Milton's "Lycidas."* The Hague: Mouton.

Tillyard, E. M. W. (1930). "Later Horton Period and 'Lycidas.'" In *Milton* (pp. 76–85). London: Chatto and Windus.

General

Creaser, John (1981). "*Lycidas*: The Power of Art." *Essays and Studies of the English Association* (n.s.) 34: 123–47.

Franson, J. Karl (1989). "The Fatal Voyage of Edward King, Milton's Lycidas." *Milton Studies* 25: 43–67.

French, J. Milton (1953). "The Digressions in Milton's 'Lycidas.'" *Studies in Philology* 50.3: 485–90.

Leonard, John (1991). "'Trembling ear': The Historical Moment of *Lycidas*." *Journal of Medieval and Renaissance Studies* 21.1: 59–81.

Madsen, William G. (1963). "The Voice of Michael in *Lycidas*." *Studies in English Literature* 3.1: 1–7.

Shinskey, Clare M. (1981). "*Lycidas*: Milton's Doric Song." *Notes and Queries* (n.s.) 28: 202–5.

A MASK (COMUS) (See also chapter 7)

Textual studies

Diekhoff, John S. (1937). "The Text of *Comus*, 1634 to 1645." *Publications of the Modern Language Association* 52.3: 705–27.

Grierson, Herbert J. C. (1925). "Preface." In Herbert J. C. Grierson, *The Poems of John Milton, English, Latin, Greek and Italian*. London: Chatto and Windus.

Lewis, C. S. (1932). "A Note on *Comus*." *Review of English Studies* 8.2: 170–6.

Lockwood, Laura (1910). "Milton's Corrections to the Minor Poems." *Modern Language Notes* 25.7: 201–5.

Macklem, Michael (1949–50). "Love, Nature, and Grace in Milton's Poetry." *Queen's Quarterly* 56.4: 534–7.

Shawcross, John T. (1960). "Certain Relationships of the Manuscripts of *Comus*." *Papers of the Bibliographical Society of America* 54: 35–56, 293–4.

Smith, George W., Jr (1979). "Milton's Revisions and the Design of *Comus*." *English Literary History* 46: 56–80.

Stevens, David Harrison (1927). "The Bridgewater Manuscript of *Comus*." In *Milton Papers* (pp. 14–20). Chicago: University of Chicago Press.

Genre

Barber, C. L. (1965). "*A Masque Presented at Ludlow Castle*: The Masque as a Masque." In Joseph H. Summers (ed.), *The Lyric and Dramatic Milton* (pp. 35–63). New York: Columbia University Press.

Martin, Jeanne S. (1977). "Transformations in Genre in Milton's *Comus*." *Genre* 10: 195–213.

Treip, Mindele A. (1989). "*Comus* and the Stuart Masque Connection, 1632–34." *American Notes and Queries* 2.3: 83–9.

Context

Adams, Robert Martin (1955). "Reading Comus." In Robert Martin Adams (ed.), *Ikon* (pp.1–34). Ithaca: Cornell University Press.

Berkowitz, M. S. (1979). "An Earl's Michaelmas in Wales: Some Thoughts on the Original Presentation of *Comus*." *Milton Quarterly* 13: 122–5.

Brown, Cedric C. (1987). "Presidential Travels and Instructive Augury in Milton's Ludlow Masque." *Milton Quarterly* 21.4: 1–12.

Flannagan, Roy (ed.) (1987). "Comus: Contexts." *Milton Quarterly* 21.4 (special issue).

Hunter, William B., Jr (1972). "The Liturgical Context of *Comus*." *English Language Notes* 10: 11–15.

Lloyd, David (1987). "Ludlow Castle." *Milton Quarterly* 21.4: 52–8.

Marcus, Leah S. (1987). "The Earl of Bridgewater's Legal Life: Notes toward a Political Reading of *Comus*." *Milton Quarterly* 21.4: 13–23.

Marcus, Leah S. (1988). "Justice for Margery Evans: A 'Local' Reading of Comus." In Julia Walker (ed.), *Milton and the Idea of Woman* (pp. 66–85). Urbana: University of Illinois Press.

Mortimer, Anthony (1984). "Comus and Michaelmas." *English Studies* 65.2: 111–19.

Mundhenk, Rosemary K. (1975). "Dark Scandal and the Sun-clad Power of Chastity: The Historical Milieu of Milton's *Comus*." *Studies in English Literature* 15.1: 141–52.

Sensabaugh, George F. (1944). "The Milieu of *Comus.*" *Studies in Philology* 41.2: 238–49.

Schwyzer, Philip (1997). "Purity and Danger on the West Bank of the Severn: The Cultural Geography of *A Masque Presented at Ludlow Castle, 1634.*" *Representations* 60: 22–48.

Taafe, James G. (1969). "Michaelmas, the 'lawless hour', and the Occasion of Milton's 'Comus.'" *English Language Notes* 6: 257–62.

Wilding, Michael (1985). "Milton's *A Masque Presented at Ludlow Castle, 1634*: Theatre and Politics on the Border." *Trivium* 20: 147–79; repr. in *Milton Quarterly* 21.4: 35–51; expanded in *Dragon's Teeth: Literature in the English Revolution* (pp. 28–88). Oxford: Clarendon Press, 1987.

Chastity

Bennett, Joan S. (1987). "Virgin Nature in *Comus.*" *Milton Studies* 23: 21–32.

Christopher, Georgia B. (1976). "The Virginity of Faith: *Comus* as a Reformation Conceit." *English Literary History* 43: 479–99.

Evans, J. Martin (1998). "Virtue and Virginity." In *The Miltonic Moment* (ch. 2, pp. 39–70). Lexington: University of Kentucky Press.

Kendrick, Christopher (1987). "Milton and Sexuality: A Symptomatic Reading of *Comus.*" In Mary Nyquist and Margaret W. Ferguson (eds), *Re-membering Milton* (pp. 43–73). New York: Methuen.

Miscellaneous

Baruch, Franklin R. (1973). "Milton's *Comus*: Skill, Virtue, and Henry Lawes." *Milton Studies* 5: 289–308.

Cunnar, Eugene R. (1987). "Milton, the Shepherd of Hermas, and the Writing of a Puritan Masque." *Milton Studies* 23: 33–52.

Dyson, A. E. (1955). "The Interpretation of *Comus.*" *Essays and Studies of the English Association* (n.s.) 8: 89–114.

Fish, Stanley E. (1975). "Problem Solving in *Comus.*" In Earl Miner (ed.), *Illustrious Evidence* (pp. 115–31). Berkeley: University of California Press.

Patterson, Annabel (1988). "'Forc'd fingers': Milton's Early Poems and Ideological Constraint." In Claude J. Summers et al. (eds), *"The Muses Common-weale"* (pp. 9–22). Columbia: University of Missouri Press.

Woodhouse, A. S. P. (1941). "The Argument of Milton's *Comus.*" *University of Toronto Quarterly* 11.1: 46–71.

Woodhouse, A. S. P. (1950). "*Comus* Once More." *University of Toronto Quarterly* 19.3: 218–23.

PROSE (See also chapter 1)

Background

Corns, Thomas N. (1992). *Uncloistered Virtue: English Political Literature, 1640–1660*. Oxford: Clarendon Press.

Fish, Stanley Eugene (1972). *Self-Consuming Artifacts: The Experience of Seventeenth Century Literature*. Berkeley: University of California Press.

Hill, Christopher (1977). *Milton and the English Revolution*. New York: Viking Press.

Patrick, J. Max et al. (1966). *Style, Rhetoric and Rhythm: Essays by Morris Croll*. Princeton: Princeton University Press.

Siebert, F. S. (1952). "The Control of the Press during the Puritan Revolution." In *Freedom of the Press in England, 1476–1776* (pp. 107–64). Urbana: University of Illinois Press.

Webber, Joan (1968). *The Eloquent "I": Style and Self in Seventeenth Century Prose*. Madison: University of Wisconsin Press.

Williamson, George (1951). *The Senecan Amble: A Study in Prose Form from Bacon to Collier*. Chicago: University of Chicago Press.

Style

Corns, Thomas N. (1982). *The Development of Milton's Prose Style*. Oxford: Clarendon Press.

Gilman, Wilbur Edwin (1939). *Milton's Rhetoric: Studies in his Defense of Liberty*. Columbia: University of Missouri.

Hamilton, K. G. (1967). "The Structure of Milton's Prose." In R. Emma and J. Shawcross (eds), *Language and Style in Milton* (pp. 304–42). New York: F. Ungar.

Limouze, Henry S. (1981). "Joseph Hall and the Prose Style of John Milton." *Milton Studies* 15: 121–41.

Neumann, J. H. (1945). "Milton's Prose Vocabulary." *Publications of the Modern Language Association* 60: 102–20.

Stavely, Keith W. (1975). *The Politics of Milton's Prose Style*. New Haven: Yale University Press.

Thompson, E. N. S. (1935). "Milton's Prose Style." *Philological Quarterly* 14: 1–15.

General criticism

Egan, James Joseph (1973). "Public Truth and Personal Witness in Milton's Last Tracts." *English Literary History* 40: 231–84.

Kendrick, C. (1986). *Milton: A Study in Ideology and Form*. New York: Methuen.

Kranidas, Thomas (1965). *The Fierce Equation: A Study in Milton's Decorum*. The Hague: Mouton.

Lieb, Michael and Shawcross, John T. (eds) (1978). *Achievements of the Left Hand*. Amherst: University of Massachusetts Press.

Loewenstein, D. and Turner, J. G. (eds) (1990). *Politics, Poetics and Hermeneutics in Milton's Prose*. Cambridge: Cambridge University Press.

Patterson, Annabel (1975). "The Civic Hero in Milton's Prose." *Milton Studies* 8: 71–101.

Richardson R. C. and Ridden, G. M. (eds) (1986). *Freedom and the English Revolution*. Manchester: Manchester University Press.

Saillens, Émile (1964). *John Milton: Man, Poet, Polemicist*. New York: Barnes and Noble.

Anti-prelatical tracts

Cooley, Ronald W. (1991). "Iconoclasm and Self-Definition in Milton's *Of Reformation*." *Religion and Literature* 23: 23–37.

Fish, Stanley Eugene (1971). "Reasons that Imply Themselves: Imagery, Argument and the Reader in Milton's *Reason of Church Government*." In Earl Miner (ed.), *Seventeenth Century Imagery* (pp. 83–102). Berkeley: University of California Press.

Kranidas, Thomas (1971). "'Decorum' and the style of Milton's Antiprelatical Tracts." In Stanley Fish (ed.), *Seventeenth-Century Prose* (pp. 475–88). Oxford: Oxford University Press.

Kranidas, Thomas (1982). "Words, words, words, and the Word: Milton's *Of Prelatical Episcopacy*." *Milton Studies* 16: 153–66.

Lieb, Michael (1978). "Milton's *Of Reformation* and the Dynamics of Controversy." In M. Lieb and J. Shawcross (eds), *Achievements of the Left Hand* (pp. 55–82). Amherst: University of Massachusetts Press.

Rosenberg, D. M. (1973). "Style and Meaning in Milton's Anti-episcopal Tracts." *Criticism* 15: 43–57.

Via, John A. (1973). "Milton's Antiprelatical Tracts: The Poet Speaks in Prose." *Milton Studies* 5: 87–127.

Divorce tracts

Barker, Arthur (1940). "Christian Liberty in Milton's Divorce Pamphlets." *Modern Language Review* 35: 153–61.

Biberman, Matthew (1999). "Milton, Marriage, and a Woman's Right to Divorce." *Studies in English Literature* 39: 131–53.

Boyette, Purvis (1969). "Milton's Divorce Tracts and the Law of Marriage." *Tulane Studies in English* 17: 73–92.

Cable, Lana (1981). "Coupling Logic and Milton's Doctrine of Divorce." *Milton Studies* 15: 143–59.

Fallon, Stephen M. (2000). "The Spur of Self-Concernment: Milton in his Divorce Tracts." *Milton Studies* 38: 220–42.

Hodgson, Elizabeth (1994). "When God Proposes: Theology and Gender in *Tetrachordon*." *Milton Studies* 31: 133–54.

Kirby, R. Kenneth (1984). "Milton's Biblical Hermeneutics in *The Doctrine and Discipline of Divorce*." *Milton Quarterly* 18: 116–25.

McCready, Amy R. (1992). "Milton's Casuistry: The Case of *The Doctrine and Discipline of Divorce*." *Journal of Medieval and Renaissance Studies* 22: 393–428.

Political tracts

Achinstein, Sara (1992). "Milton Catches the Conscience of the King: *Eikonoklastes* and the Engagement Controversy." *Milton Studies* 29: 143–63.

Fink, Z. (1942). "The Theory of the Mixed State and the Development of Milton's Political Thought." *Publications of the Modern Language Association* 57: 705–36.

Helgerson, Richard (1987). "Milton Reads the King's Book: Print, Performance, and the Making of a Bourgeois Idol." *Criticism* 29: 1–25.

Lewalski, Barbara (1959). "Milton: Political Beliefs and Polemical Methods, 1659–60." *Publications of the Modern Language Association* 74: 191–202.

Loewenstein, David (1989). "'Casting down imaginations': Milton as Iconoclast." *Criticism* 31: 253–70.

Radzinowicz, Mary Ann (1978). "'Occasions drew me': Political Intention in Milton's Prose." In Mary Ann Radzinowicz (ed.), *Toward Samson Agonistes* (pp. 145–66). Princeton: Princeton University Press.

Sirluck, Ernest (1964). "Milton's Political Thought: The First Cycle." *Modern Philology* 61: 209–24.

Stavely, Keith W. (1973). "The Style and Structure of Milton's *Readie and Easie Way*." *Milton Studies* 5: 269–87.

Stewart, Stanley (1984). "Milton Revises *The Readie and Easie Way*." *Milton Studies* 20: 205–24.

Areopagitica

Burt, Stephen (1998). "To the Unknown God: St. Paul and Athens in Milton's *Areopagitica*." *Milton Quarterly* 32: 23–31.

Evans, John X. (1966). "Imagery as Argument in Milton's *Areopagitica*." *Texas Studies in Literature and Language* 8: 189–205.

Illo, John (1988). "*Areopagitica's* Mythic and Real." *Prose Studies* 11: 3–23.

Kendrick, Christopher (1983). "Ethics and the Orator in *Areopagitica*." *English Literary History* 50: 655–91.

Long, Anne B. (1974). "'She may have more shapes than one': Milton and the Modern Idea that Truth Changes." *Milton Studies* 6: 85–99.

J. Martin Evans

Price, Alan F. (1952). "Incidental Imagery in *Areopagitica*." *Modern Philology* 49: 217–22.
Rajan, Balachandra (1975). "Cunning Resemblance." *Milton Studies* 7: 29–48.
Read, Herbert Edward (1945). "The *Areopagitica*." In *Coat of Many Colours* (pp. 333–46). London: Routledge and Kegan Paul.
Smallenburg, Harry R. (1976) "Contiguities and Moving Limbs: Style as Argument in *Areopagitica*." *Milton Studies* 9: 169–84.
Whitaker, Juanita (1976). "The Wars of Truth: Wisdom and Strength in *Areopagitica*." *Milton Studies* 9: 185–201.
Wilding, Michael (1986). "Milton's *Areopagitica*: Liberty for the Sects." *Prose Studies* 9: 7–38.
Williams, Arnold (1944). "*Areopagitica* Revisited." *University of Toronto Quarterly* 14: 67–74.
Wittreich, Joseph (1972). "Milton's *Areopagitica*: Its Isocratic and Ironic Contexts." *Milton Studies* 4: 101–15.

Educational works (See also chapter 4)

Coiro, Ann Baynes (1988). "'To repair the ruins of our first parents': *Of Education* and Fallen Adam." *Studies in English Literature* 28: 133–47.
Herendeen, Wyman H. (1995). "Milton's *Accedence Commenc't Grammar* and the Deconstruction of Grammatical Tyranny." In P. G. Stanwood (ed.), *Of Poetry and Politics*. (pp. 295–312). Binghampton, NY: Medieval and Renaissance Texts and Studies.
Hamilton, Gary D. (1990). "*The History of Britain* and its Restoration Audience." In D. Loewenstein and J. G. Turner (eds), *Politics, Poetics, and Hermeneutics in Milton's Prose*. (pp. 241–55). New York: Cambridge University Press.
Thompson, E. N. S. (1918). "Milton's *Of Education*." *Studies in Philology* 15: 159–75.
Viswanathan, Gauri (1998). "Milton, Imperialism, and Education." *Modern Language Quarterly* 59: 345–61.

Latin tracts

Campbell, Gordon et al. (1997). "The Provenance of *De Doctrina Christiana*." *Milton Quarterly* 17: 67–121.
Fallon, Robert T. (2000). "*A Second Defence*: Milton's Critique of Cromwell?" *Milton Studies* 39: 167–83.
Hoffman, Richard L. (1971). "The Rhetorical Structure of Milton's *Second Defence of the People of England*." *Studia Neophilologica* 43: 227–45.
Hunter, William B. (1992). "The Provenance of the *Christian Doctrine*." *Studies in English Literature* 32: 129–42.

254

Lewalski, Barbara K. (1992). "Milton's *Christian Doctrine.*" *Studies in English Literature* 32: 143–54.

Loewenstein, David (1990). "Milton and the Poetics of Defense." In David Loewenstein and J. G. Turner (eds), *Politics, Poetics, and Hermeneutics in Milton's Prose* (pp. 171–92). New York: Cambridge University Press.

PARADISE LOST

General

Fish, Stanley Eugene (1965). "The Harassed Reader in *Paradise Lost.*" *Critical Quarterly* 7: 162–82.

Rumrich, John P. (1990). "Uninventing Milton." *Modern Philology* 87: 249–65.

Milton's plans

Gilbert, Allan H. (1947). *On the Composition of* Paradise Lost. Chapel Hill: University of North Carolina Press.

Hunter, George K. (1980). *Paradise Lost* (esp. pp. 1–95, chs 1–3). London: Allen and Unwin.

McColley, Grant (1940). *Paradise Lost, An Account of its Growth and Major Origins* (esp. pp. 269–325, chs 11–12). Chicago: Packard.

Epic elements

Aryanpur, Manoocher (1967). "*Paradise Lost* and *The Odyssey.*" *Texas Studies in Literature and Language* 9: 151–66.

Blessington, Francis C. (1979). Paradise Lost *and the Classical Epic*. London: Routledge and Kegan Paul.

Boltwood Robert M. (1952). "Turnus and Satan as Epic Villains." *Classical Journal* 47: 183–6.

Bowra, C. M. (1945). *From Virgil to Milton*. London: Duckworth.

Bush, Douglas (1952). "Virgil and Milton." *Classical Journal* 47: 178–82.

Condee, Ralph W. (1949). *Milton's Theories Concerning Epic Poetry: Their Sources and Their Influence*. Urbana: University of Illinois Press.

Connely, Willard (1923). "Imprints of the *Aeneid* on *Paradise Lost.*" *Classical Journal* 18: 466–76.

Di Cesare, Mario A. (1969). "*Paradise Lost* and Epic Tradition." *Milton Studies* 1: 31–50.

Gransden, K. W. (1967). "*Paradise Lost* and the *Aeneid.*" *Essays in Criticism* 17: 281–303.

Greene, Thomas M. (1963). *The Descent from Heaven*. New Haven: Yale University Press.

J. Martin Evans

Harding, Davis Philoon (1962). *The Club of Hercules*. Urbana: University of Illinois Press.

Lewis, C. S. (1942). *A Preface to* Paradise Lost. Cambridge: Cambridge University Press.

Martindale, Charles (1986). *John Milton and the Transformation of Ancient Epic*. London: Croom Helm.

Mueller, Martin (1969). "*Paradise Lost* and the *Iliad*." *Comparative Literature Studies* 6: 292–316.

Rajan, Balachandra (1983). "*Paradise Lost*: The Uncertain Epic." *Milton Studies* 17: 105–19.

Richardson, J. (1962). "Virgil and Milton Once Again." *Comparative Literature* 14: 321–31.

Spaeth, Duncan J. (1945). "Epic Conventions in *Paradise Lost*." *Elizabethan Studies in Honor of George F. Reynolds*. Boulder: University of Colorado Press.

Spencer, T. J. B. (1968). "*Paradise Lost*: The Anti-epic." In C. A. Patrides (ed.), *Approaches to* Paradise Lost (pp. 81–98). Toronto: University of Toronto Press.

Steadman, John N. (1968). "The Classical Hero: Satan and Ulysses." In *Milton's Epic Characters* (pp. 194–208). Chapel Hill: University of North Carolina Press.

Steadman, John N. (1976). *Epic and Tragic Structure in* Paradise Lost. Chicago: University of Chicago Press.

Tillyard, E. M. W. (1949). "Milton and the Epic." In *The Miltonic Setting* (pp. 141–204). New York: Macmillan.

Tillyard, E. M. W. (1954). *The English Epic and its Background*. London: Chatto and Windus.

Webber, Joan (1979). *Milton and his Epic Tradition*. Seattle: University of Washington Press.

Dramatic elements

Barker, A. E. (1949, 1965). "Structural Pattern in *Paradise Lost*." *Philological Quarterly* 28: 17–30; and in *Milton, Modern Essays in Criticism* (pp. 142–55). New York: Oxford University Press.

DeMaray, John G. (1980). *Milton's Theatrical Epic: The Invention and Design of* Paradise Lost. Cambridge, MA: Harvard University Press.

Gilbert, Allan H. (1920). "Milton and the Mysteries." *Studies in Philology* 17: 147–69.

Hanford, J. H. (1917). "The Dramatic Element in *Paradise Lost*." *Studies in Philology* 14: 178–95.

Ramsay, R. L. (1918). "Morality Themes in Milton's Poetry." *Studies in Philology* 15: 123–58.

Style

Adams, Robert A. (1955). "Milton's Verse: Efforts at a Judgment." In Robert Martin Adams (ed.), *Ikon* (pp. 177–211). Ithaca: Cornell University Press.

Berek, Peter (1970). "'Plain' and 'Ornate' Styles and the Structure of *Paradise Lost*." *Publications of the Modern Language Association* 85: 237–46.

Broadbent, John B. (1968). "Milton's 'Mortal Voice' and his 'Omnific Word.'" In C. A. Patrides (ed.), *Approaches to* Paradise Lost (pp. 99–118). Toronto: University of Toronto Press.

Bush, Douglas (1945). "The Poetical Texture." In Paradise Lost *in our Time* (pp. 88–117). Ithaca: Cornell University Press.

Davie, Donald (1960). "Syntax and Music in *Paradise Lost*." In Frank Kermode (ed.), *The Living Milton: Essays by Various Hands* (pp. 70–84). London: Routledge and Kegan Paul.

Eliot, T. S. (1936). "A Note on the Verse of John Milton." *Essays and Studies* 21: 32–40.

Eliot, T. S. (1947). "Milton." *Proceedings of the British Academy* 33: 61–79.

Emma, Ronald (1964). *Milton's Grammar*. The Hague: Mouton.

Emma, R. D. and Shawcross, J. T. (eds) (1967). *Language and Style in Milton*. New York: F. Unger.

Hale, John K. (1997). *Milton's Languages: The Impact of Multilingualism on Style*. Cambridge: Cambridge University Press.

Harding, Davis Philoon (1962). "Answerable Style!" In *The Club of Hercules* (pp. 114–34). Urbana: University of Illinois Press.

Leavis, F. R. (1936). "Milton's Verse." In *Revaluation: Tradition and Development in English Poetry* (pp. 42–67). London: Chatto and Windus.

Leavis, F. R. (1938, 1952). "In Defense of Milton." *Scrutiny* 7: 104–14; and in *The Common Pursuit* (pp. 33–43). London: Chatto and Windus.

Leavis, F. R. (1952). "Mr Eliot and Milton." In *The Common Pursuit* (pp. 9–32). London: Chatto and Windus.

Lewis, C. S. (1942). *A Preface to* Paradise Lost (esp. pp. 39–60, chs 7–8). New York: Oxford University Press.

Pearce, D. R. (1965). "The Style of Milton's Epic." In A. R. Barker (ed.), *Milton: Modern Essays in Criticism* (pp. 368–85). New York: Oxford University Press.

Rajan, Balachandra (1947). "The Style of *Paradise Lost*." In Paradise Lost *and the Seventeenth Century Reader* (pp. 108–34). Ann Arbor: University of Michigan Press.

Ricks, Christopher (1963). *Milton's Grand Style*. Oxford: Clarendon Press.

Samuel, Irene (1969). "Milton on Style." *Cornell Library Journal* 9: 39–58.

Stein, Arnold (1953). "Answerable Style." In *Answerable Style* (pp. 119–62). Minneapolis: University of Minnesota Press.

J. Martin Evans

Tillyard, E. M. W. (1938). "A Note on Milton's Style." In *The Miltonic Setting* (pp. 105–40). New York: Macmillan.

Language

Belsey, Catherine (1988). *John Milton: Language, Gender, Power.* Oxford: Blackwell.
Clark, Everett M. (1956). "Milton's English Poetical Vocabulary." *Studies in Philology* 53.2: 220–38.
Corns, Thomas N. (1990). *Milton's Language.* Oxford: Blackwell.
Darbishire, Helen (1957). "Milton's Poetic Language" *Essays and Studies* 10: 31–52.
Leonard, J. (1990). *Naming in Paradise: Milton and the Language of Adam and Eve.* Oxford: Clarendon Press.
Rajan, Balachandra (1966). "The Language of *Paradise Lost.*" In Louis L. Martz (ed.), *Milton* (pp. 56–60). Englewood Cliffs, NJ: Prentice-Hall.
Wright, B. A. (1962). "Diction." In *Milton's Paradise Lost* (pp. 62–85). New York: Barnes and Noble.
Wright, B. A. (1967). "A Note on Milton's Diction." In Amadeus P. Fiore (ed.), *Th'Upright Heart and Pure* (pp. 143–9). Pittsburgh: Duquesne University Press.

Prosody

Banks, Theodore H. (1927). "Miltonic rhythm." *Publications of the Modern Language Association* 42: 140–5.
Bridges, Robert (1921, 1965). *Milton's Prosody.* Oxford: Clarendon Press.
Cook, Albert (1960). "Milton's Abstract Music." *University of Toronto Quarterly* 29: 370–85.
Hunter, William B. (1949). The Sources of Milton's Prosody. *Philological Quarterly* 28: 125–44.
Sprott, S. Ernest (1953). *Milton's Art of Prosody.* Oxford: Blackwell.
Stein, Arnold (1953). "Structures of Sound in Milton's Verse." *Kenyon Review* 15: 266–92.
Watkins, W. B. C. (1955). *An Anatomy of Milton's Verse.* Baton Rouge: Louisiana State University Press.

Similes

Bedford, R. D. (1975). "Similes of Unlikeness in *Paradise Lost.*" *Essays in Criticism* 25: 179–97.
Fish, Stanley Eugene (1967). "Yet Never Saw." In *Surprised by Sin* (pp. 22–37). London: St Martin's Press.
Gregerson, Linda (1980). "The Limbs of Truth: Milton's Use of Similes in *Paradise Lost.*" *Milton Studies* 14: 135–52.

258

Hartman, Geoffrey (1965). "Milton's Counterplot" In A. E. Barker (ed.), *Milton* (pp. 386–97). New York: Oxford University Press.

Lerner, L. D. (1954). "The Miltonic Simile." *Essays in Criticism* 4: 297–308.

Jones, R. I. S. (1976). "Eighteenth-Century Criticism of the Miltonic Simile." *Milton Quarterly* 10: 113–19.

Whaler, J. (1931). "The Miltonic Simile." *Publications of the Modern Language Association* 46: 1034–74.

Whaler, J. (1931). "Grammatical Nexus of the Miltonic Simile." *Journal of English and Germanic Philology* 33: 327–34.

Whaler, J. (1931). "Compounding and Distribution of Similes in *Paradise Lost*." *Modern Philology* 28: 313–27.

Widmer, K. (1958). "The Iconography of Renunciation." *English Literary History* 25: 258–69.

Classical allusions

Browning, Judith (1991). "Sin, Eve, and Circe: *Paradise Lost* and the Ovidian Circe Tradition." *Milton Studies* 26: 135–57.

Bush, Douglas (1961). "Ironic and Ambiguous Allusion in *Paradise Lost*." *Journal of English and Germanic Philology* 60: 631–40.

Collett, Jonathan H. (1970). "Milton's Use of Classical Mythology in *Paradise Lost*." *Publications of the Modern Language Association* 85: 88–96.

DuRocher, Richard (1985). *Milton and Ovid*. Ithaca: Cornell University Press.

Farrison W. E. (1933). "The Classical Allusions in *Paradise Lost*." *English Journal* 22 (College Edition): 650–3.

Harding, Davis Philoon (1946). *Milton and the Renaissance Ovid*. Urbana: University of Illinois Press.

Herbst, E. L. (1934). "Classical Mythology in *Paradise Lost*." *Classical Philology* 29: 147–8.

Osgood, Charles Grosvenor (1900). *Classical Mythology of Milton's English Poems*. New York: Holt.

Porter, William M. (1993). *Reading the Classics and* Paradise Lost. Lincoln: Nebraska University Press.

Rudat, Wolfgang E. H. (1981). "Milton's Dido and Aeneas: The Fall in *Paradise Lost* and the Virgilian Tradition." *Classical and Modern Literature* 2: 33–46.

Biblical allusions (See also chapter 8)

Conklin, George N. (1949). *Biblical Criticism and Heresy in Milton*. New York: King's Crown Press.

Potter, George (1911). "Milton's Bibles." *Notes and Queries* 3: 70.

Williams, Arnold (1948). *The Common Expositor: An Account of the Commentaries on Genesis 1527–1633*. Chapel Hill: University of North Carolina Press.

Theology (See also chapter 8)

Bauman, Michael (1987). *Milton's Arianism*. Frankfurt: Peter Lang.

Boswell, Jackson Campbell (1967). "Milton and Prevenient Grace." *Studies in English Literature* 7: 83–94.

Campbell, Gordon (1979). "The Mortalist Heresy in *Paradise Lost.*" *Milton Quarterly* 13: 33–6.

Conklin, George N. (1949). *Biblical Criticism and Heresy in Milton*. New York: King's Crown Press.

Danielson, Dennis (1978). "Milton's Arminianism and *Paradise Lost.*" *Milton Studies* 12: 47–73.

Danielson, Dennis (1982). *Milton's Good God: A Study in Literary Theodicy*. Cambridge: Cambridge University Press.

Empson, William (1962). *Milton's God*. London: Chatto and Windus.

Fiore, Peter Amadeus (1981). *Milton and Augustine*. University Park: Pennsylvania State University Press.

Fish, Stanley Eugene (1967). *Surprised by Sin: The Reader in* Paradise Lost. New York: St Martin's Press.

Fixler, Michael (1964). *Milton and the Kingdoms of God*. London: Faber and Faber.

Frye, Roland N. (1960). *God, Man, and Satan*. Princeton: Princeton University Press.

Hunter, William B., Patrides, C. A. and Adamson, J. H. (eds) (1971). *Bright Essence: Studies in Milton's Theology*. Salt Lake City: University of Utah Press.

Joseph, Sister Miriam (1954). *Orthodoxy in* Paradise Lost. Quebec: Les Presses Universitaires Laval.

Kelley, Maurice (1941). *This Great Argument: A Study of Milton's* De Doctrina Christiana *as a Gloss upon* Paradise Lost. Princeton: Princeton University Press.

Kerrigan, William (1975). "The Heretical Milton: From Assumption to Mortalism." *English Literary Renaissance* 5: 125–66.

O'Keefe, Timothy (1982). *Milton and the Pauline Tradition*. Washington, DC: University Press of America.

Sewell, Arthur (1939). *A Study of Milton's* Christian Doctrine. London and New York: Oxford University Press.

Williamson, George (1935). "Milton and the Mortalist Heresy." *Studies in Philology* 32: 553–79.

God and angels (See also chapter 8)

Blessington, Francis C. (1979). "Above the Olympian Mount." In Paradise Lost *and the Classical Epic* (pp. 19–49). Boston: Routledge and Kegan Paul.

Broadbent, J. B. (1960). "Heaven." In *Some Graver Subject* (pp.135–61). New York: Barnes and Noble.

Chew, Samuel Claggett (1947). *The Virtues Reconciled: An Iconographic Study.* Toronto: University of Toronto Press.
Christopher, Georgia (1982). "The Improvement of God's 'Character' in *Paradise Lost.*" *Renaissance Papers*: 1–8.
Hamilton, Gary D. (1972). "Milton's Defensive God: A Reappraisal." *Studies in Philology* 69: 87–100.
Peter, John Desmond (1960). "God and his Angels." In *A Critique of* Paradise Lost (pp. 9–30). New York: Columbia University Press.
Riggs, William (1970). "The Poet and Satan in *Paradise Lost.*" *Milton Studies* 2: 59–82.
Samuel, Irene (1957). "The Dialogue in Heaven." *Publications of the Modern Language Association* 72.4: 601–11.
Traver, Hope (1907). *The Four Daughters of God.* Philadelphia: J. C. Winston.
Webber, Joan (1973). "Milton's God." *English Literary History* 40: 514–31.
West, Robert (1955). *Milton and the Angels.* Athens: University of Georgia Press.

Doctrine of the Fall (See also chapter 9)

Blackburn, Thomas (1971). "Uncloister'd Virtue." *Milton Studies* 3: 119–35.
Diekhoff, John S. (1944). "Eve, the Devil, and *Areopagitica.*" *Modern Language Quarterly* 5: 429–34.
Hyman, Lawrence (1972). "Dogma and Poetry in *Paradise Lost* IX–X." In *The Quarrel Within: Art and Morality in Milton's Poetry* (pp. 56–74). Port Washington, NY: Kennikat Press.
Lewis, C. S. (1942). *A Preface to* Paradise Lost. Cambridge: Cambridge University Press.
Ogden, H. V. S. (1957). "The Crisis of *Paradise Lost* Reconsidered." *Philological Quarterly* 36: 1–19.
Tillyard, W. N. W. (1951). "The Crisis of *Paradise Lost.*" In *Studies in Milton* (pp. 8–52). London: Chatto and Windus.
Waldock, A. J. A. (1947). "The Fall." In Paradise Lost *and its Critics* (pp. 25–64). Cambridge: Cambridge University Press.

Felix culpa [The Fortunate Fall] (See also chapters 9 and 10)

Bell, Millicent (1953, 1955). "The Fallacy of the Fall in *Paradise Lost.*" *Publications of the Modern Language Association* 68: 863–83.
Danielson, Dennis (1982). "*Paradise Lost* and the Unfortunate Fall." *In Milton's Good God* (pp. 202–27). Cambridge: Cambridge University Press.
Lovejoy, A. O. (1937). "Milton and the Paradox of the Fortunate Fall." *English Literary History* 4: 161–79.
Madsen William B. (1959). "The Fortunate Fall in *Paradise Lost.*" *Modern Language Notes* 74: 103–5.
Marshall, W. H. (1961). "*Paradise Lost, felix culpa,* and the Problem of Structure." *Modern Language Notes* 76: 15–20.

J. Martin Evans

Miner, Earl (1968). "*Felix culpa* in the Redemptive Order of *Paradise Lost*." *Philological Quarterly* 47: 43–54.

Mollenkott, Virginia (1972). "Milton's Rejection of the Fortunate Fall." *Milton Quarterly* 6: 1–5.

Patrides, C. A. (1963). "Adam's Happy Fault and Seventeenth-Century Apologetics." *Franciscan Studies* 23: 238–43.

Taylor, Dick (1959). "Milton and the Paradox of the Fortunate Fall Once More." *Tulane Studies in English* 9: 35–52.

Ulreich, John C. (1971). "A Paradise Within: The Fortunate Fall in *Paradise Lost*." *Journal of the History of Ideas* 32: 351–66.

Satan (See also chapter 8)

Benet, Diana Trevino (1989). "Hell, Satan, and the New Politician." In D. T. Benet and M. Lieb (eds), *Literary Milton* (pp. 91–113). Pittsburgh: Duquesne University Press.

Bennett, Joan (1987). "God, Satan, and King Charles." *Publications of the Modern Language Association* 102: 441–57.

Blessington, Francis C. (1979). "Pellax Ulysses." In Paradise Lost *and the Classical Epic* (pp. 1–18). Boston: Routledge and Kegan Paul.

Empson, William (1961). "Satan." In *Milton's God* (pp. 36–90). London: Chatto and Windus.

Evans, J. Martin (1968). "Hellish Hate and Heavenly Love." In *Paradise Lost and the Genesis Tradition* (pp. 223–41). Oxford: Clarendon Press.

Gardner, Helen (1965). "Satan and the Theme of Damnation in Elizabethan Tragedy." In Arthur Barker (ed.), *Milton* (pp. 205–17). New York: Oxford University Press.

Gilbert, A. H. (1942). "The Theological Basis of Satan's Rebellion." *Modern Philology* 40: 19–42.

Hodge, Robert (1978). "Satan and the Revolution of the Saints." *Literature: History* 7: 20–33.

Lewis, C. S. (1942). "Satan." In *A Preface to* Paradise Lost (pp. 92–100). Cambridge: Cambridge University Press.

Musgrove, S. (1945). "Is the Devil an Ass?" *Review of English Studies* 21: 302–15.

Peter, John Desmond (1960). "Satan and his Angels." In *A Critique of* Paradise Lost (pp. 31–62). New York: Columbia University Press.

Rajan, Balachandra (1947). "The Problem of Satan." In Paradise Lost *and the Seventeenth-Century Reader* (pp. 93–107). Ann Arbor: University of Michigan Press.

Revard, Stella (1973). "Satan's Envy of the Kingship of the Son: A Reconsideration of *Paradise Lost*, Book 5, and its Theological Background." *Modern Philology* 70: 190–8.

262

Riggs, William (1970). "The Poet and Satan in *Paradise Lost.*" *Milton Studies* 2: 59–82.

Steadman, John M. (1976). "The Idea of Satan as the Hero of *Paradise Lost.*" *Proceedings of the American Philosophical Society* 120: 253–94.

Stoll, E. E. (1944). "Give the Devil his Due." *Review of English Studies* 20: 108–24.

Summers, Joseph H. (1962). "Satan, Sin, and Death." In *The Muse's Method* (pp. 32–70). Cambridge, MA: Harvard University Press.

Waldock, Arthur John Alfred (1947). "Satan and the Technique of Degradation." In Paradise Lost *and its Critics* (pp. 65–96). Cambridge: Cambridge University Press.

Werblowsky, R. J. Z. (1952). *Lucifer and Prometheus: A Study of Milton's Satan.* New York: Routledge and Kegan Paul.

Williams, A. (1945). "The Motivation of Satan's Rebellion in *Paradise Lost.*" *Studies in Philology* 42: 253–68.

Adam and Eve (See also chapter 9)

Froula, Christine (1983). "When Eve Reads Milton: Undoing the Canonical Economy." *Critical Inquiry* 10: 321–476.

Froula, Christine (1984). "Pechter's Spectre: Milton's Bogey Writ Small, or Why Is He Afraid of Virginia Woolf?" *Critical Enquiry* 11: 171–8.

Gallagher, Philip J. (1979). "Milton's Bogey." *Publications of the Modern Language Association* 94: 319–21.

Gallagher, Philip J. (1984). "Creation and Genesis in *Paradise Lost.*" *Milton Studies* 20: 163–204.

Gilbert, A. H. (1920). "Milton on the Position of Women." *Modern Language Review* 15: 240–64.

Gilbert, Sandra M. (1978). "Patriarchal Poetry and Women Readers: Reflections on Milton's Bogey." *Publications of the Modern Language Association* 93: 368–82.

Juhnke, Anna K. (1988). "Remnants of Misogyny in *Paradise Lost.*" *Milton Quarterly* 22: 50–7.

Kerrigan, William and Braden, Gordon (1986). "Milton's Coy Eve: *Paradise Lost* and Renaissance Love Poetry." *English Literary History* 53: 27–51.

Landy, Marcia (1972). "Kinship and the Role of Women in *Paradise Lost.*" *Milton Studies* 4: 3–18.

Landy, Marcia (1976). "'A Free and Open Encounter': Milton and the Modern Reader." *Milton Studies* 9: 3–36.

Lewalski, Barbara K. (1974). "Milton on Women: Yet Once More." *Milton Studies* 6: 3–20.

McColley, Diane K. (1983). *Milton's Eve.* Urbana: University of Illinois Press.

McColley, Diane K. (1989). "Milton and the Sexes." In Dennis Danielson (ed.), *The Cambridge Companion to Milton* (pp. 147–66). Cambridge: Cambridge University Press.

Miller, Dorothy D. (1962). "Eve." *Journal of English and Germanic Philology* 61: 542–47.

Nyquist, Mary (1984). "Reading the Fall: Discourse and Drama in *Paradise Lost.*" *English Literary Renaissance* 14.2: 199–229.

Nyquist, Mary (1987). "Gynesis, Genesis, Exegesis, and the Formation of Milton's Eve." In Marjorie Garber (ed.), *Cannibals, Witches and Divorce* (pp. 147–208). Baltimore: Johns Hopkins University Press.

Parker, William R. (1978). "Eve, Evening and the Labor of Reading in *Paradise Lost.*" *English Literary Renaissance* 9: 319–42.

Pechter, Edward (1984). "When Pechter Reads Froula Pretending She's Eve Reading Milton." *Critical Inquiry* 11: 163–70.

Revard, Stella (1973). "Eve and the Doctrine of Responsibility in *Paradise Lost.*" *Publications of the Modern Language Association* 88: 69–78.

Shullenberger, William (1986). "Wrestling with the Angel: *Paradise Lost* and Feminist Criticism." *Milton Quarterly* 20: 69–84.

Siegel, Paul N. (1950). "Milton and the Humanist Attitude toward Women" *Journal of the History of Ideas* 11: 42–53.

Walker, Julia M. (ed.) (1988). *Milton and the Idea of Woman.* Urbana: University of Illinois Press.

Webber, Joan M. (1980). "The Politics of Poetry: Feminism and *Paradise Lost.*" *Milton Studies* 14: 3–24.

Wittreich, Joseph A. (1987). *Feminist Milton.* Ithaca: Cornell University Press.

Separation (See also chapters 8 and 9)

Benet, Diane (1983). "Abdiel and the Son in the Separation Scene." *Milton Studies* 18: 129–43.

Bennett, Joan S. (1983). "Milton's Antinomianism and the Separation Scene in *Paradise Lost.*" *Publications of the Modern Language Association* 98: 388–404.

Bowers, Fredson (1969). "Adam and Eve and the Fall in *Paradise Lost.*" *Publications of the Modern Language Association* 84: 264–73.

Evans, J. Martin (1984). "Mortals' Chiefest Enemy." *Milton Studies* 20: 111–26.

Farwell, Marilyn R. (1982). "Eve, the Separation Scene, and the Renaissance Idea of Androgyny. *Milton Studies* 16: 3–20.

Low, Anthony (1968). "The Parting in the Garden in *Paradise Lost.*" *Philological Quarterly* 47: 30–5.

McColley, Diane K. (1972). "Free Will and Obedience in the Separation Scene in *Paradise Lost.*" *Studies in English Literature* 12: 103–20.

Revard, Stella (1973). "Eve and the Doctrine of Responsibility in *Paradise Lost.*" *Publications of the Modern Language Association* 88: 69–78.

Safer, Elaine B. (1972). "'Sufficient to have stood': Eve's Responsibility in Book IX." *Milton Quarterly* 6: 10–14.

Tillyard, E. M. W. (1951). "The Crisis in *Paradise Lost*." In *Studies in Milton*. (pp. 8–52). London: Chatto and Windus.

Marriage (See also chapter 9)

Aers, David et al. (1979). "'Rational Burning': Milton on Sex and Marriage." *Milton Studies* 13: 3–33.

Fido, Martin (1966). "Milton on Love." *Oxford Review* 3: 47–66.

Fresch, Cheryl H. (1982). "'And brought her unto the man': The Wedding *in Paradise Lost*." *Milton Studies* 16: 21–33.

Halkett, John C. (1970). *Milton and the Idea of Matrimony: A Study of the Divorce Tracts and* Paradise Lost. New Haven: Yale University Press.

LeComte, Edward (1978). *Milton and Sex*. London: Macmillan.

Lewis, C. S. (1942). "Adam and Eve." In *A Preface to* Paradise Lost. (pp. 112–17). Cambridge: Cambridge University Press.

Pezenik, F. (1984). "Fit Help: The Egalitarian Marriage in *Paradise Lost*." *Mosaic* 17.1: 29–48.

Summers, Joseph H. (1962). "The Two Great Sexes." In *The Muse's Method*. (pp. 87–111). Binghamton, NY: Center for Medieval and Early Renaissance Studies.

Willis, Gladys J. (1984). *The Penalty of Eve: John Milton and Divorce*. New York: P. Lang.

Garden of Eden (See also chapter 10)

Armstrong, John (1969). *The Paradise Myth*. New York: Oxford University Press.

Comito, Terry (1978). *The Idea of the Garden in the Renaissance*. New Brunswick: Rutgers University Press.

Demaray, Hannah D. (1974). "Milton's 'Perfect' Paradise and the Landscapes of Italy." *Milton Quarterly* 8: 33–41.

Duncan, Joseph Ellis (1972). *Milton's Earthly Paradise*. Minneapolis: University of Minneapolis Press.

Garber, Majorie B. (1975). "Fallen Landscape: The Art of Milton and *Poussin*." *English Literary Renaissance* 5: 96–124.

Giamatti, A. Bartlett (1966). *The Earthly Paradise and the Renaissance Epic*. Princeton: Princeton University Press.

Hunt, John D. (1981). "Milton and the Making of the English Landscape Garden." *Milton Studies* 15: 81–105.

Hyams, Edward (1964). *The English Garden*. New York: H. N. Abrams.

Knott, John R. (1971). *Milton's Pastoral Vision: An Approach to* Paradise Lost. Chicago: University of Chicago Press.

Koehler, G. Stanley (1975). "Milton and the Art of Landscape." *Milton Studies* 8: 3–40.

Otten, Charlotte F. (1973). "'My Native Element': Milton's Paradise and English Gardens." *Milton Studies* 5: 249–67.

Stewart, Stanley (1966). *The Enclosed Garden: The Tradition and the Image in Seventeenth-Century Poetry.* Madison: University of Wisconsin Press.

Strong, Roy (1979). *The Renaissance Garden in England.* London: Thames and Hudson.

Politics

Armitage, David (1990). "John Milton: Poet against Empire." In David Armitage, A. Himy and Q. Skinner (eds), *Milton and Republicanism* (pp. 206–25). Cambridge: Cambridge University Press.

Evans, J. Martin (1996). *Milton's Imperial Epic:* Paradise Lost *and the Discourse of Colonialism.* Ithaca: Cornell University Press.

Hill, Christopher (1977). *Milton and the English Revolution.* London: Faber and Faber.

Hodgkins, Christopher (2002). *Reforming Empire: Protestant Colonialism and Conscience in British Literature.* Columbia: University of Missouri Press.

Lewalski, Barbara (2000). "*Paradise Lost* and Milton's Politics." *Milton Studies* 38: 141–68.

Quint, David (1993). *Epic and Empire: Politics and Generic Form from Virgil to Milton.* Princeton: Princeton University Press.

Radzinowicz, Mary Ann (1987). "The Politics of *Paradise Lost.*" In Kevin Sharpe and Steven Zwicker (eds), *The Politics of Discourse* (pp. 204–9). Berkeley: University of California Press.

Rajan, Balachandra and Sauer, Elizabeth (eds) (1999). *Milton and the Imperial Vision.* Pittsburgh: Duquesne University Press.

Stevens, Paul (1996). "*Paradise Lost* and the Colonial Imperative." *Milton Studies* 34: 3–21.

Worden, Blair (1990). "Milton's Republicanism and the Tyranny of Heaven" In G. Buck, Q. Skinner, and M. Viroli (eds), *Machiavelli and Republicanism* (pp. 225–45). Cambridge: Cambridge University Press.

Worden Blair (1998). "John Milton and Oliver Cromwell". In I. Gentles, J. Morrill, and B. Worden (eds), *Soldiers, Writers and Statesmen of the English Revolution* (pp. 243–64). Cambridge, Cambridge University Press.

Zwierlein, Anne-Julia (2001). *Majestick Milton: British Imperial Expansion and Transformations of* Paradise Lost, *1667–1837.* Munster: Lit Verlag.

PARADISE REGAINED (See also chapter 11)

Genre

Condee, Ralph (1970). "Milton's Dialogue with Epic: *Paradise Regained* and the Tradition." *Yale Review* 59: 357–75.

Curran, Stuart (1983). "*Paradise Regained*: Implications of Epic." *Milton Studies* 17: 209–24.

Guss, Donald L. (1971). "A Brief Epic: *Paradise Regained.*" *Studies in Philology* 68: 223–43.

Hero

Fisher, Alan (1980). "Why is *Paradise Regained* So Cold?" *Milton Studies* 14: 195–217.

Hughes, Merritt Y. (1938). "The Christ of *Paradise Regained* and the Renaissance Heroic Tradition." *Studies in Philology* 35: 254–77.

Jordan, Richard D. (1976). "*Paradise Regained* and the Second Adam." *Milton Studies* 9: 261–75.

Knoppers, Laura L. (1992). "*Paradise Regained* and the Politics of Martyrdom." *Modern Philology* 90 200–19.

Langford, Thomas (1982). "The Nature of Christ in *Paradise Regained.*" *Milton Quarterly* 16: 63–7.

Robson, W. W. (1960). "The Better Fortitude." In Frank Kermode (ed.), *The Living Milton: Essays by Various Hands* (pp. 124–37). London: Routledge and Kegan Paul.

Temptations

Bredbeck, Gregory W. (1991). "Milton's Ganymede: Negotiations of Homoerotic Tradition in *Paradise Regained.*" *Publications of the Modern Language Association* 106: 262–76.

Christopher, Georgia B. (1980). "The Secret Agent in *Paradise Regained.*" *Modern Language Quarterly* 41: 131–51.

Lewalski, Barbara K. (1960). "Theme and Structure in *Paradise Regained.*" *Studies in Philology* 57: 186–220.

McAdams, James R. (1972). "The Pattern of Temptation in *Paradise Regained.*" *Milton Studies* 4: 177–93.

Rollinson, Philip (1995). "The Homoerotic Aspect of Temptation in *Paradise Regained.*" *English Language Notes* 33.2: 31–6.

Rushdy, Ashraf H. A. (1990). "'In dubious battle': Skepticism and Fideism in *Paradise Regained.*" *Huntington Library Quarterly* 53.2: 95–118.

Summers, Claude J. (1997). "The (Homo)sexual Temptation in Milton's *Paradise Regained.*" *Journal of Homosexuality* 33: 45–69.

Woodhouse, A. S. P. (1956). "Theme and Pattern in *Paradise Regained.*" *University of Toronto Quarterly* 25: 167–82.

General discussions

Arye, Northrop (1956). "The Typology of *Paradise Regained.*" *Modern Philology* 53: 227–38.

J. Martin Evans

Forsythe, Neil (1985). "Having Done All to Stand: Biblical and Classical Allusion in *Paradise Regained*." *Milton Studies* 21: 199–214.
Stein, Robert A. (1970). "The Sources and Implications of the Jobean Analogies in *Paradise Regained*." *Anglia* 88: 323–33.

SAMSON AGONISTES (See also chapter 12)

Hellenic and Hebraic elements

Jebb, R. C. (1907–8). "*Samson Agonistes* and the Hellenic Drama." *Proceedings of the British Academy* 3: 341–8.
Parker, William R. (1934). "The Greek Spirit in Milton's *Samson Agonistes*." *Essays and Studies* 20: 21–44.
Parker, William R. (1937). *Milton's Debt to Greek Tragedy*. Baltimore: Johns Hopkins University Press.
Stollman, S. S. (1971). "Milton's Samson and the Jewish Tradition." *Milton Studies* 3: 185–200.
Stollman, S. S. (1972). "Milton's Understanding of the Hebraic in *Samson Agonistes*." *Studies in Philology* 69: 334–47.
Tinker, Chauncey B. (1955). "*Samson Agonistes*." In Cleanth Brooks (ed.), *Tragic Themes in Western Literature* (pp. 59–76). New Haven: Yale University Press.

Religion

Gossman, Ann (1962). "Milton's Samson as the Tragic Hero Purified by Trial." *Journal of English and Germanic Philology* 61: 528–41.
Sadler, Lynn V. (1970). "Typological Imagery in *Samson Agonistes*." *English Literary History* 37: 195–210.
Wilkes, G. A. (1963). "The Interpretation of *Samson Agonistes*." *Huntington Library Quarterly* 26: 363–79.

Politics

Achinstein, Sharon (1996). "*Samson Agonistes* and the Drama of Dissent." *Milton Studies* 33: 135–58.
DiSalvo, Jackie (1973). "The Lords Battells: *Samson Agonistes* and the Puritan Revolution." *Milton Studies* 4: 39–62.
Guillory, John (1988). "*Samson Agonistes* in its Historical Moment." In Mary Nyquist and Margaret Ferguson (eds), *Re-membering Milton* (pp.148–76). New York: Methuen.
Hill, Christopher (1972). *Milton and the English Revolution*. London: Faber.
Hill, Christopher (1984). *The Experience of Defeat: Milton and Some Contemporaries*. Harmondsworth: Penguin.

268

Hill, Christopher (1990). *"Samson Agonistes* Again." *Literature and History* 1: 24–39.

Lewalski, Barbara K. (1988). "Samson and the 'new acquist of true [political] experience." *Milton Studies* 24: 233–51.

Radzinowicz, Mary Ann (1965). *"Samson Agonistes* and Milton the Politician in Defeat." *Philological Quarterly* 44: 454–71.

Worden, Blair (1955). "Milton, *Samson Agonistes,* and the Restoration." In G. MacLean (ed.), *Culture and Society in the Stuart Restoration Literure, Drama, History* (pp. 111–36). Cambridge: Cambridge University Press.

General discussions

Fish, Stanley Eugene (1969). "Question and Answer in *Samson Agonistes.*" *Critical Quarterly* 9: 237–64.

Fish, Stanley Eugene (1989). "Spectacle and Evidence in *Samson Agonistes.*" *Critical Inquiry* 15: 556–86.

Grenander, N. E. (1955). *"Samson's* Middle: Aristotle and Dr Johnson." *University of Toronto Quarterly* 24: 377–89.

Kerrigan, William (1974). *The Prophetic Milton.* Charlottesville: University of Virginia Press.

Kirkconnell, W. (1964). *That Invincible Samson: The Theme of* Samson Agonistes *in World Literature with Translations of the Major Analogues.* Toronto: University of Toronto Press.

Mollenkott, Virginia R. (1970). "Relativism in *Samson Agonistes.*" *Studies in Philology* 67: 89–102.

Parker, William R. (1949). "The Date of *Samson Agonistes.*" *Philological Quarterly* 28: 145–66.

Roston, Murray (1968). *Biblical Drama in England: From the Middle Ages to the Present Day.* Evanston: Northwestern University Press.

On stage

Haskin, Dayton (1985). *"Samson Agonistes* on the Stage at Yale." *Milton Quarterly* 19: 48–53.

Shaw, William P. (1979). "Producing *Samson Agonistes.*" *Milton Quarterly* 13: 69–79.

Index

DH